SELLING THE ROPE
TO HANG CAPITALISM?

Pergamon Titles of Related Interest

Collins U.S.–SOVIET MILITARY BALANCE

Davis ASYMMETRIES IN U.S. & SOVIET STRATEGIC DEFENSE PROGRAMS

Deibel & Gaddis CONTAINING THE SOVIET UNION: A CRITIQUE OF U.S. POLICY

Denoon CONSTRAINTS ON STRATEGY: THE ECONOMICS OF WESTERN SECURITY

Pfaltzgraff NATIONAL SECURITY: ETHICS, STRATEGY, AND POLITICS—A LAYMAN'S PRIMER

Goldstein FIGHTING ALLIES: TENSIONS WITHIN THE ATLANTIC ALLIANCE

Related Journals*

DEFENSE ANALYSIS

DEFENCE ATTACHE

*Free specimen copies available upon request.

SELLING THE ROPE
TO HANG CAPITALISM?

The Debate on West-East Trade & Technology Transfer

Edited by

Charles M. Perry
and
Robert L. Pfaltzgraff, Jr.

A Joint Publication of the

International Security Studies Program
The Fletcher School of Law and Diplomacy, Tufts University
and the

Institute for Foreign Policy Analysis, Inc.
Cambridge, Massachusetts, and Washington, D.C.

PERGAMON-BRASSEY'S
International Defense Publishers

WASHINGTON · NEW YORK · LONDON · OXFORD
BEIJING · FRANKFURT · SÃO PAULO · SYDNEY · TOKYO · TORONTO

14966318

U.S.A. (Editorial)	Pergamon-Brassey's International Defense Publishers, 8000 Westpark Drive, Fourth Floor, McLean, Virginia 22102, U.S.A.
(Orders)	Pergamon Press, Maxwell House, Fairview Park, Elmsford, New York 10523, U.S.A.
U.K. (Editorial)	Brassey's Defence Publishers, 24 Gray's Inn Road, London WC1X 8HR
(Orders)	Brassey's Defence Publishers, Headington Hill Hall, Oxford OX3 0BW, England
PEOPLE'S REPUBLIC OF CHINA	Pergamon Press, Room 4037, Qianmen Hotel, Beijing, People's Republic of China
FEDERAL REPUBLIC OF GERMANY	Pergamon Press, Hammerweg 6, D-6242 Kronberg, Federal Republic of Germany
BRAZIL	Pergamon Editora, Rua Eça de Queiros, 346, CEP 04011, Paraiso, São Paulo, Brazil
AUSTRALIA	Pergamon-Brassey's Defence Publishers, P.O. Box 544, Potts Point, N.S.W. 2011, Australia
JAPAN	Pergamon Press, 8th Floor, Matsuoka Central Building, 1-7-1 Nishishinjuku, Shinjuku-ku, Tokyo 160, Japan
CANADA	Pergamon Press Canada, Suite No. 271, 253 College Street, Toronto, Ontario, Canada M5T 1R5

First edition 1987

Library of Congress Cataloging in Publication Data
Selling the rope to hang capitalism?
"A joint publication of the International Security Studies Program, the Fletcher School of Law and Diplomacy, Tufts University, and the Institute for Foreign Policy Analysis, Inc., Cambridge, Massachusetts and Washington, D.C."
Includes index.
1. East-West trade (1945-) 2. Technology transfer—Soviet Union. 3. Technology transfer—United States. I. Perry, Charles M. II. Pfaltzgraff, Robert L. III. Fletcher School of Law and Diplomacy. International Security Studies Program. IV. Institute for Foreign Policy Analysis.
HE1412.S45 1987 382'.091713'01717 86-30401

British Library Cataloguing in Publication Data
Selling the rope to hang capitalism?: the debate on West-East trade and technology transfer.
1. East-West trade (1945-)
I. Perry, Charles M. II. Pfaltzgraff, Robert L. III. Fletcher School of Law and Diplomacy, *International Security Studies Program.* IV. Institute for Foreign Policy Analysis.
382'.09171'301717 HF499

ISBN 0-08-034959-5

Printed and bound in Great Britain by
Hazell Watson & Viney Limited,
Member of the BPCC Group,
Aylesbury, Bucks

PREFACE

On September 23-24, 1985, the Institute for Foreign Policy Analysis, Inc., and the International Security Studies Program of the Fletcher School of Law and Diplomacy, Tufts University, cosponsored a meeting in the ISSP's Forum series whose purpose was to address the strategic dimensions of technology transfer from the West to the Soviet Union. This conference brought together policymakers from the Reagan administration as well as persons from the academic community outside government and from industry. Included were members of the various executive departments and agencies of the U.S. government charged with the administration of the legislation and regulations governing the transfer of technologies to the Soviet Union. Considerable emphasis, moreover, was placed on congressional perspectives on the West-East technology flows.

Participants addressed such issues as the adequacy of existing U.S. technology export controls, together with technology transfer as an alliance issue confronting the United States and NATO-European countries as well as Japan. A principal focus of the forum was the role of illicit means—espionage and theft—in the West-East transfer of sensitive technologies. Last but not least, considerable attention was given to the impact of technology transfer upon the Soviet economy, especially its military sector. Although the conference provided the occasion for an in-depth analysis of a broad range of political, economic, and legal issues confronting the United States and its allies, the overarching theme of the forum was the *strategic* context and the security implications of West-East technology transfer. From the conference emerged a range of policy options.

The present volume represents an outgrowth of this forum. Its purpose is to make available to a broader audience, within government and outside, in the academic policy community and industry, the analysis and policy implications generated by formal presentations and the discussions that took place at the meeting. Each of the chapters has been revised to take account not only of the dialogue that occurred during the forum sessions, but also subsequent events.

v

Included is a chapter entitled "Technology Transfer to China: Where is the United States Headed?" by Denis Simon, commissioned after the conference in keeping with the editors' belief that China, especially in light of its extensive modernization program, is likely in the years ahead to play a role of increasing importance as an international actor and, in particular, to become a greater importer and exporter of technology. The editors have contributed a concluding chapter to assess both the emerging Soviet technology acquisition agenda and to summarize and synthesize the range of policy options that were discussed at the forum itself and are reflected in various chapters contained in this volume.

The editors express their deep appreciation to the J. Howard Pew Freedom Trust and to the Sarah Scaife Foundation, Inc., for the generous support and encouragement that made possible both the forum and this publication.

CONTENTS

PART 5: RECENT DEVELOPMENTS IN U.S. EXPORT CONTROL POLICY

PART 6: TECHNOLOGY TRANSFER AND U.S.–ALLIANCE RELATIONS

PART 7: CONCLUSIONS

PART 1

TECHNOLOGY TRANSFER AS A SECURITY PROBLEM

1

THE STRATEGIC IMPACT OF
TECHNOLOGY TRANSFERS

Richard N. Perle

Preparation of a book on this subject—much less one treating the subject in such great depth, as reflected by the contents of this volume—would not have been undertaken even as recently as three or four years ago. Yet it is a terribly important topic, and should have been on the national agenda a good deal earlier. The fact that so many people are devoting their time and energy to an examination of this topic is a tribute both to the importance of the issue and, if I may say so, to the work of the present administration in placing this issue on the national agenda.

The first and most important point about this subject is that our defense, and the defense of the Western Alliance generally, depends on the quality of our military technology. We are not now able, and we will not be able in the future, to keep pace with the Soviet Union tank for tank, artillery piece for artillery piece, or plane for plane. We have depended, and I believe we will continue to depend, on weapons systems that, gun for gun, tank for tank, plane for plane, are superior to their Soviet equivalents. Without that margin of technical superiority, without the ability to turn out weapons systems that are competent to do the task for which they are designed efficiently and effectively, we will face a continually deteriorating military balance.

It is particularly troubling, therefore, that the more we observe the Soviet program to acquire Western technology for military purposes, the more closely and intensively we examine the Soviet structures devoted to this purpose and evaluate the threat thus created, the more concerned we have become. In releasing a report on this subject prepared by a number of different agencies,[1] Secretary of Defense Caspar Weinberger noted that until we had acquired the information on which this report is based, we had no idea how extensive the

3

Soviet collection effort has been. Perhaps more significantly, we had no idea how successful that effort has been.

The study introduced by Secretary Weinberger is based (as I think any careful reader of it will observe) on a close examination of documentary evidence. I would note that the study was prepared by a group of government agencies that sometimes disagree with one another; on the substance of this report, however, they agreed entirely. The report relies heavily on what I think are startling facts, such as the evident use of Western technology in over 5,000 Soviet military research and development projects *in a single year*. This we know from Soviet sources. We know how extensively and in what detail the Soviets are able to target Western companies and institutions—down to the design teams within individual corporate entities—in order to acquire the technology they need to advance their own military purposes. We know how they assign responsibility, and how they select from among the KGB and the GRU (the specialized institutions working for the military-industrial complex [the VPK], the Academy of Sciences, and exchange programs) to assemble a tailor-made acquisition strategy for each individual target. We know also how they target human resources with great precision and sophistication to bring back to the Soviet Union the technology they need—technology we now increasingly see in first-line Soviet battle systems. The Soviets use a variety of devices. From time to time cases come to light that illustrate these techniques. Some of you may recall that within the last year or so a number of sophisticated pieces of data processing equipment embargoed for sale to the Soviet Union were intercepted en route, via a circuitous path that began in South Africa and would have ended in the Soviet Union had they not been discovered in Sweden and West Germany. It turned out that these shipments had been organized by a West German businessman, Richard Mueller, through a front organization located in South Africa. At last count, this was one of 77 such front organizations run by this one individual. Our estimate is that there are hundreds of these organizations throughout the Free World—some organized for a week, or a month, or a year—with the exclusive purpose of concluding a transaction that would be prohibited were the governments involved fully aware of the ultimate destination of the goods or services. We are, then, dealing with a massive Soviet effort involving literally thousands of individuals from dozens of Soviet intelligence organizations.

Soviet success has been considerable. Two or three months ago we released another study. It was contracted out by the Department of Defense for the purpose of making some estimate of the value to the Soviet Union, and thus the cost to the West, of Soviet technology acquisition efforts. The group that conducted the study used an interesting technique. They examined all of the licenses that had been requested for the transfer of high-technology equipment to the Soviet bloc over a 12-month period, license requests that had ultimately been rejected. We are not talking here about egregious cases where the Soviets at the outset would know that they would be forced to resort to illegal acquisition. From the beginning, the selection included the borderline cases in which the exporter thought there was a chance he might get a license.

This selection was winnowed down to about 70-odd specific license denials. Those cases were then analyzed to see what the impact on the relevant Soviet military-industrial capabilities would have been had the licenses been approved. Wherever assumptions had to be made (and in a study of this sort, of course, a number of assumptions must be made), they were conservative, at our insistence. Thus, only first-order effects on the Soviet military-industrial base were considered, and not the second- and third-order effects that would ensue.

The study concluded that over the lifetime of the technologies that would have been transferred *in a single year* had the licenses been granted, the Soviets would have saved some $13 billion in investment. The cost to the United States and its allies of improving our own military forces in order to overcome these Soviet advances would have been another $13 or $14 billion. That would have meant a net swing of $27 billion. Now, this was a very limited sample; it omitted some of the most interesting and important potential transfers. But we may safely conclude that the scope of the Soviet effort is great indeed.

It might be helpful to illustrate this point by citing some specific examples of losses that have occurred. We depend very heavily on air-to-air missiles. The AIM 9-L, a missile developed in the United States, was copied so perfectly by the Soviet Union that a design flaw in that missile was incorporated into the Soviet copy. What is striking about the Soviet acquisition of what was at the time our most advanced air-to-air missile (and which is, in its most recent versions, still a first-line air-to-air missile) is that the Soviets could neither have manufactured nor reverse-engineered it. They could not have replicated it at all *without* the production-line equipment necessary to make the sensors, the microprocessors, and the subassemblies. Upon close examination, these prove to have been exact copies of Western equipment.

We have satellite photographs of the Soviet space shuttle. In due course, I have no doubt that we will see the Soviets' own photographs of their space shuttle. You will be astonished when you see how similar it is to the U.S. space shuttle. This is hardly surprising; it is copied largely from our shuttle, even down to the surface tiles. This was the result of what, in my view, has been a wholly improvident publication policy on the part of the National Aeronautics and Space Administration (NASA), which has for years seen the global diffusion of advanced space technology as its mission. Thus the Soviet Union has had the benefit of a large part of our space program, and this access has been primarily used for military purposes.

The backbone of the Soviet computer system—the Ryad series of computers—is a copy of the IBM 360 series. As far as we can tell, the Soviets have continued their practice of basing advanced data processing equipment on American designs, and building them with American production line equipment. Though we do not always get intelligence of this sort, we have procured, in at least one case familiar to me, a photograph of the interior of a Soviet intelligence collection station, which is, even at this writing, intercepting military and other communications emanating from West Germany. When one looks at the array of equipment in that station, one finds our major microelectronics firms well represented. We only found out about this station when the Soviets had the gall to ask Hewlett-Packard to upgrade a piece of equipment they had acquired illegally. By sheer good luck, when this piece of equipment went back to the United Kingdom for upgrade, someone noticed it was not quite right. This led to its own conclusions, and the subsequent discovery of the equipment's true owners.

In the Soviet Union there is a city that enjoys the distinction of being the microelectronics capital of the communist world. It could not exist without production line equipment acquired in the United States, Japan, West Germany, Switzerland, Britain, and France. Without the 15 or so major production lines in Zelenograd, our military task would be vastly easier. The budgets available for our own military would produce a far more effective defense—which would, in my view, lead to a far more stable relationship between East and West.

When this administration came to office in 1981 and began looking at the system of export controls by which previous governments had sought to cope with this problem, we were, in varying degrees, horrified. First of all, we found an administrative and bureaucratic ineptitude that had justly earned the contempt of the American businessman. It was not in the least unusual for the system to lose files, make capricious decisions, or lose track of the status of license requests. It was understaffed, overworked, undermanaged, and appallingly inefficient.

We found upon our arrival that there was not a single computer dedicated to the purpose of administering the system of export controls in the United States. This in spite of the fact that the government was dealing with over 120,000 license applications a year. These applications were dealt with in hard copy, with couriers taking them back and forth. The average time to process a case was never less than 90 days, and often closer to six months to a year.

We have tried to improve this situation, and I think we have made considerable progress. We now have computers in a variety of roles; for example, tracking license requests, tracking intelligence about known diverters, and "alert list" monitoring computers programmed to pay special attention to technologies known to be high on the Soviet priority list. It is the job of this last section to detect anomalies when they occur. To illustrate the importance of this task, I will give you an example of an anomaly detected in this way. Eighty-seven helicopters manufactured by Hughes Helicopters wind up in North Korea. These helicopters are externally identical to the military helicopters operated by South Korean forces. The result of this, of course, is that South Korea has to send its own helicopters south, away from the demilitarized zone, to be sure that any helicopter seen flying in or south of the zone is hostile. The appropriate officials at Hughes believed they were selling these to a West German middleman, who in turn said he was selling them to an unidentified African country intending to use them for oil exploration. On the face of it, this was a wildly implausible story. Yet no license was required in this case, and approvals were given up and down the line.

Henceforth, this sort of anomaly should be far less frequent. We are now in a position to integrate the information we have about Soviet operations with requests for applications. In the past, many Soviet acquisitions have been based on commercial transactions. Now both the private and public sectors are doing a better job of preventing such acquisitions. The government is giving better service to the export community; exporters can now depend on reliable answers to their inquiries, furnished in record time. We now have an electronic bulletin board in the Department of Defense so that any exporter can, through a computer link, check the status of a license request pending for review by the department. A few years ago this was unheard of. We have also greatly increased the number of people in the Department of Defense working on export licenses. When I assumed this responsibility, there were only a handful of people in the department. We now have 110 people involved in the administration of export controls. With a little luck, this number will increase to the point where we will be able to do a competent job expeditiously.

Other departments of the government have been challenged by the energy shown in this area by the administration, and they too have adopted management reforms. As a result, we are now in a position to implement a policy with which there has been little disagreement. As I travel around the country and to various allied capitals, I have discovered that the biggest single complaint about the Western system of export controls is *not* the principle of denying to our enemies the means with which to magnify the threat they have imposed upon us. It is instead that this principle is meted out with such a cumbersome and inept administrative system. We have worked hard to gain the confidence of the business community. Without their support, it would be pointless to administer any system, regardless of its principles. By improving our own administrative practices, I believe we have regained their confidence.

Three years ago, the Central Intelligence Agency (CIA) had no unit whose sole responsibility was to look after Soviet bloc technology acquisitions. Today we have the Technology Transfer Intelligence Committee, to which 22 departments of the government contribute manpower and other resources. This committee is centered in the Central Intelligence Agency and has provided, for the first time, a systematic process for collecting and disseminating information.

Let me conclude with a word about the role of our allies and the efforts of this administration to address with them the question of technology security. The institution devoted to allied coordination of the commercial embargo on high technology to the Soviet Union is located in a once-obscure office in Paris (actually, an annex of the American Embassy). The Coordinating Committee—or, as it is more commonly known, "CoCom"—was founded 35 years ago.[2] Three or four years ago, CoCom had an annual operating budget of half a million dollars. This was for the *only* organization in the Western Alliance that brought together our advanced industrial societies in an attempt to coordinate controls on the flow of technology to the Soviet Union. Three years ago, CoCom had what must have been the last hand-cranked mimeograph machine in Western Europe. The staff was not sufficient for simultaneous translation, so it took twice as long to do everything, as the French insisted that all documentation be done in both French and English. It was an antiquated institution.

Though not noted for its endorsement of big bureaucracies, this administration has, nevertheless, been trying to strengthen this minuscule bureaucracy in Paris, and not unsuccessfully. We have added staff and have begun to professionalize the institution. We now communicate with CoCom by electronic means, instead of sending couriers over and back and spending two or three weeks in the process.

Additionally, our allies have begun to take the problem far more seriously than before. They have always agreed, in principle, that it makes little sense to make militarily sensitive technologies available to the Soviet Union. Because they lacked the knowledge and expertise which comes after years of studied concern, however, they seldom agreed on which technologies required control, and rarely came to the same conclusions at which we had long ago arrived. We have, therefore, encouraged our allies, and they have responded. If you go to London, you will now find a technology transfer unit in the Ministry of Defence that did not exist as recently as two years ago. There are 15 to 18 people busy at work there. The same thing is happening in Paris and in other European capitals. The result, in my view, is that the much-exaggerated tension between the United States and its West European allies on this issue is gradually dissipating, through continuing dialogue and through the information we are able to share with them.

Our allies have been struck, as we have, by the extent to which the Soviets have been successful predators, siphoning off their technology. The departure from France of 47 Soviet intelligence agents in April 1983, and of 31 such agents from the United Kingdom in the fall of 1985 (as well as similar departures from virtually every country in Europe), suggests that our allies are finally coming to grips with the problem of technological espionage.

Despite some critics, then, the United States is not destroying the alliance over the issue of technology controls. Indeed, apart from the very unfortunate controversy over the pipeline and the complicated aftermath of the Polish sanctions, the discussions we are having with our allies on the question of strategic trade controls have, on the whole, produced a very high degree of unity. Primarily because of U.S. Department of Defense urging, CoCom has established, for the first time, a group of defense experts within its own framework. This group will help give CoCom members the practical technical military assessments needed to ensure our control over those emerging technologies that would otherwise be used against us.

NOTES

1. *Soviet Acquisition of Militarily Significant Western Technology: An Update* (Washington, D.C.: U.S. Government Printing Office, September 1985).
2. CoCom stands for the Coordinating Committee of the Consultative Group of Nations, which coordinates trade controls over the export of strategic items to communist bloc countries. It is composed of all NATO countries (except Iceland) and Japan.

2

TECHNOLOGY TRANSFER AND NATIONAL SECURITY: FINDING THE PROPER BALANCE

Stephen Bryen

Had I been writing this paper six years ago, I would have given a very brief statement on the nature and scope of the problem of technology transfer, because, quite honestly, six years ago there was little recognition of the problem at high levels. This is not to say that there were not a number of people working in government who were both aware of and alarmed at the problem. In those days, however, these people lacked the capability to do anything with their knowledge. It is the hope of the Reagan administration that, if any changes have been made successfully in the past six years, it has been to provide that capability. In this way, we think we have made it possible to address a complex and difficult problem, one with enormous implications for our national security.

At the end of World War II, the United States was in the unique position of being able to resume a normal and healthy economic life while having the capability of defending our interests worldwide. This capability was the byproduct of our substantial wartime investment in scientific research, which paid off handsomely both in terms of military capabilities and commercial developments in the 1950s and on through the 1960s.

In consequence, we developed some interesting habits. One of them, which persists to this day, has come to characterize our national defense program in many ways. It is our heavy emphasis on a far more *compact* military, compact in terms of men and equipment. This emphasis has been based largely on our belief that the capacity and quality of our field equipment was vastly superior to that of any potential adversary—indeed, so superior as to afford the rather significant luxury of a far less burdensome military organization. One does not need to point out how nicely this fits with the traditional attitude held by democracies (strongly so in the American case) toward the proper amount of emphasis to place on the national defense.

Since that time, a great deal has changed. One very significant change is that the burden of research, placed for the most part on the military sector immediately after World War II, has now shifted decisively into the civilian sector. We have today the reverse of the situation that prevailed at the end of World War II. Rather than drawing on military research for commercial products, we are now drawing on commercial research for military products. Contrary to what one might think, there is a real gap between the sort of technology in fielded military weapons systems and the sort of technology immediately available to civilians in the United States and elsewhere throughout the world. For example, an IBM personal computer (or its equivalent) with large-scale integrated circuits and enormously advanced software capabilities can be bought in most computer stores. This computer will most likely have a higher capability than the small computers at work in most military systems. There is no question that the home computer is *technologically* better, simply by virtue of the fact that its development is far more recent. This sort of gap has created some challenging problems.

With this in mind, return for a moment to the end of World War II, and consider the circumstances faced by the Soviet Union. Technology-wise, the situation was not entirely dissimilar for the Soviets. Of course, they emerged from the war rather differently than did we. Their economy was devastated; millions and millions of their people had died.

The Soviets, seeing before them an enormous reconstruction effort, began acquiring a great deal of technology at the end of the war. Some of it was ours, given through Lend-Lease and other programs. Some of it was German, acquired through a program to transfer physically, and in some cases bodily, a large portion of the Nazi scientific establishment to the Soviet Union. Whole factories were removed to locations east of the border. The Zeiss factory, for example, was packed up brick by brick (the bricks were numbered) and shipped to the Soviet Union.

From this position, the Soviets began the reconstruction of their productive capacity. The difference, however, was—and remains—that they focused their efforts on the rapid development of their military capabilities. In our own case, though the technological edge remained in defense-related technology, our emphasis on growth and development was in the civilian sector.

The final result of this was the situation that prevails today—that is, the technological edge has itself shifted, as one would expect, into the area of higher growth, the civilian sector. I suggest that this situation has presented us with a number of challenges. Most significant among these is that the Soviets themselves realize that this shift has taken place. They are aware of the tremendous technological richness of the Western civilian sector; they are equally aware that this sector is, to a certain extent, accessible. This accessibility is very important to them. The primary motive driving the Soviets to take advantage of this accessibility is a desire to match, if not exceed, the capabilities of our military programs. From the Soviet perspective, the achievement of technological parity is essentially the achievement of military superiority. This is so because they will field a far larger number of weapons systems than will we. They will put more of each weapon in the field, and will make them far more available to allies and surrogates.

Fundamentally, if the Soviet Union is able to improve the technological capacity of its weapons systems, serious implications for our security, and the security of those who depend on us, will result. Moreover, the large capacity of the Soviet military infrastructure—clearly demonstrated in solving the logistical problems of resupply during the 1973 Arab-Israeli War—vastly outstrips our ability to produce high-technology weapons systems quickly and deliver them to friends in need. We must make the difficult choice of meeting their needs by depleting our own supply base, or of offering very little more than moral support.

With this background, we can turn to an examination of the Soviet program to acquire Western technology. Perhaps the best way to begin is with some examples. In 1970, the United States was well along on what could be called the "semiconductor revolution." We were producing a large variety of integrated circuits, which were being utilized in both military and civilian pursuits. In fact, the first military use of integrated circuits was in our strategic rocket arsenal, where they were part of the on-board guidance system of the Minuteman missile.

The Soviets realized that to achieve similar levels of accuracy and performance, in strategic missiles as well as conventional systems, it would be necessary to use integrated circuits. In 1970, there was no factory in the Soviet Union capable of producing integrated circuits. Moreover, both the United States and Western Europe had in place a system of export barriers intended to prevent the transfer of these kinds of capabilities.

A number of appeals were made by the Soviet Union directly, and on behalf of its Eastern allies, to loosen these restrictions, thus allowing some transfer of information and training (perhaps even some factories) to produce integrated circuits for civilian use. In 1973 and 1974, the Soviets were able to convince Western leaders that this would be consistent with the logic of détente, that it would help to "weave a web of golden threads" (to use some famous, or infamous, words) around the raw elements of the superpower struggle. This web of commercial interests would then serve to lessen, or at least contain, the conflict of political interests, leading inevitably to some sort of unified single system brought about by a merger of these two rather disparate systems.

The result of all this was the approval, at the very highest levels of the U.S. government, of projects to transfer to the Soviet Union the capacity to build semiconductor factories. First, the French sold one to Poland; then, the British sold one to Hungary. Finally, the United States sold to everybody. In consequence, within the space of a decade—from 1970 to 1980—the Soviets built more than 20 such factories, each running at full steam. They are now able to produce at least medium-scale integrated circuits and, in certain cases, more than this.

What does this mean in military terms? Roughly 90% of the output of these factories goes into either Soviet weapons systems *directly,* or into the industries needed to produce these weapons, thus greatly assisting productivity. Precious little is left over for those civilian projects we were originally sold on—wristwatches, "intelligent" sewing machines, and so forth.

This also means that the increment of technological sophistication between our arsenal and theirs—that gap upon which we have staked so much of our security—has narrowed considerably. Another case in point will serve to illustrate. Around 1973, we developed a "look-down, shoot-down" radar system. This system was first deployed in the F-15 aircraft. As one would imagine, it was comprised of integrated circuits—medium-scale circuits, to be precise. This system gave our aircraft the ability to fly over adversary aircraft, using the radar to look down. Conventional radar had always been limited in its effectiveness by the problem of noise, or ground clutter, which obscured what was being tracked. The on-board computer in the look-down, shoot-down system can sort out this extraneous information, leaving only the track of the adversary's aircraft. One can get an idea of its importance by recalling that in 1980, Israeli aircraft equipped with the system had occasion to use it against Syrian aircraft not so equipped. The scorecard in this engagement ended up at 80 to zero.

There are 4,778 integrated circuits in the computer that runs the look-down, shoot-down system. The Soviets now have this capability because we gave them the techniques to produce these integrated circuits, as well as the ability to assemble them into the required configuration. That they have this capability is a result of the fact that we gave them the techniques to produce the circuits in the first place. In real terms, this means that in any future conflict between Soviet and Western air forces, an advantage in this crucial area no longer exists. We are now faced, at considerable expense, with finding some way to recapture the advantage.

The difficulty here is that as the difference in technological capabilities becomes even smaller, it also becomes increasingly expensive to redress. We are currently embarked on a program to rectify the loss of the look-down, shoot-down system with the Very High-Speed Integrated Circuit program (VHSIC). This system will be a tremendous financial investment, however, and will not even be available for deployment until the beginning of the next decade. In the meantime, Congress levels accusations about the tremendous cost of modern weapons systems, and the seeming failure of these systems to perform the missions for which they were designed—at least, for as long as they were intended to fulfill those missions. But this should not surprise anyone, given an understanding that the "window of technology" is indeed closing.

The Soviets understand precisely the difficult dilemma facing Western governments, which are continually seeking cost-effective methods of resolving their own security problems. The Kremlin has embarked on a large, two-part effort to acquire Western technology. One part of it is run by the Soviet Military-Industrial Commission, known by its Cyrillic initials as the "VPK." Its purpose is to collect everything from classified documents to proprietary information about and from Western companies. Drawings, blueprints, one-of-a-kind examples of various systems—whatever we leave lying around is fair game.

U.S. systems are the first and most important target in this effort; European developments rank a close second. The Soviets maintain a staff of over 100,000 people just to translate Western documents. This certainly does not indicate a dearth of Western documents. While it may seem huge, this effort has, by their own estimates, saved them billions of rubles. We have also attempted to compute the value of this project in dollars, and have arrived at a figure of roughly $10 billion. This is not only a savings in resources available for scientific research. It also allows the Soviets to redirect the focus of this research to areas that we cannot at the moment address. In short, they no longer have to spend time and effort reinventing the wheel. They have the freedom to develop technologies that pose real challenges for us—new types of cruise missiles, new types of strategic missiles, new types of submarines, and so forth.

The second aspect of the Soviet program is probably the one most familiar to those studying these issues. It is run by the Ministry of Foreign Trade, with the cooperation of the intelligence services. The intelligence services are part of the VPK effort as well. The purpose of this second dimension is to acquire the wherewithal to exploit the technologies once they have been acquired. This involves building up the necessary infrastructure, developing the required facilities, locating the necessary software, and other related efforts.

This aspect of the Soviet effort has met with considerable success. However, we also have enjoyed considerable success of late in closing down their avenues of access to Western computers, microelectronic manufacturing equipment, and other sensitive manufacturing techniques. We have certainly halted many of the legal transactions. An important point to emphasize here is that we no longer allow whole factories to be transferred to the Soviet Union. This point may appear to be so obvious as not to merit attention. In my view, however, this will be an accomplishment of which, in the long term, we and our allies will justifiably be proud.

After all, it is one thing to steal a piece of high technology, and quite another to make it work. There are bugs to ferret out and spare parts to be found. The Kama River Truck Factory, with which many are familiar, is not operating at nearly the level for which it was designed. In fact, it is achieving only about 25% of its capacity. The reason for this is clear enough—there are far fewer Western technicians and engineers there to bring the plant up to full capacity. This difficulty is compounded in cases where direct threat is involved.

That is the positive side. There is, of course, a negative side. It is that, in response to the closing down of legal avenues of transfer, the Soviets have substantially increased their targeting of Western materiel through illegal means—both in terms of the volume of technology now sought and the resources devoted to its acquisition. And they are taking advantage of the disparities that exist in enforcement systems between alliance nations and other friendly countries.

We have developed a number of responses to this problem. The first has been our effort to strengthen the international Coordinating Committee, or CoCom, based in Paris. In this area, I believe real progress has been made. A second step has been encouraging the CoCom nations to strengthen their own enforcement systems. Here the results have been mixed. Those nations which have responded to our encouragement are now playing a truly vital role. Special note must be taken of our British colleagues, who have apprehended one of the two biggest "technobandits" in this business. Werner Bruchhausen is now sitting in a British jail, thanks to the increasingly vigilant efforts of our British allies.

Domestically, we have begun to take steps to increase greatly the penalty to Western businessmen involved with the KGB. We feel that this will be an effective deterrent to "future Werner Bruchhausens." Some of our CoCom partners have pursued a similar course, and, again, Britain should be singled out as notable among them.

A second aspect of our response has been in relations with non-CoCom countries. There are a large number of non-CoCom countries through which high technology passes. With some of the neutral countries, we have reached arrangements whereby these sensitive items no longer pass through with such ease. As these neutral countries have in the past been major conduits for Western materiel going East, these are significant steps indeed. In some few cases, we have actually managed to get prosecutions under the laws of these countries. Sweden has jailed two individuals for attempting to pass technology to the Soviet bloc; Austria has passed a new law making it illegal to traffic in such defense-related materials.

There is still, however, a long way to go. Recognizing the sophistication of the Soviet program, and the implications for us, we must not lose sight of the complex and difficult challenges we are called upon to answer. We must staunch the flow of this most valuable and unique Western resource. This administration is resolved to meet the challenge. We are determined to broaden and strengthen our efforts to assure the inviolability of the technological achievements upon which our security depends.

TECHNOLOGY TRANSFER AND SOVIET MILITARY R&D

Jack Vorona

The all-too-successful efforts of the Soviet Union to obtain scientific knowledge and advanced hardware from the West have been highlighted by Secretary of Defense Caspar Weinberger's release of a special report on the subject, entitled *Soviet Acquisition of Militarily Significant Western Technology: An Update.* This chapter has as its focus the system within which the Soviet Union assimilates the technology that it acquires, regardless of source, into new weapons. There are those who are inclined to believe that the great influx of Western technology into the USSR will confuse if not choke them. On the contrary: The purpose of this chapter is to demonstrate that the Soviet Union has evolved a process that is highly effective in evaluating and exploiting our technology.

To begin with, it is a system driven from the top. The Soviet leadership views science and technology as bearing directly on national power—economic, political, and military. In addressing the Twenty-third Party Congress in 1966, Secretary-General Leonid Brezhnev stated, "Science and technology have made it possible for us to create a powerful, qualitative new material and technical base. Our superiority in the latest types of military technology is a fact, comrades, and one can't escape facts." Several years later, Brezhnev, in his 1971 address to the Soviet Academy of Sciences, stated: "One can say without exaggeration that it is in this field, in the field of scientific and technical progress, that one of the main fronts of the historic contest of two systems lies today—at the present stage, questions of scientific and technical progress acquire, to put it bluntly, a decisive importance." The top echelon of Soviet management comes to this appreciation quite naturally—75% of the Politburo and an even greater portion of the Council of Ministers have technical backgrounds.

As the sector receiving the highest priority, military R&D receives large and regular infusions of capital investment, and is provided the latest, most advanced equipment from domestic and foreign sources. Moreover, it handpicks the best science and engineering graduates for its programs. Through an unparalleled commitment of national resources, the Soviet Union has produced an impressive variety of technologically advanced weaponry. Its national resources include, in a vital way, Soviet intelligence collection assets.

Acquisition of Western military equipment was an essential Soviet policy in the mid-1930s, expanded during the Lend-Lease era of World War II, and brought to the state of a fine art during the past 20 years. In effect, the USSR has institutionalized what amounts to industrial espionage and has put it on a rigorous, business-like basis replete with annual cost-benefit analyses. This is not to imply that the Soviet Union is mindlessly dependent on the Free World to advance its industrial base and military capabilities. While this was probably an accurate description during the 1940s and 1950s, it does not approximate today's (or tomorrow's) reality. The Soviets react to a specific requirement by first amassing data on the best technical approaches. Then, based on their military doctrine, assessed limitations in supporting technologies, and perceived difficulties in production and maintenance, a weapons system uniquely Russian is born. In some instances, its Western parentage is obvious; in others, one could only tell by detailed examination.

It is necessary to provide some insight into the development process of the Soviet weapons system and the important players. The allocation and control of Soviet R&D resources is carried out by two intertwined bureaucracies, the Communist Party and the government. Ultimately, the Politburo of the Communist Party makes the key policy decisions on directions for Soviet military R&D. The Council of Ministers, the top executive organ of the government, is responsible for its day-to-day operations.

The Soviet economy is functionally managed by over 30 major ministries. Nine of these are the prime performers of military-related research, development, testing, and production, with each responsible for a selected family of weapons. Each strives for self-sufficiency to improve chances for meeting its all-important annual and Five-Year Plan goals. To this end, each ministry has its own research institutes, design bureaus, and production facilities. Although legendary inefficiency permeates Soviet civil industry, bureaucratic impediments are, to a large extent, absent in the defense sector.

The military is deeply involved in every aspect of the weapons acquisition process. Each of the military services has one or more directorates charged with managing its weapons developments. To support this function, these directorates maintain their own research institutes, which provide the technical expertise to manage weapons programs. These institutes link the military consumer, his requirement, and the weapon developer. In so doing, they appear to act as a means to stimulate contact among the various functional elements of the ministry.

The premier establishments of the civilian science sector are the 200 research institutes of the Soviet Academy of Sciences. Their primary focus is on basic and exploratory research. We have detected a trend of increasing Academy involvement with the Ministry of Defense—implying to us a greater emphasis by the military on state-of-the-art hardware and technological breakthroughs. In fact, this is not at all surprising because, as science progresses, the boundary between research and engineering becomes increasingly blurred.

The Council of Ministers has created several special commissions concerned with important sectors of the economy. The most powerful of these is the Military Industrial Commission, the VPK. As monitor and coordinator of all military R&D and production, the VPK reviews new weapons proposals both for technical feasibility and production requirements. The VPK is also instrumental in planning and supervising major programs with military application, such as the development and manufacture of integrated circuits. In addition, it is particularly important that the VPK actually manages the acquisition of Free World technology for all military programs. It coordinates and validates requirements for Western technological know-how and equipment, which will be used to advance the state-of-the-art of Soviet weaponry. It receives these requirements from the defense industrial ministries, levies them on the appropriate collection organizations—be they the KGB, the GRU, the Academy of Sciences, or the Ministry of Foreign Trade—and closely monitors and evaluates their satisfaction.

The value the VPK places on Free World technology is illustrated by a document released by France in the spring of 1985. This report was based on a classified Soviet study, one of several acquired by the French government, and which led directly to the expulsion from France of 47 Soviet agents in April 1983. It shows the savings in rubles (in this case 48.6 million) achieved in just one year, 1979, by one ministry—the Ministry of the Aviation Industry—by the use of Western technology. The disclosure went on to say, "Among the fighter aircraft whose construction was accelerated thanks to stolen Western technologies are the MiG-29, the Su-27, and the Su-25. The Soviet report said that engineers had succeeded in using Western techniques to overcome development problems on the Su-25 fighter, which was put into service at the beginning of the decade by assisting in the construction of a high-performance wing." The Su-25 is the Soviet version of our ground-attack bomber, the A-10, and has been undergoing combat trials in Afghanistan.

The State Committee for Science and Technology (GKNT), another special commission, was established to plan and monitor scientific R&D and to coordinate the introduction of technological innovations throughout the economy. It appears that, with respect to technology transfer, the GKNT has a complementary role to that of the VPK, coordinating the collection and efficient use of dual-purpose Western hardware for industrial applications. It is also instrumental in arranging for S&T bilateral agreements with individual Western nations—a technique that we have come to recognize as yet another means of satisfying the VPK's collection requirements.

With respect to the actual weapons development cycle, there is a logical sequence of research, requirement, design, engineering, and testing that is followed by both the United States and the Soviet Union. It is possible to identify a number of similarities in the processes each nation uses, including a research base, top management review of each development phase, formal documentation for each major phase, and rigorous testing throughout.

Despite these commonalities, the Soviet military R&D system is inherently different from that of the United States in several important ways.

1. It is totally government owned and controlled.
2. In the U.S. process, the major approval of resources to proceed with full-scale development is the Milestone II decision of the Defense System Acquisition Review Council. In the Soviet Union, it is the Joint Decree of the Central Committee and Council of Ministers. It is important to note that the Joint Decree is the *only major approval* required in the Soviet process, and it occurs at the beginning of the development cycle. Conversely, the Milestone II decision is just one of three major approvals required by the United States.
3. While U.S. resource commitments for defense programs are revisited on an annual basis because of congressional budgetary approval requirements, Soviet resources are committed for the full program to include development, testing, and production by the issuance of the single Joint Decree.

Soviet weapons development is, however, characterized by an inherently conservative approach. Although we are seeing increasingly advanced technologies appearing in the newer Soviet weapons, one of the salient characteristics of their system continues to be the control and minimization of risk. An important technique the Soviets use to control risk is a formal process outlining the steps to be taken by any development project. Formally codified in the late 1960s in a series of national-level State Standards (GOST), these procedures establish inflexible requirements for all forms of research, design, and production. Included are specific directives on each step of the process from requirement generation through draft and engineering designs, development of blueprints and prototypes, several levels of testing, and production. These standards are closely adhered to by the defense industry, and the criteria emphasized are completely consistent with observed Soviet weapon characteristics. Every project progresses according to a stipulated sequence that specifies tasks to be carried out in each phase, review procedures by the consumer, and state acceptance trials. With each succeeding step, the technical alternatives become more narrowly defined, and less research-oriented.

An important aspect of the Soviet military R&D environment is the fact that the major customer, the Ministry of Defense, closely monitors the product throughout its development cycle. This is a unique privilege not accorded to any other sector of the Soviet economy. The military can demand that a project be delivered as promised and on schedule. Although vigorous negotiations precede a ministry's acceptance of a project, the responsible organization is expected to deliver the weapons system on time and according to specification. As a result, the top programmatic priority in Soviet weapons acquisition is meeting project schedules. Because of this imperative, their weapons designers are understandably reluctant to inject unproven technology into their programs. But they place great confidence in the ability of American R&D to help solve their problems.

When the Soviets initiated design of the AN-124 (their version of the C-5A) in the early 1970s, they were lacking a critical technology—that of a high-thrust, high-bypass ratio engine. Still, they pursued the aircraft's development, obviously counting on acquiring the know-how from outside sources. They attempted to buy both the Rolls-Royce RB211 and GE CF6 engines, as well as the ceramic core turbine blade-casting technology, and were unsuccessful on all counts. This case represents a success story for Western control efforts, because it was not until the 1985 Paris Air Show that the AN-124 finally appeared with a high-thrust, high-bypass ratio engine. Betting on the outcome as they did must have given the Antonov Design Bureau many anxious moments.

On the whole, technology transfer has unfortunately been a Soviet success story. The Soviet commitment to develop and field airborne pulse Doppler radar technology on their newest-generation fighter aircraft was probably made in the early 1960s. The significance of such a radar is its ability to detect low-flying targets otherwise invisible against ground clutter. But to do this requires sophisticated signal processing—impossible in an airborne platform without the benefit of microelectronics. Relying solely on their indigenous and primitive microelectronics industry would have been a very high-risk prospect for Soviet decisionmakers. The evidence strongly indicates that their decision to proceed correctly assumed acquisition from the West, which allowed the Soviets to leapfrog in time and technology. Actually, they had no other choice if they wished to field a defense against low-flying penetrators as soon as possible.

Although Soviet design philosophy typically calls for evolutionary improvement, the Soviets can, on occasion, be innovative where they perceive the need. There is evidence that there are parallel design processes and organizational structures used in the cases of high-risk/high-payoff ventures. The titanium-hulled Alpha submarine with its high-propulsion density, liquid metal-cooled nuclear reactor was one such example. Work on designing this high-speed boat must have begun during the mid-1950s—at that time a very chancy venture.

Due to the pressures of the timeline, Soviet designers face strong incentives to use proven technologies that can be counted on to perform to acceptable, though perhaps not state-of-the-art, standards. Design handbooks, produced by the research institutes in close coordination with the design bureaus, closely control the choice of technologies, components, and manufacturing techniques. They are, in fact, the designer's bible. But even with such a document in hand, the designer is required to conduct a comprehensive investigation of the worldwide state-of-the-art in all candidate technologies applicable to the system under consideration. If an indigenous off-the-shelf technology is not available, the designer will seek a proven foreign capability. If, and only if, a designer cannot find a proven domestic or imported technology will he seek to develop a new one through the Soviet R & D community. No doubt this was the philosophy which drove them to acquire the Western microelectronics design and production know-how just mentioned.

Translating new technology into Soviet weapons systems is thus complicated by two seemingly incompatible factors: the intrinsic conservatism of Soviet design practices versus their increasing inclination to optimize system performance by exploiting new technology. To resolve this dichotomy, the Soviets generally implement new technology by continuous modification of existing systems—a procedure which is entirely consistent with their evolutionary approach to weapons development. Although conceivably they could inject new technologies at nearly any stage of the development process, in practice they tend to freeze the level of technology considerably earlier in the design cycle than does the United States. They do this knowing full well that new technology will be applied to follow-ons when that technology is mature and risk is greatly reduced. In some cases, these modifications are at work even before the parent system is fielded.

The special report mentioned earlier contains literally hundreds of examples cited by the Soviets in which their weapons systems have benefited from the exploitation of Western technology. It is a distressing litany that includes the T-64, T-72, and T-80 tanks, an advanced fire-control radar for their new fighters, new aircraft carrier catapults, submarine-quieting equipment, radar-absorbing coatings, navigation satellites, carbon-carbon nose tips for reentry vehicles, fiber optics, ASW torpedoes, and advanced electronics for on-board weapons systems. In particular, of all the many examples described in the U.S. government report, microelectronics and computers have had the most pervasive impact. Not only do they greatly enhance weapons system performance, but they are also an invaluable tool to the engineer in developing even more optimal designs. It is readily apparent that the Soviets have evolved a research, development, and acquisition process ideally suited for exploitation of the West's technology. To feed this system, they have created an intricate and effective collection apparatus that can be vectored, in pinpoint fashion, against Western targets. They have done their homework well.

Forty years ago, the Soviets simply replicated Western hardware. Their TU-4 bomber was a slavish copy of the B-29 down to the bumps and dents. During the past 10 to 20 years, along with a growing technical sophistication, the Soviet Union has become much more selective in its acquisitions. For example, U.S. microelectronics has given Soviet ground-based air defense systems significant and unique capabilities. Most recently, we have seen an increasing tendency on the part of the Soviets to target academic institutions where the more basic science is done,. It would appear that Soviet collection efforts are looking further back along the research trail; this implies to us a greater tendency on their part toward increasingly innovative weapons systems.

In sum, we have long recognized that technology transfer is used by the Soviet Union to improve its defense posture. However, only in recent years have we come to appreciate the extent and importance of such transfer. By incorporating the West's R&D advances, they have greatly magnified the effectiveness of their weapons and countermeasures designers. The Soviets are not 12 feet tall, but they do achieve additional stature by standing in our shoes. We know that virtually every Soviet long- and short-term research project for military systems, numbering well over 5000 in the early 1980s, is benefiting from Western documents and hardware, and this knowledge is causing the U.S. intelligence community to rethink old shibboleths. One of these is the dictum never to mirror image, unless all else fails. Now it appears that—at least as a first-order response—it might not be such a bad idea. Without a doubt, the Soviets have been very clever and methodical in all of this. The huge and still growing Soviet military R&D structure could not sustain itself at its present level of effectiveness without the benefit of Western input. The formidable task facing the West now is to respond in such a way that the Soviet Union is forced to rely more heavily on its own assets. Otherwise, we are likely to confront increasing examples of technological crossover, whereby the assimilation of U.S. technology results in Soviet weapons systems superior to our own.

PART 2

SOVIET NEEDS AND ACQUISITION METHODS

4

GORBACHEV'S DOMESTIC ECONOMIC STRATEGY AND EAST-WEST COMMERCIAL CONNECTIONS

John P. Hardt

OVERVIEW

Gorbachev as a Leninist Modernizer[1]

Mikhail Gorbachev represents the post-World War II generation in the USSR. By invoking the style of Lenin, he is attempting to rekindle the perceived revolutionary élan that had previously imbued many Soviet citizens and leaders alike with enthusiasm, discipline, and optimism; he may also be preparing the ideological and political grounds for significant changes in the economic system.

- Ideologically, Gorbachev's new strategy resembles that of Lenin during the New Economic Policy of the early 1920s, which emphasized a withdrawal of central planning to the "commanding heights" of a more decentralized system based on increased top leadership guidance and oversight.
- Gorbachev's rule may usher in a new stage or epoch for the Soviet economy: a shift from Stalinist extensive development to intensive growth. The adoption of modernization and efficiency as economic criteria may result in

increases in quality, as well as increases in quantity. If economic modernization is the principal aim of the Gorbachev leadership, the USSR might, in time, join the Western industrial nations as an economic and technological superpower.

- In order to approach Western levels of efficiency in a market-stimulating economy, changes would need to be introduced within the Marxist-Leninist political system, which guides and controls the Soviet economy. The twin objectives of improved economic efficiency and maintenance of the political system may prove to be mutually exclusive in the future as they have seemed to be in the past. Devolution of ministerial and regional party responsibility and authority to economic enterprises appears to be essential to this change in management.
- Such a new Gorbachevian economic formula would require a new environment conducive to technological dynamism, an information revolution, and increased efficiency in the manner in which imported Western technology is absorbed, adapted, and integrated into the Soviet economic system. This would be facilitated by a heightened emphasis on economic modernization rather than on continued, rapid military growth—that is, a change in the classic "guns, growth, or butter" choice.
- The current Gorbachev strategy appears to emphasize short-term gains over long-term improvements: priority to Western regions with preexisting but aging capital, plants, and infrastructure over developing eastern and southern regions with abundant material and human resources; renovation of existing facilities over new, modern complexes. Sectors such as machine building are to be strengthened, while other sectors important to modernization are to be given lessened priorities. Moreover, the short-term strategy seems to center on energizing and potentially strengthening the ministerial system and local party role in the economy, which in the long term must be changed to effectuate the reforms Gorbachev has been calling for.

If, indeed, a politically acceptable growth rate is to be achieved in the foreseeable future on the basis of politically attainable change and if, subsequently, fundamental reform in the economic system is undertaken, it seems reasonable to assume that hard choices will be faced by the new leadership. Such choices may involve a shake-up of the major underpinnings of the Stalinist system, and the Soviet economy might then begin to enter what may be called the "economic modernization stage of Leninist development."

Psychologically, many in the new leadership would like to return to the Leninist image. Gorbachev presents himself as an intellectual favoring a newly rekindled Soviet spirit, calling for hard work and dedication from leaders and workers alike, and establishing new economic responsibility and accountability for the managers and workers as the ministers and regional political leaders recede toward what Lenin called "the commanding heights." Vladimir Ilyich Lenin, in a tactically brilliant speech which led to the Bolshevik seizure of power in 1917, promised the Russian people peace, bread, and land. If Gorbachev as Lenin's successor were now to offer

- a redirection of the heavy defense allocations to the peaceful purposes of modernizing the economy [peace];
- a significant improvement in meat, housing, and other attractive consumer goods [bread];
- an improved incentive system for plants and farms that gives the citizen a stake in the outcome of his economic enterprise [land],[2]

then the traditional essence of Leninism, as seen by many of the Bolsheviks in 1917, might be recaptured. Whatever formula Gorbachev ultimately chooses to follow, it should be assumed that it is likely to be couched in this Marxist-Leninist Soviet tradition. Lenin was not a Westernizer or a capitalist.

Gorbachev's strategy for the domestic economy is important in terms of both style and substance. The style is to project the Leninist image of intellectualism and to revive the Soviet spirit; in effect, to create a new Gorbachevian "efficient technocrat," a professional who upholds a work ethic, a competent manager who is accessible to subordinates, demanding, but fair.

The substance of the Gorbachev strategy is more complex. For each proposed economic change there appear to be offsetting costs, institutional and political. Style is not easily translated into substance, words to deeds; overcoming inertia and deep-seated skepticism is extremely difficult. However, if Gorbachev appears to be successful—and if he is lucky—he may develop what early Soviet leaders referred to as the "smell of success," which will enable him to command support in the party, the government, and among the populace. Success may facilitate a translation of style into substance. Economic success may assist Gorbachev in establishing himself firmly enough in power to risk significant systemic changes.

In the short run, perhaps through most of the next Five-Year Plan (1986-1990), Gorbachev's short-term strategy may show results. By putting professionally efficient and motivated people in charge and generating a work ethic in the Soviet society based on the increasing appearance of reward for accomplishment, the current system may be energized. Through a short-run strategy of centralizing economic policy and planning in the hands of handpicked Gorbachevian lieutenants, of selectively pruning the overgrown ministerial system, and of devolving some authority and responsibility to enterprises and collective farms, the performance of the system may be enhanced in terms of the growth of output and improved productivity measures.

Rising growth rates may give the impression of enhanced quality of performance. Centralization and computerization may give an impression of movement within the scientific and technical community and provide some results. Moreover, Soviet society may accept the idea that the system is moving toward a more just and responsive society.

Any short-term improvements, however, must be considered against the exceptionally low levels of performance of recent years and the comparatively low level of Soviet productivity by international standards. Recently, weather has had an especially negative effect on harvests and construction; industrial growth has been at a post-World War II low. And the popular spirit, the way of life, has been as depressed as the Kremlin's uninspiring, aged leaders.

Short-term economic success may, paradoxically, reduce the pressure for, and likelihood of, beneficial long-term changes in the system. Systemic changes require the effective adoption of new success indicators:

- Better allocation of resources requires accurate measures of cost and revenues, and simulation of a marketplace—essentially, a price system.
- Rationalization and decentralization of management should be based on profitability criteria that provide the central planning authorities with an effective measure of accountability and oversight.
- A scientific and technical environment that fosters innovation and scientific communication and rewards those responsible for technological advancement requires criteria such as the world market provides Western industrial economies.

Faced with the problems of reforming the economic bureaucracy, especially streamlining the formidable ministerial system and curbing the regional and local party organs from intervening in the management system, Gorbachev may not stop short of pursuing the fundamental changes necessary for putting the USSR in the ranks of modern industrial economies. He may use the power accumulated by personnel changes and political success to realize a vision of an efficient, technologically dynamic economy. Or, like Khrushchev, despite early successes, he may squander his political capital in other political-economic changes that do not provide long-term aid to the economy. In attempting to reform the economic, governmental, and party bureaucracy, he has one great advantage over most of his predecessors: The institutions he must change will be populated by his chosen cadres. By the time of the 27th Communist Party Congress in February 1986, many of the key economic administrators were Gorbachev's choices. Gorbachevian "efficient technocrats" may be able and willing to accept market-stimulating change. They may give Gorbachev the option of reconstituting the roles of government and party in the Soviet economy, and they may aid him in exercising that option. Gorbachev's appointees may represent a new class of economic bureaucrats not only able to perform in a changed environment but committed to the process of economic change—an interest group for reform.

Ironically, the pressure that pushes Gorbachev to make the necessary systemic changes may be generated by the United States. Only by basic, long-term changes can the Soviet Union keep up in the scientific and technological race as an economic superpower. Moreover, in view of the dynamic character of military technology, falling further behind in the scientific and technological revolution would erode the long-term security of the USSR as a military superpower.

Gorbachev's Preferred Commercial Strategy: Eastern Consensus and Trade Facilitation

As Gorbachev continues to establish and solidify his domestic power, he will probably attempt to reassert Soviet control over the East European allies, which had been loosened during the interregnum. In this process he faces policy dilemmas not dissimilar to those faced by leaders in the West: How should the trade advantages of closer East-West interdependence be weighed against the diplomatic gains that might be achieved through exploiting political-economic differences among developed countries in the West? How should the economic benefits of closer Western economic relations be weighed against the security problems of Eastern dependency and vulnerability resulting from interdependence?

Gorbachev's cost-benefit calculus for relating trade and diplomacy, trade and security will be related in part to the priority given to domestic economic and technological improvement; that is, how high does improvement in economic performance in the USSR and throughout Eastern Europe rank in his strategy for enhancing his own position? What foreign economic strategy will be most advantageous for furthering his domestic economic priorities? The commercial policy most advantageous to Gorbachev's domestic strategy would be a policy of East-West trade facilitation based on a bilateral U.S.-Soviet understanding on trade. The Soviet Union, like the United States, can more easily persuade its allies to adhere to a policy of trade facilitation than a policy of trade restriction.

One must also ask how the contributions of the Council for Mutual Economic Assistance (CMEA) allies relate to the above Soviet dilemmas. Is Eastern Europe a burden or an asset in economic and security terms? What must Gorbachev do to improve his net Eastern European assessment? The CMEA-Six tend to favor economic détente and limited usage of trade in Eastern diplomacy; they tend to prefer more East-West economic interrelation, and are less concerned than the Soviet Union about vulnerability and dependency on trade relations with the West.

Political gains may flow, to be sure, from exploiting a divided Western policy. These gains, however, might be more than offset by the commercial losses generated by a mixed Western policy of restriction and facilitation.

A preferred Gorbachev commercial strategy that complements his domestic strategy would be one that facilitated expanding trade with the United States and other Western countries. A stable trade facilitation policy encouraging both an Eastern and Western consensus might include the following:

- A delineation of Eastern import needs, sensitive to Western security concerns, that deemphasizes noncommercial transfers, especially industrial espionage;
- Long-term agreements involving assurances of contract sanctity and government-private commercial partnerships; and
- A shift in import policy from materials to machinery and from products to systems.

Gorbachev's Domestic and Commercial Strategies Important to U.S. Policy Formulation

With his ascendancy to the pinnacle of Soviet power, Mikhail Gorbachev brings a new look to Soviet foreign as well as domestic economic policy. His general political-economic approach is important because it will affect even the details of commercial policy changes, that is, the determination of contracts for imports, exports, and credits. Moreover, Gorbachev may directly initiate and consummate foreign economic transactions. His Western counterparts in Washington and elsewhere may influence—that is, facilitate or restrict—trade, but are usually not directly involved in negotiating commercial contracts or transfers of technology. The Soviet leadership, following its own perceived interests, decides whether to put oil or other commodities or products on the world market. It also makes the decisions that determine which part of the domestic programs will be supplied by foreign imports. If Gorbachev decides not to buy from or sell to the United States, there will not be a Soviet market for American goods. To paraphrase Ronald Reagan, "It takes two to trade." Therefore, any assessment of U.S. commercial relations with the USSR should give major consideration to the premises and parameters of Soviet commercial policy.

Because of large domestic and CMEA production and wide foreign availability of supplies, the Soviet leadership has a broad range of choices for the twelfth Five-Year Plan (1986-1990). There is usually some source in the West willing to supply nonmilitary imports. As the major Soviet exports—oil, gas, arms, and gold—are not purchased by the United States, the pattern of Soviet sales to the West is, by and large, not directly influenced by the United States. Soviet exports and imports are tradeable with many other Western countries. If the United States follows a restrictive policy, the Soviet Union may use trade policy as an instrument to divide further Western policy. American policy may be most effective in conditioning or responding to Soviet policy, if there is a Western consensus and coordinated action. A Western consensus on commercial policy appears more likely under circumstances of trade facilitation than trade restriction.

GORBACHEV'S DOMESTIC STRATEGY

Modernization of Planning and Management—the Emergence of the "Efficient Technocrat"

Stalin said "cadres are everything." Gorbachev's cadres may not only be his people, dependent on his support for power, but also a different type of economic bureaucrat. Gorbachev's choices may signal new role models for his economic bureaucracy.

There has been a relatively quiet purge of the Soviet economic bureaucracy: A new team is being brought in at most of the highest levels, as well as throughout the ministerial and enterprise bureaucracy. Part of the change, of course, has been political, that is, bringing in cadres and top leadership dependent on Gorbachev for their positions. But the change seems to be more than just political in nature. If the Brezhnev cadre may fairly be characterized as *ideologically loyal apparatchiks,* then the role model of the new Gorbachev cadre may be characterized as *efficient technocrats.*[3]

Gorbachev comes to power at an unprecedented time of change within the top leadership. The "Oaks of Party Tradition" (i.e., Brezhnev, Chernenko, Ustinov, Kirilenko, Kosygin, Suslov, Gromyko, Tikhanov) have all fallen from the pinnacle of power, physically or politically. His major rivals have been removed, such as Romanov. With new "Barons," the institutional and regional party cadres are open to change. The regional Leningrad and Ukrainian apparatuses seemed set for conversion to the Gorbachev image when, soon after taking over in March 1985, Gorbachev made key policy statements in Leningrad and Kiev.

The generation of men which came to power with Brezhnev 20 years ago has clung tenaciously to power, not only at the highest levels of party leadership, but throughout the party hierarchy and government bureaucracy, and as directors of enterprises and institutes nationwide, protected by the gerontocracy in the Kremlin. Now actuarial inevitability is being accelerated by the political pressure of the younger Gorbachevian men at the top who seek to bring their allies, colleagues, and protégées into positions of power, as Brezhnev and his clique did two decades ago. The result is a period of rapid nationwide personnel turnover from top to bottom. Since the convening of the 27th Party Congress in February 1986, the party membership may be well on its way toward becoming Gorbachevian. If this proves to be true, Gorbachev might be said to have accomplished in the short time of two or three years what Stalin took almost a decade to achieve—that is, choose his own party and governmental cadres, the result of which led some to call Stalin's 17th Party Congress in 1934 the "Congress of the Victors."

Will such a generational change have genuine political-economic significance? Many of those who say "yes" believe that the new generation of leaders will be better educated, more pragmatic, dynamic, result oriented, and less obsessed with the trauma of World War II. Gorbachev is the first superpower leader too young to have fought in World War II, and the first Soviet leader since Lenin with a formal higher education. In spite of the appearances of change, many others feel that Gorbachev and his lieutenants are products of the system and not likely to be basically different from their predecessors.

Based on their careers and their dossiers to date, those tapped by Gorbachev for leadership positions may still be ideologically and politically fragmented. Gorbachev, however, may be able to overcome those differences through the new Party Program and certain other new rules. The first Party Program in 1919 was an ideological guide for Lenin's party. The second, introduced by Khrushchev in 1961, did not live up to its opportunity or promise. The third Soviet Party Program, initiated by Andropov,[4] may succeed in providing an ideological framework for instituting Gorbachev's long-term economic strategy and the development of a new type of economic system. Some of its major features will probably include:

- A redefinition of democratic centralism to give ideological support to decentralization of economic planning and management, as in Lenin's early NEP.
- Socialist democracy to invite more participation from outside the party and government.

Ministers in key sectors such as energy (oil, electric power, electric equipment) have been removed, often with public criticism.[5] Politburo candidate member Dolgikh, a purported early rival of Gorbachev, served as party spokesman in several of those cases. New appointments and encouraged retirements provide Gorbachev with major opportunities for personnel change. He appears to be implementing the purge said to have been intended by Yuri Andropov.[6] New party and government role models seem to have emerged. Although the Soviet system may not be keyed to revolutionary change, the fear of purge and the resultant desire and ability to conform to new guidelines may convert many economic bureaucrats to new ways. Some Brezhnev "ideological *apparatchiki*" may become Gorbachevian "efficient technocrats." Gorbachev has been actively and systematically exercising his power over cadres. His appointment power over personnel wielded by his right-hand man, Ligachev, may be reinforced by success.

Gorbachev seems to be positioned for short-term success. Domestically, the new leader may benefit from greater activism and discipline on the part of the populace, and the appearance of success from the dynamism of a younger, healthy leader. Abroad, negotiations and summits may provide Gorbachev with an appearance of power, legitimacy, and success.

The appearance of success and the absence of failure may help Gorbachev establish his power and accelerate the acceptance of his programs by the remaining Brezhnev ideologues. Thirty years ago, good weather, the apparent success of the "New Lands Program," and Sputnik, together with the absence of apparent domestic or foreign policy failures, helped solidify Khrushchev's power in his early years and provided him with options not initially available. Khrushchev, however, seemed to squander opportunities opened through his early successes by failing to adopt effective economic programs and appoint professionally capable people who could have helped improve the economic system in the long run. Resulting failures in domestic and foreign policy contributed to Khrushchev's demise. Gorbachev may learn from Khrushchev's mistakes.

Centralization and Decentralization of the Bureaucracy: Targeting the Ministerial System and Regional Party

Adopting the Leninist policy of the "commanding heights" calls for more centralization of policy in the hands of the top political leadership, as well as more responsibility for, and accountability of, the enterprises and their managers. The target is change in the planning and management responsibilities of the large ministerial bureaucracy. The party and top government organs have taken on greater responsibility for central policy determination. This may require heightened horizontal integration and broader political-economic prerogatives for the top political leaders.

Increased centralization of planning responsibilities is being carried out at the Politburo, Party Secretariat, and Council of Ministers level. The enhanced role of such groups as the Party Secretariat's Economics Department, initially under Gorbachev's key economic manager Nikolai Ryzhkov, is a significant change. Nikolai Ryzhkov, Chairman of the Council of Ministers, and Nikolai Talizan, Chairman of the State Planning Commission, are full and corresponding members of the Politburo, respectively. These new economic lieutenants of Gorbachev, high in the party and government hierarchy by historical standards, occupy key positions with Gorbachev on the economic "commanding heights." It may also be noted that Aliev, Dolgikh, Zaikov, and other Politburo members have the portfolios for transport, energy, defense industries, and other sectors and have been given enhanced responsibilities for their sectoral success. Councils intended to combine ministerial responsibility within broad sectors (e.g., agriculture) have been formed at the Council of Ministers level. These senior governmental coordinating groups are intended to bring together sectoral policymaking, which has been fragmented among a multiplicity of ministries. Previously, there has been a lack of horizontal coordination, especially the coordination of agriculture, energy, and machine building. Centralization of power may include initially the emergence of "super ministries" with broad coordinating responsibilities. The purposes of this increased centralization appear to include more direct involvement of top party leaders in the key economic policy decisions, in order to develop broad strategies, reduce the planning role of the ministerial bureaucracy, and provide more effective management oversight by the top party leaders. This would assure more effective coordination of broad economic strategies, such as in energy, machine building, and agriculture. Elite involvement in top planning decisions could also reinforce a devolution of management authority and responsibility from the ministries to the enterprises. Note how often in his speeches Gorbachev has directly and specifically criticized the functioning of the ministerial system. For example, he made the following statement:

The true independence and responsibility of enterprises and associations can obviously be achieved when the rights and obligations of each level of management are correctly defined. We will not resolve the problem of independence if a director, in each instance, has to have dozens of things approved and discuss everything from A to Z. The resolution of every problem cannot be drawn to the center. The level of our economic management cadres fully allows many problems to be resolved on the spot. We only need to remove the fetters of poor and superfluous instructions from them, decisively decrease accountability of higher organs and free ourselves from the paper chase, which will at the same time contribute to a reduction of the management apparatus. This concerns both ministries and All-Union Industrial Associations.[7]

Supporting Gorbachev's criticism, albeit delivered before his accession to power, was a damning critique of the ministerial system by academician Nikolai Federenko, the senior academic economist in the Academy of Sciences. Federenko criticized the 4,000 major product categories used by the State Planning Commission, the 40-50,000 specifications of ministries, and the 1,000,000 specialized specifications of the State Committees for Supply.[8] Were such overmanagement at the center not the practice, noted Federenko, there could be a reduction in the central management apparatus in the ministries. If top party and government officials were more involved in key planning decisions and oversaw the devolution of detailed managerial decisions at the ministerial level, there might be fewer ministries and a much smaller ministerial bureaucracy in Moscow.

Moving the decisionmaking down from the ministries and out to the enterprises does not necessarily strengthen the regional and local party role in the economy. Although Gorbachev has been less critical of the regional and local party economic activities as a group, the requirement of autonomy of the enterprise directors implies a restriction of the party's right to intervene on economic matters. Were regional and local party officials less involved in the day-to-day functioning of economic enterprises, they could probably exercise more effective oversight and political control through the functioning of the *nomenklatura* system of personnel management. Of course, the *nomenklatura* system would have to be adjusted to take technical proficiency into account. Party reforms discussed during the past two years may prove helpful, if adopted and enforced.

A change in declarative policy in support of the principle of reward for accomplishment would contribute to a positive attitude toward a vigorous "work ethic," from worker to manager to minister to top party leaders. The range of negative to positive incentives, moral to material stimulii, might be the metaphoric replacement of the alcoholic with a "workaholic" image for the Gorbachevian worker and manager. According to a well placed Western diplomat, such a work ethic pattern was established when the Central Committee members assembled from the provinces in March 1985 for Chernenko's funeral, elected Gorbachev, and then were sent by Gorbachev directly back to work with "no rest and recreation" in Moscow. Although possibly apocryphal, the story caught the Moscow mood when Gorbachev took the reins of power in March 1985,[9] and has continued since then.

Gorbachev has raised expectations for increased autonomy, responsibility, and authority among enterprise managers. Financial autonomy means that managers whose enterprises earn more could retain the profits and have wide discretion over their use.[10] Conversely, managers of unprofitable enterprises would face the imminent prospect of replacement for failure with some enterprise reorganization, a process similar to bankruptcy in the West. He has increased the expectation that the productive workers and managers will be rewarded, and the unproductive penalized. If he does not follow through along these lines, questions may be raised: Why did he raise expectations? Will not the cynicism of many Soviet elites and citizens alike be strongly reinforced?

Decentralization within the economic system is to be implemented through the extension of the "experiment" to "activated" enterprises and collectives, and by increased party participation.[11] The sharing of rights and responsibilities between enterprises and ministries is now in the process of being redefined, with a definite shift of authority projected from the ministries to enterprises, and from Moscow to the republics.

In the short run, horizontal integration may be improved, some reduction in the number and staffing of the ministerial system may take place, and the governmental bureaucracy may be energized through the actions of Gorbachev and his new appointees. Energy, machine building, agriculture, and other sectors have been poorly coordinated in the past; horizontal integration has been lacking. The creation of "super-ministries" and the pruning of some redundancies in staffing may streamline the system. Gorbachevian ministers may be more active in exhorting and stimulating increased productivity. The frequent "field trips" of the General Secretary to trouble spots have an influence on the intensity of effort at the localities, as well as at the center.

In the long run, reform requires spelling out in detail and implementing changes in the economic institutions that reflect in practice the philosophy that Gorbachev has been preaching, that is, that enterprises should have clearly delineated responsibility and accountability for decisions on production, supply, investment, and marketing. If revenue exceeds costs, for example, the enterprise managers after reform should be able to distribute their retained profits through a degree of financial autonomy.

In order for this system of devolution from the ministers to enterprises to be effective, new performance criteria are necessary, and active oversight from party and government officials above the ministerial level is needed to ensure that the spirit of the decrees is carried out, and to monitor the performance of the enterprises. Finally, a physical shift from the center to the locality is necessary—commuters from Moscow to the localities do not make good local managers. This shift out of Moscow raises the need for central oversight to avoid "localism," "family-ness," even corruption. Were the clarification on new powers and responsibilities reinforced by institutional changes, the ministerial system would be dramatically changed. However, if the ministers retain their old organizations and personnel, even with directives changing their responsibilities and accountability, the ministerial system might stage a comeback. The lessons of the Paris Commune would be appropriate—the old ministerial system has to be destroyed for Gorbachev's long-term reforms to be successful.

In devolution of responsibility and accountability to the regional and local party, distinction should be made between the political role exercised through the *nomenklatura* system and the economic role exercised through intervention in the day-to-day functioning of the economy. The latter would need to go; the former is central to the retention of the primacy of the party and is likely to be retained for effective channels of oversight as to the efficient functioning of the economy. In order to effect these basic changes in recentralization and decentralization, the state must be able to enforce the needed changes. Such a basic change is not without uncertainty, as Oleg Bogomolov, Director of the Institute of World Socialist Economies, noted: "We still do not always and thoroughly know the society in which we live."[12]

The initiation of direct, two-way communication between the top leader and the two million enterprise directors and brigade leaders may be said to illustrate the new policy of socialist democracy and self-management. This new "town meeting" approach to managerial problems appears to be a stimulating new departure in the USSR.[13] In these unusually frank exchanges between Gorbachev and leaders of industrial and agricultural enterprises, a bill of particulars—including detailed criticisms—was drawn up against the ministerial system. In these forums, the precedents were established for direct top party oversight and involvement in the efficient functioning of the economy, devolution of responsibility to the enterprise, and the operation of an active reward system based on productivity and merit rather than on status and privilege. Gorbachev has repeatedly stressed the need to implement the directives of the "experiment" to give rights and responsibilities to managers and brigade leaders, and to reward them for good performance. Moreover, he invited the managers and brigade leaders to inform him and his retinue of top lieutenants if his wishes were not being carried out.

Gorbachev is especially identified with promoting institutional change in agriculture, giving more authority to local collective farm directors and "brigade chiefs" to control local production as well as the farm-market process. He has expressed the view that major improvement can be achieved in agriculture through the more efficient use of existing resources. Although it is not yet precisely clear how the implementation of the new agricultural managerial system would be carried out, the expressed intent is to move decisions on planting, contracting for farm inputs, harvesting, and marketing down to the productive unit, and to tie rewards to the resulting success or failure of that unit.

Earlier programs for the reform of the economy previously approved by the party but not implemented with vigor may now be pursued, including programs originally introduced during Brezhnev's early years. It has been said that Andropov intended to implement them in spirit as well as form. The "treadmill of reform" resulted, some Soviets say, because decrees were not implemented. The Ministry of Finance, the State Construction Committee, and the State Bank were all said to have resisted attempts to implement the expansion of the rights of enterprises and to reallocate authority and responsibility from the ministries to the enterprises.[14] Efforts to activate the formal decrees were evident in the early Andropov period, and have been resumed by Gorbachev.

The increasing inclination toward oversight on the part of the top leadership is illustrated in almost every one of Gorbachev's speeches. For example, in speaking to the oil workers in Tyumen on September 6, he criticized the ministries, the republic and regional research institutes, and the *oblast'* party chairman for not following effective policies and for not being productive.[15] Of course, criticism not followed by remedial action would be unproductive, even counterproductive.

Computerization of the Economy

In a concerted effort to deal with the scientific and technological revolution (STR), which has been such an integral part of change in the Western industrialized economies, the "computerization of the economy" is now being pursued within the Soviet system. Only glimpses of the measures being taken to deal with the complex problem are available, but Gorbachev's concern is evident. To date, the enhanced effort seems to be imposed largely from above. Even a partial list of what is needed to bring the Soviet Union into the information revolution is long and challenging:

• Adequate computer education in secondary schools, including vocational training, is needed.
• Industrial plant managers must have an electronic information network.
• The transport networks (air, water, railroad, and truck) need complex computerization.
• Service industries—for example, banks and agricultural supply stations—need information networks.
• Health care and medical processes should have complex information links.
• Research institutes should not only be computerized, but interconnected.

In his major speech on June 11, 1985, Gorbachev stressed the need for the development of new technology, and the failure of enterprises to implement new methods devised by the research institutions. He also raised questions on the role and place of the State Committee for Science and Technology.[16] The State Committee is in charge of setting scientific priorities and budgets for research, encouraging the application of new methods, supervising the development of the S&T information base, and coordinating with foreign scientific establishments. How one central organization can effectively handle such a wide range of responsibility seems to be under question. Decentralization of the computer-assisted system of research also runs counter to the pattern of control inherent in the secretive Soviet system. Wide dissemination of research data needed for effective scientific inquiry would require substantial steps toward data declassification.

Gorbachev's criteria of technological change and application of science—for example, in Siberia—seem to stress the need for more flexible, decentralized, applied research.[17] The requirements for an effective information revolution are such that fundamental changes in the system, rather than simply an adjustment of its priorities, are in order.

By pressuring the current centralized system, more hardware may become available in the critical areas. However, the adoption of flexible systems that facilitate scientific communication and information-sharing may be set back. In the short run, energizing the centralized scientific establishment through the infusion of more resources may work toward enhancing some of its managerial and planning operations. In the long run, however, such an approach seems contrary in nature to the goal of achieving more effective information systems. The Soviets' problem may be what Marshall Goldman called "the systems trap"[18]—that is, the pressure for catching up with or entering the technological revolution may be great enough to generate short-term ad hoc changes, but these changes may actually reinforce the current rigid, centralized system. They would thereby postpone the necessary transition to a new decentralized environment conducive to technological dynamism, an information revolution, and increased efficiency in the absorption, adaptation, and integration of Western technology.

Investment Strategy

For the twelfth Five-Year Plan, the minimum acceptable growth rate is to be 4% per year—the highest since the early 1970s.[19] The Gorbachev investment line was succinctly stated as the following:

The party requires funds and resources to be invested where the greatest return can be obtained in the shortest space of time; and not by increasing the number of workers, but by creating fundamentally new, highly efficient machinery and technology.[20]

How is this high growth rate to be attained? Soviet economic performance is expected to improve significantly and to meet the targeted rates of growth for the next five-year plan as the result of a number of specific changes soon to be introduced into the Soviet economic mechanism. These changes merit further examination.

First of all, investment is to be targeted on the reconstruction and modernization of existing plants, especially in European Russia. The high overall investment growth is to be concentrated on a doubling of machinery and equipment output keyed to completion and modernization of existing plants in order to improve the quality of output and reduce inputs of energy, metals, and labor. While investment priorities in the agricultural and energy sectors are to be generally maintained, they are to be keyed to machine-building aspects of those sectors, for example, agricultural equipment and energy-efficient machinery. By emphasizing machinery, agricultural and energy investment shares will thus be restructured or reduced; in fact, the resulting increase in machine-building industries will be at the direct expense of the agricultural and energy sectors. Likewise, all other sectors will be maintained at second-level priorities. No equal sharing of investment resources is intended.

Second, pressing issues of regional development policy also confront the new leadership. Development of Siberia implies a priority for the energy sector and requires construction of new, big projects in the East, rather than renovation of older, established enterprises in the Western industrial core area. Development of the southern part of the USSR, where there is surplus labor, calls for water supplies from irrigation and river diversion projects. In an economy strapped for investment capital, these regional development projects are in direct competition with priority short-run modernization requirements. Gorbachev's specific regional preferences are not all clear, but his general time preference is short. Most major projects in Central Asia will be delayed, and large-scale projects for East Siberia—such as the Baikal-Amur Railroad project (BAM)—are likely to be deferred.[21] The BAM railroad is to be completed to Yakutia, but accompanying development projects planned for the Baikal-Amur region seem likely to be postponed until the 1990s. The interregional water supply diversion canal to Central Asia, the *Sibaral,* may be on again.[22] If so, this large project would seem to be an exception. In spite of the importance of West Siberian oil and gas, capital investment may not be allocated at the past rate for the integrated development of that key energy province. As Gorbachev noted in his speech to the energy workers in West Siberia, the capital construction for oil and gas development in that region "is unparalleled. Each year the volume of work is like building two Volga motor vehicle works, and a BAM every two years."[23]

A third key factor in Gorbachev's economic strategy relates to Soviet-East European relations. Specifically, imports from the CMEA-Six are to feature higher quality machinery and consumer goods. The Soviet price of oil and gas to Eastern Europe is likely to go up further, with greater requirements for payment in "hard goods," that is, machinery and consumer goods marketable in the West.[24]

Fourth, and finally, there may be significant change in Soviet defense spending. In recent years, the rate of increase in Soviet military spending has apparently slowed from 4 or 4.5% to about 2% real growth per annum, with procurement leveling off. According to CIA estimates, the lower priority for military procurement began in 1976. Although there is some difference of view within the U.S. intelligence community, this trend generally appears to be continuing into the Gorbachev period. While there are questions about the dollar value of weapons production in the DIA estimate, CIA and DIA analysts agree that physical weapons procurement programs have not materially accelerated since military procurement leveled off during the 1976-1981 period.[25] The preference for short-term civilian investment may mean a delay or stretch-out in military procurement programs and military R&D, perhaps leading to a discussion of the use of militarily related manpower in civilian activities. Long-run improvement in Soviet R&D may be more beneficial to the military, but it would be a tenuous agreement.

Modest economic growth still confronts the regime with difficult choices on resource allocation: "guns, growth, or butter." Gorbachev has tended to favor increased capital investment leading to growth and increased production of consumer goods, as a means of reviving economic performance. If the rate of growth of Soviet defense spending has decreased to 2% annually, as the CIA claims, Gorbachev may seek to hold it at that relatively low level, deferring increases in military procurement. This shift in relative emphasis between guns and growth may influence other key decisions on the share of R&D for military and civilian programs, the level and use of manpower for military service or the civilian labor force, and on projects of military or civilian construction. Military and civilian procurement, R&D, and manpower utilization are all among the primary "guns" or "investment" choices latent in the Gorbachev strategy.

Consumption Strategy

Consumption is also expected to increase: The gap between purchasing power and the value of goods available is expected to narrow; the quality of consumer goods is expected to improve; and the state subsidies for subsistence items are expected in the short run to continue.[26] This pro-consumption policy appears to have continued from Andropov through Chernenko to Gorbachev.

Subsidies for meat, butter, milk, rent, subways, and so forth—all considered essential—are to remain intact for the time being. These subsidies are estimated to be very large. Gorbachev complained in his Tselinograd speech about the high level of meat subsidies of 20 billion rubles a year.[27] Prices for nonessential commodities are to increase, albeit with some improvement in quality. The gap between supply and effective demand is also expected to be narrowed through more production of consumer goods and increased imports from CMEA.[28] Some more effective integration of the "informal" or "second economy" into the formal economy is possible, for example, making some private production and services legal as is the case in Hungary.

A consumption strategy stressing more goods is a short-run policy. Maintenance of subsidies for "essentials" is likewise a short-run policy. In the longer term, prices should be adjusted to clear the market and provide profits for efficient producers. Incomes tied to productivity should be convertible to goods and services desired. The short-term adjustments in the current consumption policy, however, may not make the implementation of the needed long-term reform easier.

Increased value of consumer goods output may appear to provide progress in the availability of goods to satisfy and stimulate the populace. However, the short-run consumption strategy leaves unresolved gaps in implementing an effective incomes policy:

- Subsistence goods will still be heavily subsidized. The cost of providing bread, housing, and medical services will not be captured by revenue, particularly since agricultural procurement prices have recently been raised.
- Income based on need would be necessary to provide an effective consumption policy. Quality-of-life needs, including adequate medical care, would require a fivefold to sevenfold increase in medical expenditures even to approach Western standards.[29]
- Purchasing power created will not be absorbed fully by available goods, even if prices of nonsubsistence items are inflated, ostensibly to reflect higher quality.
- Availability of goods and services will need to be obtained from both the formal and informal market. Coordination of these markets would facilitate goods and services availability and consumer satisfaction.
- Payment by accomplishment would require a change in the entire system of privilege and status. Moreover, equality of opportunity and payment by accomplishment would give substance to the egalitarian rhetoric of the Soviet nationality policy, as well as to the official policy of nonsex discrimination. As demographic trends reduce the number of preferred Great Russian males, the opportunity cost of continuing a policy of ethnic and sex discrimination escalates.

Prospects for Gorbachev's Domestic Strategy

Gorbachev's short-term economic strategy may well be judged successful during the next few years. By professionalizing, rationalizing, and energizing the economic system, performance may improve, even materially—especially if the weather and other exogenous factors are favorable. Improvement in the harvest and delivery of additional food to the market seems attainable, and significant improvement in the conservation of scarce oil and quality metals appears to be a reasonable possibility. Heightened efficiency and productivity of planners, managers, scientists, and workers are possible with more qualified people in control, a closer correlation between performance and rewards, and some rationalization of tasks. Good weather for harvests and construction in the next year or two together with greater discipline and pressure for performance within the system may create the possibility of exploiting the wellspring of untapped efficiencies currently lost in the Soviet economic system. Judging by the wide gap that exists between the USSR and other industrial nations of a comparable level, the Soviet system ought to produce better with less.

This is not to say that the "experiment" in decentralization of management or other Gorbachev programs for improving the economic mechanism will convincingly improve the manner in which industrial enterprises or collective farms are managed, or materially change the system for the long term. Nor need one expect that centralization and computerization of planning will modernize the central decisionmaking process in applied science and bring about a scientific-technological revolution. It is not clear that currently projected changes in the economic mechanism will improve the long-term performance of the Soviet economic system. However, *incremental* improvements within the system may provide substantial short-term improvements: Citizens may perceive themselves as being better off in the next few years; economic growth figures could be impressively higher; and the scientific R&D community may be perceived as dynamic and more effective. The general image of dynamic socialism under Gorbachev may well be accepted at home and abroad.

However, short-term success may both mask the need for long-run change and hold back its accomplishment: The short-term preference in investment strategy may trade short-term for long-term results. Projects such as the BAM, needed for the 1990s, may now be deferred; short-term hardware-related computerization may delay a long-term "information revolution."

Some of the basic systemic changes required in the long run include:

- A rational system of allocation by value of inputs and outputs—a market-simulating price system.
- The modernization and rationalization of the planning process to use available economic techniques and correlate policy and planning across major areas.
- The clear delineation of responsibility and authority of managers of economic enterprises operating under rational profitability criteria.

• Scientific and technical progress in an environment that fosters innovation, scientific communication, and rewards those responsible for technological improvement.[30]

The political resistance to such necessary long-term systemic change resides, first of all, in the economic bureaucracy—especially the ministerial system—and in those elements of the party which act as interveners in the administration of planning and management. Were this long-term change to occur, Gorbachev's slogan might, in essence but not in rhetoric, be "laissez faire, laissez passer." The Soviet system needs to get the dead hand of ministerial bureaucracy and the regional party out of the day-to-day management of the economy, and find its version of an impartial domestic system, an "unseen hand," and a more open economy. Gorbachev seems to recognize this problem of Soviet neomercantilism and has clearly identified the ministerial bureaucracy as a target. But will he be able and willing to proceed toward implementation of fundamental changes, especially if he appears to have politically painless short-term economic successes? Is Gorbachev not only a pragmatist and an efficient technocrat, but also the visionary and strategist probably necessary to initiate and carry through the fundamentalist reforms required to strengthen the Soviet system?

The difficulties in making the needed fundamental changes may be summarized as follows in the political imperatives of reform of the economic system.

Restructuring the economic bureaucracy would mean nothing less than taking power and position from the vast ministerial system with the devolution of that power, responsibility, and accountability to a new group of industrial and agricultural managers. The top party leaders would need to be more involved, responsible, and accountable for overall policy and assure that decentralization had been carried out in letter and spirit. Will top party leaders take on this broadened responsibility and be held accountable? Can the large and powerful economic ministerial bureaucracies be dismantled? Will local enterprises effectively discharge their new responsibilities and be held accountable?

The regional and local party's role would have to be redefined as less economic and more narrowly political. Specifically, the party's right to intervene in the day-to-day functioning of the economy would be restricted. While Gorbachev seems to be criticizing the regional and local party officials for not performing, and implies a need for restricting their power, will he move to take away their economic management responsibility and accountability? Will the party system, once energized for short-term economic improvement, not seem essential for carrying out the long-term wishes of the General Secretary?

As both of these changes in the economic bureaucracy and the party threaten not only the power and prerogatives of important power holders, but in many cases the political survival of many powerful people, they cannot be assumed to be easily attainable, even if pushed by Gorbachev. The appeal of returning to the "commanding heights" policy of Lenin in the early NEP is an attractive image, but is it an effective program for Gorbachev? It would seem easy for us to conclude that fundamental changes will prove too difficult and costly for Gorbachev. Indeed, this may turn out to be true. Nonetheless, there are a number of considerations suggesting that fundamental changes may take place under the new Soviet leadership:

1. *Gorbachev's appointees may be suited for adjustment and committed to change to a new economic mechanism.* If the short-term results are as good as the leadership expects, a Gorbachevian cadre—in place and successful—may be prepared to accept the role of "efficient technocrats" in a reformed system of planning and management. Some of his new appointees may make up a constituency for reform—a new "interest group."

2. *Gorbachev may have learned the lesson of Khrushchev.* Khrushchev, too, had early success in political and economic programs: the "new lands" program and good weather provided good harvests and an improvement in consumption; *Sputnik* made it appear that the Soviet Union was competitive with the United States in military technology; labor-force problems were surmounted by military modernization and reduction of military manpower. But instead of addressing the systemic problems of the economic bureaucracy and the party role in the economy, Khrushchev aggravated them. He himself became the prime party intervener in economic matters, with which he was ill equipped to deal. Indeed, he reverted to the "cult of the personality" in economic affairs, as, for example, in his corn production program.

According to a Czech Communist Party leader who knew Gorbachev well during this period,

Gorbachev did not regret the fall of Khrushchev and did not consider it an event that could signify a return to the past. Assessing Khrushchev primarily in terms of his domestic policies, he found that he had done harm by his erratic and ill-considered intervention in economic affairs. He blamed him particularly for the fact that he maintained the old method of arbitrary intervention by the center in the life of the whole country.[31]

Gorbachev may have a two-staged agenda with short-term growth needed to establish his power to be followed by a long-term process of economic reform.

3. *The range of debate on Soviet economic policy seems to be more open now than at any time since the 1920s.* The acceptable range of debate on economic policy has widened, and takes account of the following specific themes:[32]

- The need for optimal planning that involves a sharp reduction in the use of quotas, restricts the role of ministries, and increases the use of indirect incentives, together with financial and price policies and allowance for "slack" in planning. Optimal planning would involve forecasts of required output, prices and costs, from which plan variants would be developed.
- Changes in central wage policy and traditional wage scales
- Bankruptcy as a theoretical possibility in the USSR, and as an acceptable practice in CMEA
- The right to work
- Socialist ownership in agriculture, and an extension of brigade contracting
- Integration of "shadow" or informal service and artesan enterprises into the formal, legal economy
- The relationship of political and economic change within the economic mechanism, including discussion of issues raised in the early NEP period by Nikolai Bukharin.

From these debates may come processes of change that develop broad bases of popular support and escalating success, for example, brigade responsibility reform in agriculture and the merging of formal and informal economies in services. These programs were successful in the People's Republic of China and Hungary, respectively. A work ethic tying rewards to accomplishment and promising greater returns for improved productivity—even at the expense of reduced job security—might also receive widening support. A dynamic, successful economy would provide a better environment for replacing the "safety net" of job, income, and enterprise security with a system of payment by performance.

4. *Superpower competition may impel Gorbachev to go beyond incremental changes within the current system toward more basic systemic reform.* Paradoxically, broadening the definition of security of the Soviet state to include the development of a competitive scientific and technological system may impel Gorbachev to accept fundamental economic reform together with an attendant shift in priorities from favoring military outlays toward civilian investment and consumer incentives. It may be, as Jerry Hough and Ed Hewett suggest, that Gorbachev's concern is with the broader issue of comparative Great Power technology. The technologically inefficient Soviet economic system may be viewed as an impediment to competing with the advanced technology of the United States. Thus, the technological challenge to the USSR posed by the Strategic Defense Initiative (SDI) may be a spur to broad systemic changes (i.e., reform). As Hough and Hewett argue:

What is important here is the explicit link between economic reform and national security. Patriotism is an awesome mobilizing tool in the Soviet Union and Mikhail Gorbachev seems to be in the process of defining economic reform as "patriotic."

Gorbachev is using SDI as a very effective symbol of U.S. ability to use science and technology as a military and economic weapon, and he is seeking to construct a reform program which will allow the economy to acquire that same weapon. . . . Gorbachev needs SDI.[33]

This may not be to suggest that SDI itself, as presently projected in the United States as a military program, is the sole concern to the Gorbachev regime. SDI may be used by Gorbachev as a symbol of a growing U.S. technological advantage. The Strategic Defense Initiative may be a focal point for generating needed change in and invigoration of the Soviet scientific establishment. Even were SDI not to proceed, the increasing gap between American and Soviet technology would be a major concern of Soviet authorities. SDI currently may give them a convenient rallying point for addressing this broader problem.

GORBACHEV'S COMMERCIAL STRATEGY

The commercial strategy of the Soviet Union evolves from the overall Eastern strategy for trading with the West, and from the specific commercial needs of Gorbachev's domestic strategy.

Eastern Priorities: Policy Dilemmas

Trade and Diplomacy. Should the USSR divide the West or benefit from revival of economic détente? Should it rely on domestic technology, or accept a degree of dependency and vulnerability inherent in Western commercial relations?

Two often conflicting tendencies have dominated Soviet policy toward the West: the desire to wield political and ideological influence over a divided capitalist world, and a need to draw upon the technological resources of the economically advanced Western countries. The interplay of these tendencies has formed Soviet policy toward the West since the earliest days of the Soviet state. Divisions within the capitalist world present Soviet leaders with the opportunity to exert political and ideological influence over Western Europe. Thus, Soviet leaders have eagerly seized upon and sought to foster division within the West—either among the European countries or, particularly during the post-World War II period, between Western Europe and the United States. Efforts to enlarge or foster division between the United States and its West European allies have been a prominent feature of Soviet foreign policy. Yet, at the same time, the Soviet Union has frequently sought expanded commercial relations with the West, particularly Western Europe, in order to advance its economic goals of modernization and growth. Moreover, increased trade has often been used to advance a policy of rapprochement with the United States.

The long-term Soviet policy has been to divide and weaken the West politically while drawing on Western technological advances. In 1917, conflicts dividing the West were seen as the way to the World Socialist Revolution, but by 1928 the goal of overcoming economic backwardness made Moscow look economically toward the West. More recently, in the 1980s, the Soviets seized the opportunity to divide the NATO alliance through the peace movement and selective, economic "Westpolitik," while at the same time encouraging a much-needed Scientific-Technological Revolution with the assistance of Western technology.

These centrifugal political and centripetal economic forces have played throughout the history of Soviet policy in Europe for more than six decades. More recently, the varying policies have influenced overall East-West relations. The policies of the developed Western economies have alternatively fostered and impeded the success of these Soviet tendencies. Occasionally, Western policies have been unified, but more often divided, providing the Soviet Union a basis for choice in how to orchestrate its Western commercial and foreign policy.

The post-Brezhnev succession period found various leaders calling for degrees of independence from the West. Andropov and Chernenko generally followed the Brezhnev foreign policy line on reviving détente and trade in principle, but in practice they followed a differentiated bilateral trade policy to divide the Western allies. There were voices in the top leadership favoring a more aggressive policy of confrontation and explicit trade restriction. Ukrainian party chief Vladimir Shcherbitsky favored breaking the "U.S. technology blockade" by reliance on domestic sources.[34] Some proposed that the CMEA countries resist Western political leverage by relying on Soviet supplies of advanced technology.

Trade and Security. Should Moscow increase integration within the CMEA and rely on commercial espionage and third-country transfers, or should it foster CMEA trade with the West and accept political vulnerability and dependency?

Political factors dominate Soviet policy in the 1980s, as in the past.[35] During the post-Brezhnev era, however, issues of political economy, such as commercial relations with Western Europe and alliance relations in Eastern Europe, have also been high on the policy agenda. To be sure, when the Soviet leadership perceives threats to political or military security, national sovereignty, or systemic continuity, issues of political economy do not take precedence. During the 1970s, major threats to these values were not perceived, and the Soviet leaders were able to concentrate on the needs of the domestic economy and on the agenda of political economy generally. The turn to the West for technology, grain, and credit was central to Moscow's policy of economic modernization.

In alliance relations, the Soviet leaders sought to retain their hold over Eastern Europe by economic as well as military levers. In the era of détente, Moscow gave the East European countries leeway to build up their own economic bridges to Western Europe and the United States. Soviet authorities hoped that the East European regimes could thereby foster economic modernization, consumer welfare, and political stability. An equally important reason for the granting of this leeway was to reduce the drain on scarce Soviet energy and other raw materials. Soviet leadership during the post-Brezhnev interregnum may have also been unwilling or unable to exercise the degree of control many in the Moscow leadership may have preferred.

Because of the continued division within the West on relations with the East, Soviet leaders have been tempted to exploit political divisions and move closer to an autarkic system. Within Soviet leadership circles, reducing the level of interdependence with the West and increasing CMEA integration have always had an appeal; such steps, it was thought, could reduce CMEA's dependency and vulnerable exposure to economic leverage by the West.

Market Constraints: Economics over Politics? Oil prices and growth in the advanced Western economies influence the prospects for Soviet hard currency earnings. If economic growth in the West and limits on alternative supplies combine, the price of oil may increase. Were that the case, as seems likely in the 1990s, the price and demand for natural gas would also go up. In this growth scenario, supplies of Soviet nonenergy metals would also find markets and hard currency earning potential. But such has not been the case in the short run, and these major sources of foreign income have been restricted. To earn the requisite hard currency, the Soviet Union must sell more and deprive their domestic and allied markets of scarce hydrocarbons. In a time of stable or declining Soviet oil output and falling oil prices, the choices among competing claimants have been difficult. A shift away from oil and toward increased conservation in the Soviet energy balance are domestic policy options, but require time and other costs. But, especially in the long run, the market constraints on Soviet foreign economic policy are relative. With a large, richly endowed economy, if the leaders choose to export, they will. The same can be said for a wide range of imported goods and services—if the leaders give priority to imports, foreign suppliers can be found.

As a result of the coordination among the CMEA-Six and the USSR in the five-year plans for 1986-1990, the Soviet Union may receive "world standard" machinery and consumer goods imports from its allies. The Soviet Union has indicated a desire to shift the structure of imports from the CMEA toward "hard" goods and away from "soft" goods. While their concern about "technological blockade" has led them to emphasize intra-CMEA reliance, they continue to encourage some East-West interactions.

Intra-CMEA policy may permit and even encourage more interdependence with the West. The June 1984 CMEA summit did not call for full integration, that is, isolation of the CMEA-Six from the West. The major goals of the summit were increased growth in "hard goods" output and a shift to world market pricing for Soviet oil and CMEA machinery.[36] Increased availability of consumer goods is a secondary goal. Soviet bilateral trade with CMEA countries is to be "advantageous," but sharp changes in the terms of trade or the repayment of CMEA hard currency debt to the USSR is not anticipated. The USSR will not squeeze the CMEA-Six too tightly or too fast. Soviet control of CMEA partners is somewhat limited: "Requests" for more meat for oil may not be honored; the Soviets may continue to close their eyes to the CMEA-Six's practice of refining Soviet crude for resale to the West (as much as one-quarter of the current deliveries). CMEA integration on high-tech production is to be facilitated by increased commercial relations with the West, although Soviet leaders remain concerned about the vulnerability of the CMEA-Six to Western technological embargoes, for example, a cutoff of telephone system supplies.

CMEA integration still features Soviet projects. The Yamburg gas export pipeline was included in the twelfth Five-Year Plan. It will be modeled after the Orenburg gas pipeline agreement, but will include Romania. Capacity will exceed that of the Urengoi-Uzhgorod line. Details of the project—for example, route, shares, responsibilities, and so forth—are to be worked out. These should be interesting negotiations.[37] Soviet energy policy toward the CMEA-Six consists of more use of gas, electricity, and indigenous fuels, as well as improved conservation—especially with regard to oil. The GDR's success in energy policy is said to have resulted from holding down the domestic availability of energy, while at the same time the party and economic bureaucracies pressured for increased output. East Germany has the best record of improvement in energy use; Hungary is the most efficient user of energy.

CMEA relations with the West are permissible within limits. While the Andropov/Bogomolev policy of diversity in East European relations with the West (i.e., allowing for different historical, ethnic, and developmental factors in determining each country's Western relations) is still under discussion, Gorbachev came down strongly on the side of differentiation at the October Party Plenum.[38] Although some in Moscow perceive problems in the current conduct of CMEA bilateral economic relations with the West, that view is not being emphasized:

• Intra-German economic relations involving loans, favorable terms of trade, and industrial cooperation all contribute to improved output of hard goods.

Therefore, these relations are not only permitted but encouraged, but within more sharply defined political limits. Indeed, political differences have sharpened between the USSR and the GDR.

• A possible IMF/World Bank program for Poland (since Poland was admitted in 1986) would be acceptable to Moscow if austerity, rigorous reassessment of investment projects, and resumed dialogue accompanying self-management all promise improved economic performance. The official Soviet view is that Poland has put its debt and domestic economic situation back in order. The unofficial Soviet view is that Poland lacks worker discipline and direction in its industrial policy. The IMF/World Bank programs have been criticized for giving too little attention to generating exports and for not appreciating the possible adverse social consequences of some of the economic stabilization measures advocated by the IMF. Some Soviet leaders stress the importance of Poland's early repayment of debts, reestablishment of its creditworthiness, and the need for stability in world trade and credit markets. The disadvantages of sharp cuts in CMEA imports so as to facilitate improved credit positions are not acknowledged. The Vatican Bank aid for private Polish agriculture was said to be all right in principle, but not efficient, because of continued dependence on small private farms.[39]

Soviet CMEA economic policy seems to be keyed to maximizing East European output of quality goods (hard goods), especially machinery and consumer goods, that will be exchanged for Soviet oil and gas. Some increased economic relations with the West and domestic economic reforms may contribute to that aim.

In the internal debate over Soviet trade policy, integrationists favor closer ties between the USSR and Eastern Europe and seek more conformity in the East European economies to the Soviet model. Gorbachev, like Andropov, may prove to favor more diversity and experimentation in Eastern Europe, although some East European leaders fear he may seek to impose a certain measure of Moscow-oriented discipline.

Gorbachev's Evolving Commercial Strategy toward the West

Gorbachev seems to be advocating increased trade with the West within a favorable East-West political environment. His speeches suggest a policy of differentiating among West European, Japanese, and American firms according to their governments' policies toward the USSR. Although sensitive about economic sanctions, in meetings with foreign businessmen Gorbachev has favored expanded trade with the United States in nonstrategic goods if the political framework of commercial relations improves.

Specific machinery imports for selective projects. Agricultural, energy, and other equipment imports from the West are to be targeted to specific projects. These imports are generally expected to reduce significantly inputs and improve quality in key Soviet domestic economic sectors. The pattern for the Brezhnev period was set by the precedent-setting Volga plant at Togliattigrad using Fiat technology. The modernization of this plant indicates that the new pattern is to stress readjustment, for example, periodic model changes to be competitive with foreign competitors:[40]

- Foreign imports are for selective modernization of existing plants. Big projects with foreign general contractors, such as the Kama River Truck Plant (KAMAZ) and the Volga Automotive Plant (VAZ), are not the preferred strategy.
- New models, that is, changes in quality and efficiency, are planned and required to make the output competitive, both domestically and in the world market.
- Availability of hard currency for imports will be related more directly to earnings of hard currency from sales abroad.
- Gorbachev's preference for financial autonomy is to be adopted: "Independence, paying our own way, and full economic accountability— these are the three pillars on which the experiment at the Volga Automotive Plant rests."[41]

Emphasis on Machinery. There is discussion in the USSR about the shift from foodstuffs to increased machinery imports—more plants and equipment, and less grain. While this has not been the case in the past, the priority projects for imports in the twelfth Five-Year Plan indicate that machinery imports will rise in the future. The next plan emphasizes machine building, energy, and agricultural technology. The specific imports will probably represent an increase in total machinery imports with greater emphasis on the sectors listed in Table 4.1.[42]

Table 4.1.   SOVIET EQUIPMENT IMPORTS FROM THE WEST (In millions of rubles)*

	1982	1983	1984
Total Soviet imports from West	18,892.4	18,718.8	19,574.1
of which:			
Machinery and Transport Equipment	5,856.2	6,733.2	5,751.0
of which:			
• machinery and equipment for boring, geological surveying, exploration of bore holes	407.9	972.0	735.0
• equipment for the chemical industry	429.8	485.0	586.0
• metal-cutting machine tools and presses	292.7	449.7	406.7
• equipment for the wood, cellulose, and wood processing industries (excluding woodworking lathes)	182.1	175.5	293.9
• equipment for the food industry	118.0	127.0	202.0
• roadbuilding equipment	593.3	268.2	167.5
• equipment for the automotive industry	155.4	210.9	128.0
• underground and open pit mining equipment	74.4	99.1	126.0
• instruments and laboratory equipment	124.9	119.9	117.0
• steel mill equipment	176.8	143.3	86.8

*Business Eastern Europe, July 19, 1985, p. 226.

1982 R = $1.38; 1983 R = $1.35; 1984 R = $1.24

Balance of payments will be influenced by import needs and vulnerability.
The big ticket export items will continue to be oil, gas, and arms, with gold as a balancing item. Short-term balancing requires a flexible energy exports policy. The alternate means of balancing would involve credit, countertrade, and international cooperation. Again, the question will be: Should plans, and concerns about their completion, be overriding, or should debt management and limited financial vulnerability dominate import/export decisions?

Long-term commitments may induce bilateral multi-year agreements. The Soviet Union can rely on long-term agreements with assurance of contract sanctity with most of its major trading partners in the West, for example, the Federal Republic of Germany, Japan, and France. The only long-term U.S. commitments are for grain and fertilizer sales. U.S. exports to the Soviet Union in 1984 were primarily agricultural; indeed, over 80% of U.S. sales to the USSR consisted of agricultural commodities, led by corn and wheat. The limited U.S. imports ($556 million versus $3,283 million in U.S. exports) were led by ammonia and urea—the exchange under the long-term Occidental agreement for phosphoric acid.[43]

Industrial Cooperation, the Preferred Strategy. Active mechanisms for the transfer of technology would be more effective than self-sufficiency for meeting Soviet modernization needs, especially in computer technology. According to Seymour Goodman, "the overall gap between the Soviet and principal Western industries and user communities is growing." Soviet authorities have reduced the effectiveness of their absorption of Western technology by furthering a rather unreceptive economic system and an ineffective transfer process.[44]

The Soviet penchant for, or perceived necessity to use, illegal means is among the least effective approaches to active transfers. As it consumes substantial hard currency as well, its advantages over formal trade and industrial cooperation are limited. With increased Western attention to Soviet economic espionage, moreover, this particular means of transfer may be more restricted in the future.

POLICY IMPLICATIONS FOR THE WEST

Gorbachev's Domestic Strategy

Success in the short run may make the Soviet Union appear to be a more formidable competitor. We should guard against confusing short-term results and appearance of change with the necessary systemic changes needed for long-term Soviet economic and technological dynamism. Soviet economic and technological power in the long run will require more basic systemic changes, which are both less likely and harder to predict. Most of the critical choices will be determined by domestic political factors. The United States, as the other superpower, will remain a challenger to and competitor with the Soviet Union. If Soviet modernization occurs and results in part from a Soviet choice of "investment" over "guns," we may benefit in a moderation of the competition as measured by the military balance. On the other hand, if the Soviet Union is able to join the technological and information revolution and establish a firm basis for technological competition, this might be translated into more formidable Soviet military power in the longer run or more competition in the political-economic arena.

Were systemic changes to give a larger role to the Soviet manager and citizen to develop in the Soviet Union, we might find such a reformed Soviet establishment to be a more compatible system. That appeared to be what the

President's National Security Advisor was saying in his presummit speech, in November 1985, stressing incremental improvements within different systems that are more responsive to individual initiatives and which move toward a reward system based on productivity.[45]

Gorbachev's Commercial Strategy

Since Gorbachev's domestic strategy in the short and long term would benefit from enhanced commercial relations with the West, his preferred strategy for commercial relations with the West would likely be one of Eastern consensus and Western trade facilitation. The United States can limit that option by trade restriction and by selective use of trade in diplomacy. In that case, the Soviet Union would likely direct its purchases to other OECD countries and restrict economic ties that appear to involve unacceptable dependency and vulnerability. Development of a restrictive commercial policy toward the West along such lines might provide useful political gains to the USSR, but would be less attractive economically, that is, less supportive of its likely domestic economic strategy. Presumably, we could somewhat retard Soviet progress by effecting a more dynamic program of technological improvement. However, in the past their overcentralized, innovation-unfriendly system and their inability to utilize available Western technology effectively have been major stumbling blocks in attaining a scientific and technological revolution (STR) or an information revolution. Widely available technology in the West would be of substantive benefit to them if they could use it effectively, as other industrial nations have done in recent years.

NOTES

1. Gorbachev to Time, September 9, 1985: "Well, first of all, it is not my own personal style. This is something we all learned from Lenin. It goes back to Lenin."
2. Quoted in John P. Hardt, "Stages of Soviet Economic Development: The Sixty-Year Period," in Nake M. Karmany and Richard H. Day, editors, *Economic Issues for the Eighties* (Baltimore, Md.: Johns Hopkins University Press, 1980).
3. This role model distinction harkens back to the early defense distinction between "red" or "expert," but implies more political acumen and professionalism among Gorbachev's cadre, to go with their technical proficiency. *Pravda*, April 12, 24, June 12, 1985. Note also those who are listed as appearing with Gorbachev in his frequent speeches—those exercising responsibility—are joined with those from the center and locality exercising oversight.

4. Yuri Andropov, "The Teaching of Karl Marx and Some Questions of Building Socialism in the USSR," *Kommunist,* March 3, 1983. *Pravda,* June 16, 1983.

5. Jerry Hough, "Gorbachev's Strategy," *Foreign Affairs,* Fall 1985.

6. Rudolph Brancolo, "Andropov Wants to Regenerate the CPSU; Congress Brought Forward to 1985," in *La Republica,* Rome, September 21, 1983 (translation in *Foreign Broadcast Information Service (FBIS),* USSR National Affairs, September 27, 1983), pp. R6-R9.

7. *Pravda,* April 12, 1985.

8. *EKO,* No. 12, 1984.

9. I was in Moscow at the time on economic consultations.

10. See *Pravda,* April 12, 1985.

11. On January 1, 1984, five Soviet ministries embarked on a new economic "experiment." The experiment included rights of enterprises to determine output, set wages, decide on investments, and retain profits. Moreover, new success criteria keyed to profitability were to be established. The experiment was expanded to include another 26 all-union, union-republic, and republic ministries in early 1985. As Gorbachev took power, more than 11% of industrial-production—and more than 62% of machine building output—was being produced in enterprises participating in the economic experiment. In the twelfth Five-Year Plan, the "experiment" is to be economy-wide. *Pravda,* July 12, 1985.

12. Oleg Bogomolov, *Kommunist,* No. 10, July 1985. Often in Western discussions of Soviet reform one hears references to "new wine in old bottles," but with careful reading of the Bible, one's attention is drawn to the uncertainties inherent in Gorbachev's reforms and personnel changes if thorough changes are to be made. "Nor do people pour new wine into old wine-skins, else the skins burst, and wine is spilt, and the skins are ruined. But they put new wine into fresh skins, and both are saved." [Matthew 9:16-17]

13. See *Pravda,* April 12, 1985, and *Ekonomicheskaya gazeta,* No. 16, 1985, pp. 3-5.

14. In addition to consultations in Moscow, the author drew on a series of articles on planning and management in *Ekonomicheskaya gazeta* under the heading, "Khozyaystvenniy mekhanism i ekonomicheskaya rabota," dated December 1982 through March 1983. *Pravda, Literaturnaya gazeta, Izvestiya, Planovoye khozyaystvo, Izvestiya Akademii nauk SSSR, Seriya Ekonomicheskaya,* and *Voprosy ekonomiki* were also monitored. Cf. Gertrude E. Schroeder, "Soviet Economic 'Reform' Decrees: More Steps on the Treadmill," *Soviet Economy in the 1980's: Problems and Prospects,* Part 1 (Washington, D.C.: GPO, for the Joint Economic Committee of the Congress, December 1982), pp. 65-88.

15. *Pravda,* September 7, 1985.

16. *Pravda,* June 11, 1985. German Gvishiani was moved from his position as deputy chairman of the State Committee for Science and Technology to become the First Deputy Chairman of Gosplan.

17. *Pravda,* September 7, 1985.

18. Marshall Goldman, "Gorbachev and Economic Reform," *Foreign Affairs,* Fall 1985, p. 71.

19. Actually, a 4.7% growth target is implied by "doubling output by the year 2000." A. Agenbegyan, *Problemy Mira i Sotsializma,* No. 9, September 1985, pp. 13-18.

20. Vasiliy Parfenov, "Socio-Economic Review: A Time of Change," *Pravda,* August 15, 1985, p. 2.

21. See *Socialist Industry,* March 10, 1985, and *Izvestiya,* March 14, 1985.

22. *Pravda,* June 6, 1985. Reports to the U.S. Congressional delegation in September 1985 indicate that Sibaral is still in question.

23. September 6, 1985, in Tyumen, West Siberia. The Volga motor vehicle plant at Togliattigrad, the major project of the eighth Five-Year Plan (1966-1970), is now the major Soviet passenger car production facility. The Baikal-Amur Railroad, a prodigious engineering feat mainly built from 1974-1984, is part of the so-called "Project of the Century."

24. Bogomolov, op. cit.

25. For further discussion of the purported slowdown in growth in Soviet procurement, see Richard F. Kaufman, "Causes in the Slowdown in Soviet Defense," *Soviet Economy* (January-March 1985), pp. 9-41; Robert Foelber, "Estimates of Soviet Defense Expenditures: Methodological Issues and Policy Implications," Congressional Research Service, Report No. .85-131F, July 5, 1985.

26. Gorbachev, *Pravda*, May 17, 1985; Andropov, *Pravda*, April 1983; Chernenko, *Kommunist*, December 1984.

27. *Pravda*, September 8, 1985; Patrick Cockburn, *Financial Times*, May 16, 1985. "State subsidies to agriculture in the USSR rose from about 17 billion rubles in 1970 to over 37 billion in 1980, more than doubling in a decade and reaching more than 50% of the national income produced in agriculture." Vladimir G. Treml, "Subsidies in Soviet Agriculture: Record and Prospects," *Soviet Economy in the 1980's*, op. cit., Part 2, p. 171.

28. N. N. Inozemtsev, *Planovoe khozyaystvo*, No. 10, 1984.

29. Murray Feshbach, "Health in the USSR—Organization, Trends, and Ethics." Paper prepared for the International Colloquium, "Health Care Systems: Moral Issues and Public Policy," July 23-26, 1985, Bad Homburg, West Germany (to be published by D. Reidel and Co., edited by Robert U. Massey and Hans-Martin Sass).

30. Cf. Morris Bornstein, "Improving the Soviet Economic Mechanism," *Soviet Studies*, Vol. XXVII, No. 1, January 1985, pp. 1-30. Morris Bornstein provides a useful description of the economic mechanism and economic system that Gorbachev might reform: "Economic system changes seek to improve economic performance by altering some methods for carrying out given (or possibly new) economic policies. In contemporary Soviet parlance, these methods are often called the 'economic mechanism' (*ekonomicheskii-mekhanizm* or *khozyaistvennyi mekhanizm*). It consists of the means by which the government steers economic activity in regard to the choice of output; the allocation of labor, materials and fuels, machinery and equipment, and money for current production and for investment; and the distribution of personal income from participation in productive activity. This conception of the 'economic mechanism' comprises, for instance: (1) the procedures for planning production and investment; (2) the allocation of goods through 'material-supply' channels and inter-enterprise contracts; (3) the performance indicators by which the activities of enterprises, associations, and ministries are evaluated; (4) the incentives to managers and workers to strive for good performance; (5) the financial flows accompanying the movement and use of resources; and (6) the prices in which goods and services are valued. The 'economic system' includes, in addition to the 'economic mechanism,' the arrangements for the ownership of the means of production and the organizational structure to administer and conduct economic activity."
For a prescription on Soviet reform, see also "Open Letter from the World Bank: Some Polite Suggestions for Mr. Gorbachev," from A. W. Clausen, President of the World Bank, reproduced in *Financial Times*, August 14, 1985, p. 11.

31. Zdenek Mlynar—Secretary of the Czechoslovak Communist Party Central Committee during the ill-fated 'Prague Spring,' which was ended by the Soviet-led

invasion of August 1968—studied in Moscow, where he formed a close friendship with another rising young official named Mikhail Gorbachev. Now in exile, Mlynar has written two articles on the new Soviet leader, for the Italian Communist Party's newspaper and for an Austrian magazine. Gorbachev, he suggests, is a pragmatist who may be expected to recognize the need both for reforms in the Soviet system and for different communist regimes to follow their own paths of development. Kevin Devlin in *Some Views of the Gorbachev Era,* Radio Free Europe, Background Report 57, June 28, 1985.

32. Based on economic discussions in Moscow in March 1985 with N. Federenko, Ye. Kapustin, Y. Ambartsumov, Oleg Bogomolov, as well as on the writings of others.

33. Ed A. Hewett, The Brookings Institution, "Gorbachev's Emerging Strategy for Reforming the Soviet Economy." Testimony presented before the Subcommittee on Europe and the Middle East of the Committee on Foreign Affairs of the U.S. House of Representatives on "Domestic Issues in the Soviet Union," July 29, 1985, pp. 2, 17, 18. Hough, op. cit.

34. *Pravda Ukrainy,* September 24, 1984.

35. John P. Hardt and Donna Gold, "Soviet Commercial Behavior with Western Nations," in Dan Caldwell, editor, *Soviet International Behavior and U.S. Policy Options* (Lexington, Mass.: Lexington Books, 1985).

36. *Pravda,* June 16 and 21, 1985; Bogomolov, op. cit. Tass report of Gorbachev-Kadar exchange, September 25, 1985. Mikhail Gorbachev, speech to October Party Plenum, *Pravda,* October 15, 1985. John P. Hardt and Donna L. Gold, "Changes in East-West Trade: The Policy Context," in Jan Fedorowicz, editor, *East-West Trade in the 1980s: Prospects and Policies* (Boulder, Colorado: Westview Press, 1985). Cf. Wharton, *Current Analysis,* "The Results of the CMEA Summit," June 29, 1984, Vol. IV, No. 46-47.

37. For a case study on the earlier joint CMEA energy project, the Orenburg gas pipeline, see John Hannigan and Carl McMillan, "Joint Investment in Resource Development: Sectoral Approaches to Socialist Integration," in *East European Economic Assessment,* Part 2 (Washington, D.C.: GPO, 1981), pp. 274-283.

38. *Pravda,* June 15, 1985, Bogomolov, op. cit.; *Pravda,* October 15, 1985.

39. John P. Hardt and Donna L. Gold, "East-West Trade Policy and Implications for the CMEA Region," paper given at the Kennan Institute, Spring 1985, at a workshop in honor of Franklyn Holzman.

40. *Izvestiya,* July 28, 1985. "The Three Pillars of Auto VAZ." Cf. George Holliday, "Western Technology to the Soviet Automotive Industry," in Bruce Parrott, editor, *Trade, Technology and Soviet-American Relations* (Bloomington, Indiana: Indiana University Press, 1985), pp. 94, 98, 110.

41. *Izvestiya,* July 28, 1985.

42. Discussions in Moscow and in *Business East Europe,* July 19, 1985, p. 226.

43. U.S. International Trade Commission, "Forty-first Quarterly Report to the Congress and the Trade Policy Committee on Trade Between the United States and the Non-Market Countries during 1984," Washington, D.C., March 1985.

44. "...the Soviets may downgrade the value of what might otherwise be a fairly active transfer by interposing middlemen, for example, the KGB or foreign-trade organizations, in the process. While this may serve the interests of the middlemen, it limits direct feedback between the receivers and suppliers of the technology." S. E. Goodman, "Technology Transfer and Development of the Soviet Computer Industry," in Bruce Parrott, editor, op. cit., pp. 123-24. In the same vein, Thane Gustafson, commenting on the French disclosures on Soviet industrial espionage, notes that "[i]n a sense, by acquiring the technology illegally, the Soviets cheat themselves out of training, personnel, follow-up visits by the firm, etc."

Congressional Roundtable on U.S.-Soviet Relations, a project of the Peace Through Law Education Fund, 1985 Report, p. 53.

45. Robert C. McFarlane, Assistant to the President for National Security Affairs, "U.S.-Soviet Relations in the late Twentieth Century," at Channel City Club & Woman's Forum luncheon at the Miramar Convention Center, August 19, 1985.

5

ACTIVE TECHNOLOGY TRANSFER AND THE DEVELOPMENT OF SOVIET MICROELECTRONICS

Mark Kuchment

For the purposes of this essay, "active technology transfer" refers to the transfer of technologically sophisticated professionals from one country to another, as opposed to the transfer of hardware or ideas, which might be considered "passive" technology transfer. I wish to deal in particular with the careers of two American expatriates, American-educated electrical engineers known in the Soviet Union as Filipp Staros and Iosef Berg. Between 1956 and 1973, they created a very successful design bureau in the USSR, which designed and was able to produce on a limited scale the first Soviet automatically controlled small computers. Staros and Berg are also credited with establishing in the Soviet Union the new computer technology field of microelectronics, which the Russians now call *mikroelektronika.*

Approximately four years ago, in the process of interviewing Soviet émigré scientists, I encountered the unusual story of two American engineers with successful careers in the Soviet R&D community. Time and time again their names would come up—Filipp Georgievich Staros and Iosef Veniaminovich Berg—chief designer and chief engineer, respectively, of a design bureau operating in Leningrad under the auspices of the military in the 1960s and 1970s.[1] Both Staros and Berg arrived in the Soviet Union from Czechoslovakia at the end of 1955 or the beginning of 1956. Staros came with his American-born wife; Berg with his Czech wife. I will discuss in greater detail the career of Filipp Georgievich Staros, who emerged as the leader of this small American team.[2]

Staros's former colleagues maintain that his ideas gained acceptance due to three factors: (1) the support of the Soviet military, under whose auspices he worked from 1956 on; (2) the glamour of having been reared and educated in America and employed in the United States; and (3) Staros's unusual combination of abilities as a good researcher and capable manager. Here are some relevant excerpts from the interviews:

> Our director was an outstanding person. On top of being a good scientist and a strong personality, he also emanated the aura of an American. In addition, he had high-level connections. He knew Dimitry Ustinov (later Minister of Defense); he knew individuals from the Central Committee of the Communist Party of the Soviet Union, and also, I think, people from the KGB.[3]
>
> Staros was invited several times to the meetings of the Military Industrial Commission (VPK). He discussed his own projects.[4]
>
> Our Director was a consultant of the VPK.[5]
>
> Staros was not only a good professional, but also a good organizer.[6]

The military connection was an important one for several reasons: (1) the military paid more; (2) the military had access to the necessary equipment for the execution of research projects which they sponsored; and (3) because of the high priority assigned to their projects, the military had access to the higher ranks of the Soviet bureaucracy. Those in direct contact with the military-industrial commission (described rather loosely by Henry Kissinger as "a Party-State organization in charge of all the defense industries"[7]) may find themselves face to face with the Secretaries of the Central Committee of the Communist Party of the Soviet Union, Deputy Prime Ministers, top military men, and the top scientists in the country.

Staros's American background proved to be a substantial element in his successful career in the Soviet Union. Hans Rogger[8] and Kendall Bailes[9] (among others) pointed out that Soviet thinking as early as the 1920s and 1930s had shifted from a preoccupation with West European technology, which had enjoyed dominance before the Revolution, toward an increasing interest in borrowing from the American experience. After some disappointment with the American model, mostly due to the economic collapse of 1929, Soviet interest in American technology and American know-how gained new momentum during World War II and in the aftermath of the success of the Manhattan Project. These attitudes became even more prevalent following Stalin's death in 1953 and the beginning of the "thaw" period.

The final and highly substantial reason for Filipp Staros's success was his ability not only to conduct research, but also to manage effectively large research teams. This rather un-American ability (exemplified by the successes and failures of Robert Oppenheimer) fit very neatly with the mode of operation of the Soviet R&D community, where leading scientists (Abram Ioffe, Mstislav Keldysh, Igor Kurchatov, Sergei Korolev) were also successful managers of their own projects.

Staros arrived in the Soviet Union from Prague in late 1955 or early 1956, accompanied by his American-born wife, four children, and an American colleague, friend, and confidant, who later served as his deputy. "Staros," one interviewee confirmed, "had been living in Prague. . . . Khrushchev had brought [him] to the Soviet Union with his family."[10]

Though there is some question as to who invited Staros to the USSR (Eric Firdman claims it was Dementiev, then Minister of Aviation Technology), there is little doubt he was highly regarded by the Soviet authorities from the beginning. His salary of 700 rubles per month[11] was noticeably higher than the 550 rubles per month received by a deputy minister of the USSR. Staros became director of a newly created laboratory in a military research institute in Leningrad. The 1970 yearbook of the *Great Soviet Encyclopedia*[12] attests to his position as director from 1956 to 1960.

The rather mysterious, even exotic origin of Filipp Staros is reflected in the single phrase of his official Soviet biography: "In 1941, graduated from a university in Toronto and started to work as a researcher."[13] But even this phrase is misleading: attempts to confirm his degree were unsuccessful.

After nearly 18 months attempting to trace Filipp Georgievich Staros back to the United States or Canada, a breakthrough was finally achieved. Many important details of Staros's life obtained from his former Soviet colleagues closely parallel those of an American electrical engineer named Alfred Sarant, a close friend of Julius Rosenberg.[14]

Alfred Sarant received his B.S. in electrical engineering from Cooper Union College in New York City in 1941.[15] He worked in communications systems at Fort Monmouth[16] and Bell Laboratories, and as an electrical engineer in the nuclear physics laboratory of Cornell University in 1948. At Cornell he was involved in the construction of the cyclotron.[17] By 1950 he had gained substantial experience in the area of communications systems—including radars, knowledge of the first American computers and the electronic equipment of a cyclotron, and an understanding of the unique organizational structure of Bell Laboratories.

Sarant also was a member of the American Communist Party until 1944. There are indications that he and Julius Rosenberg belonged to the same party cell.[18] At Cornell he was described as a trade union organizer.[19] His sister describes him as highly idealistic.[20]

Sarant was interrogated by the FBI in the summer of 1950, immediately after the arrest of Julius Rosenberg.[21] Sarant, however, was not arrested; he was given permission to visit relatives in New York after the interrogation. There he joined a close woman friend and, using false identification, they crossed the American border into Mexico on August 9, 1950. Sarant's name then disappears from the historical record. Five years later, an American engineer named Filipp Staros came to the USSR from Czechoslovakia.

I will describe here several points which lead me to conclude that the American engineer Alfred Sarant and the Soviet professor Filipp Georgievich Staros are one and the same person.

- When I showed the photograph of Alfred Sarant taken in 1945 (given to me by his sister, Electra Jayson) to Professor Philip Morrison of MIT, Professor Morrison easily recognized him, and described Alfred Sarant as his next-door-neighbor in Ithaca, New York, between 1947 and 1950. When I showed the same photograph to Dr. Eric Firdman, he also identified the person, but claimed it was his Soviet boss, Professor Filipp Georgievich Staros, an American who had come to Russia from Czechoslovakia at the end of 1955.
- According to Eric Firdman, Staros had curly black hair, brown eyes, and was 5 feet 6 or 7 inches tall. Electra Jayson independently gave me the same description of her brother, Alfred Sarant.
- The name "Staros" sounds Greek, and, indeed, Filipp Staros claimed to be Greek-American. According to the testimony of his Soviet colleagues, he enjoyed watching Greek movies in the USSR. His Russian patronymic—Georgievich—indicates that his father's name was George. According to Electra Jayson, Alfred Sarant's father's name was Epamenonda George Sarantopoulos, changed to Nonda George Sarant. The family on both sides was Greek Orthodox.[22]
- According to Eric Firdman, Filipp Staros claimed to know Professor Hans Bethe, and claimed that Professor Bethe even presented a gift to his child. Walter and Miriam Schneir claimed that Hans Bethe "has given an article made of silver to the Sarants' newborn."[23]
- Filipp Staros mentioned to his Soviet colleagues that he had participated in the construction of an American cyclotron. Alfred Sarant did the same in 1948.[24]

The above are only several of many facts which coincide in the biographies of Alfred Sarant and Filipp Staros. There are also discrepancies. Alfred Sarant was born on September 26, 1918. Filipp Staros was born, according to the yearbook of the *Soviet Encyclopedia,* in 1917, and, as Eric Firdman claims, in the USSR they always celebrated his birthday on February 24.

The name of Alfred Sarant's girlfriend, with whom he left the United States, was Carol. The name of Mrs. Staros in the USSR was Ann. Alfred Sarant's close friend and colleague, who also disappeared in 1950, was named Joel Barr; the name of Professor Staros's deputy was Iosef V. Berg.

But these discrepancies are rather natural byproducts of the process of giving a person, or a group of people, new identities.[25]

Whatever the reasons for Sarant to assume a new identity, an American engineer named Staros managed to become an active member of the Soviet military R&D community. A Soviet scientist or engineer needed a second-class clearance from the KGB, only to find himself a subordinate of an American engineer! The ability to create an environment in which an American-trained specialist could be productive in the Soviet Union is something at which the Soviets excelled, but, as we shall see, their flexibility had its limits.

Computers designed and produced by Filipp Staros, however, received high acclaim both in the USSR and in the West. A 1964 issue of *Soviet Union* magazine[26] described a process control computer UM-1-Nkh. This 150-lb., 100-watt computer consisted of 8,000 transistors, well over 10,000 resistors and capacitors, and during the test operated for 250 hours without error. This computer was described in the American literature of the period also.[27] The designer of this computer was said by Soviet authorities to be a certain comrade "Filippov." It was not until four years later, when Staros received the State Prize, that it was publicly disclosed he had been the inventor of the UM-1-Nkh. The Pravda announcement read: "To award the State Prize of the USSR for the year 1969 to Staros, Filipp Georgievich, project director and chief designer for the development of a small-size process control computer UM-1-Nkh. . . ."[28] It is clear that Filippov was a derivative of Staros's first name—Filipp.

According to Eric Firdman, "Nkh" formally stood for "Narodnoe Khozyaistvo" (State Economy). A behind-the-scenes joke was that it also meant Nikita Khrushchev, who was a kind of godfather to Staros's design bureau and even paid a personal visit to the laboratory in the early sixties.[29]

Another machine developed by Staros attracting a great deal of attention in the West was the Elektronika K-200.[30] This was a process control computer weighing 264 lbs., which was able to perform 40,000 operations per second. The author of an American review pointed out that many of the features of the computer's design would not be considered unusual in the West, but their appearance in a Soviet computer was highly unusual. The K-200 was the first Soviet production computer that could fairly be characterized as "well engineered" and "surprisingly up-to-date." English technical jargon was also acknowledged. All of this would not have been such a surprise had the authors of the review known that the designer was a competent American electrical engineer who followed American publications on the subject on a day-to-day basis.[31]

As pointed out earlier, Staros/Sarant had limited contact with modern American computer technology, because he had left the country in 1950. (William Shockley invented the transistor in 1947.) However, he may have gained a better understanding of computer design during his stay in Czechoslovakia, where he was in touch with the leading Czechoslovakian computer specialist, Professor Antonin Svoboda. His personal opinion of Czech computer science was quite low, but his involvement in the field kept him informed.[32]

Whatever the source of his knowledge, Staros managed to achieve a series of spectacular successes during his years in the Soviet Union. According to a Soviet colleague now residing in the West, Filipp Staros deserves considerable credit for the establishment in the Soviet Union of a new area of computer technology, which the Russians now call microelectronics. The first step toward this achievement was a report on microelectronics as a new area of R&D, presented by Filipp Staros in November 1958 at a meeting of the principal designers and managers of the Soviet electronics industry. Some 15 years later, the term *mikroelektronika* was legitimized as part of the Russian language, when it appeared in Volume 16 of the third edition of the *Great Soviet Encyclopedia,* published in 1974.[33] Microelectronics was defined there as that area of computer technology dealing with functional microminiatures, integrated electronic assemblies, and units and devices such as integrated circuits. In other words, microelectronics opened the way for the creation of second- and third-generation computers in the USSR.

After 1960, Filipp Staros's position was described as chief designer of a design bureau. In 1967 he was awarded the title of Doctor of Technical Sciences (roughly equivalent to an American full professorship), and, as pointed out earlier, in 1969 he was awarded the State Prize.[34] Staros's influence increased in 1961 by the creation of a new, powerful Soviet bureaucracy—the State Committee—followed in 1965 by the creation of the Ministry of the Electronics Industry. The Minister, Alexander Shokin,[35] received his engineering degree in 1934 from Bauman Advanced Technical College in Moscow, one of the most prestigious engineering schools in the USSR. He worked for many years in the defense industry, was then Deputy Minister of the Radio-Technical Industry, and finally was able to create his own organization—the Ministry of the Electronics Industry.

The goal of the Ministry of the Electronics Industry was to improve the quality and increase the production of basic electronic components, without which the production of modern radar equipment or computers was virtually impossible. These components included various types of vacuum tubes, magnetrons, and klystrons, as well as semiconductors, transistors, resistors, and integrated circuits.[36] From the outset, the Ministry of the Electronics Industry was considered one of the most powerful among the so-called "Nine Sisters"—the nine industrial ministries most heavily involved in military production. This made Shokin's position very powerful, but it also put him under enormous pressure to produce rapid and practical results. This may also explain why he so readily supported Staros and encouraged him to expand his activities. In so doing, he inadvertently steered Staros onto a dangerous course. In staying on that course, Staros reached in a relatively short time the limits of Russian tolerance and flexibility toward foreigners in the Soviet R&D

community. The dangerous step that Staros undertook was the development of a "grand design"—a blueprint of a microelectronics center in Zelenograd, now the center of the Soviet electronics industry.

According to an eyewitness account:

All development of the project on the Center of Microelectronics was undertaken in our place by a group of five to ten people under the direction of Staros. Our project was not the result of wishful thinking. It was meticulous thought. We were young and enthusiastic. Staros knew all the relevant people, enjoyed high authority, and had carte blanche from Khrushchev. Khrushchev visited our place in 1962 and saw for himself what possibilities the development of microelectronics could open. As a result, he gave his support to a decision (*postanovlenie*) on the development of the Center for Microelectronics. Several decisions undertaken jointly by the Central Committee of the CPSU and the Council of Ministers of the USSR were initiated. All of them were classified. They were never published in the open press. Those decisions made possible the creation of a center for microelectronics [in Zelenograd]. Design bureaus were also created in Riga, Minsk, Tallin, Erevan, and Tbilisi. As a model for this center, American companies (such as IBM, TI, Raytheon) were used. English was the first language of our boss. He took American magazines home to read every day. Nobody could make an appointment with the boss without preparing himself by reading American scientific literature, which referred to the future topic of discussion.[37]

The Center for Microelectronics was to include six or seven research institutes and design bureaus, a technical college (now known as the Institut Elektronnoi Tekhniki), and a production plant. The activities of the entire superstructure were coordinated by the Director General of the Center. Staros was appointed Associate Director General of Research concurrently with his position as chief of the design bureau in Leningrad.[38] This situation set the scene for future trouble for Staros. On the one hand, he was forced to stay in Leningrad to counter the attacks of the local party bureaucracy directed against his design bureau. On the other hand, the Center in Zelenograd began to develop so rapidly and so successfully that Staros's Soviet colleagues soon realized that they could now cope with the Center—a real plum—on their own. In the summer of 1964, Staros found himself under double attack. The secretaries of the Leningrad Regional Party Committee strongly disapproved of the fact that the director of this important research organization conducting an enormous amount of work for the military was a foreigner. They—especially the regional party secretary, Grigori Romanov—likewise strongly objected to the cadre policy of Staros, who hired people mostly on merit. The result of his cadre policy was the emergence of a politically unreliable meritocracy within the Soviet military R&D community, among whom were many Jews and nonparty members.

Feeling the heat in Leningrad, Staros could not help but realize that the chances of his moving to Zelenograd were increasingly slim. As in 1950, he decided to cut the Gordian knot in his life with another bold stroke. He wrote a personal letter to Khrushchev outlining his grievances and complaining about the lack of support from the Minister of the Electronics Industry, Mr. Shokin. The letter arrived at Khrushchev's office in early October 1964. Unfortunately, Khrushchev was overthrown on October 14, 1964, and Staros's letter was forwarded to the Minister of the Electronics Industry.

The Minister's reaction was predictable. There is information that during his meeting with Staros, Mr. Shokin said the following: "Filipp Georgievich, it seems to me that you have the strange fantasy that you are the founder of Soviet microelectronics. It is all wrong. The Communist Party created Soviet microelectronics, and the sooner you realize this fact, the better it will be for you."[39]

In practice, this meant that Staros would no longer play an independent role in the Center in Zelenograd, his brainchild. In fact, he was removed from his associate directorship in 1965. In return, Shokin agreed to help him retain his position in Leningrad. For a number of years, Shokin was successful in doing this. Then, the Leningrad party boss, Tolstikov, was appointed Ambassador to China, and Grigori Romanov, whose policies toward Staros were far from friendly (as far as one can see), succeeded him in Leningrad.

"Romanov tried to push our design bureau into a merger with a big research and production unit by the name of 'Positron,' but Shokin was able to extricate Staros."[40] In other words, the Minister sitting in Moscow was still able to overrule a very powerful local party boss. This situation allowed Staros to continue his research and design successfully, to become a Doctor of Technical Sciences, and even to win the State Prize in 1969. However, by now he was aware of the very definite limits within which he could operate. Even operating within these much narrower limits, he was still able to achieve some spectacular successes.

In addition to the above-mentioned computers, concepts, and organizations, Staros is credited with several other technical achievements, such as the first Soviet integrated ferrite memory, the first MOS (metal oxide semiconductor) integrated circuits, and the first Soviet microreceiver. He also developed the first Soviet desk-top computer and the first Soviet microelectronic airborne computer.[41]

Staros widely used the Western approach to research and design, as well as Western literature and, when necessary, sensitive American technology. On at least one occasion, he initiated *direct* technology transfer: the illegal acquisition of several photorepeaters from the David Mann Company, located on Route 128 near Boston.[42] He used these photorepeaters to resolve a bottleneck in one of his programs.

Although the Soviet authorities treated him as a spent force in the last years of his life (between 1973 and 1979),[43] Staros's overall success in the USSR cannot be overestimated. Of course, Staros showed great technical, political, and administrative skills during his years in the Soviet Union. But it should also be pointed out that the Soviet authorities responded in kind, creating for Staros an environment in which he was very productive and creative for many years. This rather unique situation may be the result of the fact that Staros's design bureau belonged to the core of the Soviet military R&D community, where the achievement of a positive result in the shortest possible period of time, using all the available means at the time—a "mission-oriented approach," as John Hardt once put it—was and still is the order of the day.

NOTES

1. Mark Kuchment, *The Life and Death of Alfred Sarant/Filipp Staros and the Beginnings of Soviet Microelectronics,* Report No. 12, Russian Research Center, Harvard University, Seminar on "Soviet Science and Technology: Eyewitness Accounts," 1983.
2. On Berg, see Mark Kuchment, "Making it in the USSR," *The New York Review of Books,* March 29, 1984, p. 49.
3. "Assessment of Soviet Research and Development Capabilities: Information and Insights from the Third Immigration," Interview Project of the Russian Research Center, Harvard University (1981). Interview No. 412, p. 9. (Hereinafter cited as Interview Project).
4. Interview with Dr. Henry Eric Firdman, August 3, 1983.
5. Interview Project, Interview No. 412, p. 9.
6. Firdman interview.
7. Henry Kissinger, *White House Years* (Boston: Little Brown, 1979), pp. 1233-1234.
8. Hans Rogger, "Americanism and the Economic Development of Russia," in *Comparative Studies in Society and History,* 23:3 (1981), pp. 382-420.
9. Kendall Bailes, "The American Connection: Ideology and the Transfer of American Technology to the Soviet Union, 1917-1941," *Comparative Studies in Society and History,* 23:3 (1981), pp. 421-448.
10. Interview Project, Interview No. 209, pp. 26-27.
11. Telephone interview with Dr. Henry Eric Firdman, January 1982.
12. *Yearbook of the Soviet Encyclopedia,* 1970, p. 602 (in Russian).
13. Ibid.
14. Walter and Miriam Schneir, *Invitation to an Inquest* (New York: Pantheon, 1983), article by Alfred Sarant; Ronald Radosh and Joyce Milton, *The Rosenberg File* (New York: Holt, Reinhart, and Winston, 1983). Article: Sarant (1984 edition, article by Kuchment); Interview with Dr. Judith Reppy, July 14, 1983; Interview with Professor Philip Morrison, July 21, 1983; Interview with Electra Jayson Sarant, July 20, 1983.
15. Confirmation from Registrar's Office, Cooper Union College, July 20, 1983.
16. *The Rosenberg File,* op.cit., pp. 104-05.
17. Telephone interview with Dr. Judith Reppy, July 18, 1983.
18. *The Rosenberg File, op. cit., p. 110.*
19. Telephone interview with Dr. Judith Reppy, July 18, 1983.
20. Telephone interview with Electra Jayson Sarant, July 15, 1983.
21. *Invitation to an Inquest,* op. cit., pp. 473-474.

22. Personal letter from Electra Jayson, July 19, 1983.
23. *Invitation to an Inquest,* op. cit., p. 475. Article by Alfred Sarant.
24. Ibid., p. 474.
25. Mark Kuchment, "The Rosenberg Friend Prematurely Condemned," *New York Times,* October 20, 1983, in "Letters to the Editor."
26. *Soviet Union* magazine, No. 172, 1964, pp. 34-35.
27. Willis N. Ware and Wade B. Holland, *Rand Memo,* No. RM-4810-PR, pp. 21-31.
28. *Pravda,* November 7, 1969.
29. Mark Kuchment, "The American Connection to Soviet Microelectronics," *Physics Today,* September 1985, pp. 44-50.
30. W. Holland and W. Ware, *Soviet Cybernetics Review,* May 1972, Vol. 2, No. 3, pp. 19-30.
31. Telephone Interview with Dr. Henry Eric Firdman, January 1982.
32. Prokop Machan, "Czech Computer Policy," *Soviet Cybernetics Review,* Vol. 2, No. 3, pp. 37-43; Mark Kuchment, "Beyond the Rosenbergs," *The Boston Review,* September 1985, pp. 5-6, 23-24.
33. Henry Eric Firdman, *Decision Making in the Soviet Microelectronics Industry* (Falls Church, Va.: Delphic Associates, 1985), pp. 46-48; *Bol'shaya Sovetskaya Entsiklopedia* (Moscow), Vol. 16, pp. 246-248; *Great Soviet Encyclopedia* (New York), Vol. 16, pp. 260-262.
34. *Yearbook of The Soviet Encyclopedia,* 1970 (Moscow), p. 602 (in Russian).
35. Alexander Ivanovich Shokin, *Bol'shaya Sovetskaya Entsiklopedia,* 3rd edition, Letter "Sh," line 1336.
36. Anatol Fedoseev, "Design in Soviet Military R & D," *Papers on Soviet Science and Technology,* Paper No. 8, pp. 14-15, Russian Research Center, Harvard University (1982).
37. Interview Project, Interview No. 412, pp. 20-21.
38. Firdman telephone interview, January 1982.
39. Interview Project, Interview No. 412, Comments.
40. Ibid., Interview No. 209, p. 24.
41. Firdman, *Decision Making in the Soviet Microelectronics Industry,* op. cit., p. 1.
42. Melvern, Hebditch, and Anning, *Techno-Bandits* (Boston: Houghton Mifflin & Co., 1984), p. 48.
43. Mark Kuchment, "The Fate of Sarant," *The New York Review of Books,* November 24, 1983.

6

SOVIET AND EAST EUROPEAN ACQUISITION EFFORTS: AN INSIDE VIEW

Jan Sejna

The issue of "technology theft" from the West by the Soviet Union and its satellites is an extremely important problem, both in terms of Western security policy and in terms of overall trade relations. Yet, to steal as much as possible from the West is nothing new for Soviet leaders: They have utilized such methods since the Soviet Union first came into existence. This official policy of acquisition, however, began in the Khrushchev era. I met Khrushchev for the first time in 1954, when the Party Congress was held in Prague. Khrushchev gave a "secret speech," his first official speech; it was nothing new, the usual Marxist polemic about everything in the Soviet Union being the best and everything in the United States being the worst. But his private comments were very interesting. Khrushchev said, "Comrades, we have to get as many loans from the capitalists as possible, because the more they give us, the more new technology we can buy. If we don't have the money to buy it, the cheapest way is to steal it."

Since 1959, the decision of the Soviet Defense Council has been very clear: All intelligence services—and here I am referring to my experience in Czechoslovakia—were ordered to select the best cadres, as they are called, and to prepare them for technology-related espionage work. In Czechoslovakia, we selected the best military officers from the artillery, air force, and chemical troops, all highly educated professionals. They were then trained in intelligence work for two years, and all transferred directly to commercial organizations. The danger thus presented is that these people are not just simple agents: They are professionals, directed in their work from the highest levels. When we initially received the order from Moscow, 200 officers were selected in that first year for military intelligence alone, and this continued every year thereafter.

How does this system work, and who is responsible? Many different organizations and institutions are involved. For example, the Military-Industrial Commission and the Scientific and Technology Committee have considerable influence over Soviet acquisition policy. It is, however, the Defense Council which ultimately directs the program from the very top. Every November the Defense Council approves operational plans for the GRU and the KGB. After six months, the Defense Council evaluates how successful they have been. In particularly important cases, daily monitoring takes place—for example, with the "Concorde" (known in Czechoslovakia as "Concordsky").

In 1959, every minister in charge of industrial affairs—light industry, heavy industry, and the chemical industry—received instructions from the Defense Council to submit to the Ministers of Defense and Interior (the Czech KGB), by November of each year, lists of what they needed to acquire from the West. Two years later, the Ministers of Defense and Interior both complained about the large numbers of requests being submitted to them; carrying them out would require cutting back on other espionage work. As a result, the Defense Council decided to send these requests to the State Planning Commission (Gosplan), the main military administrative unit. Czechoslovakia's Gosplan, today headed by Lieutenant Schurka, selected the most important technology to be stolen from the West.

Of course, before that technology was selected, orders had to come from the Soviet Union. It must be remembered that the intelligence services of the satellite countries are merely branches of the Soviet intelligence services, and, from a strategic viewpoint, the Soviet Union must come first. In one of Gorbachev's most recent speeches, he said, "We have to be independent from a strategic point of view." A satellite country puts forward its plans for acquiring technology for the Soviet Union, and its own national interest comes only after that of the Soviet Union.

In order to see where the Soviet leaders will concentrate their intelligence services, their long-term plans and strategies must be understood. I think it *is* possible to anticipate very clearly where they will concentrate these thousands of agents—their own and those of the satellites. Unfortunately, many people believe that Moscow does not have any long-term policy or strategy. This is a very dangerous belief. Our intelligence services would do well, therefore, to focus their attention on the decisionmaking unit where requests for technology acquisition originate—namely, the Defense Council. In particular, we in the West need to know more about the "secret" aspects of Soviet and East European technology policy.

In the Soviet Union, Czechoslovakia, and elsewhere, parts of the budgets and State plans (one-year, five-year, or longer-term plans) are kept confidential. These plans never go to parliament—which is to say, they never go to the government. Rather, they are approved by the Defense Council and controlled by the party apparatus and the military administration at Gosplan.

Every year before Christmas, before the Defense Council approves the various plans to acquire technology from the West, the Ministers of Defense and Interior organize a show for the Defense Council and the Politburo. Ironically, in Prague it is done across the street from the American Embassy, where in three big halls they exhibit what has been taken from the West. The last time I saw this exhibition, in 1967, there were over 430 documents and pieces of technology stolen from the West and Japan by the Czech intelligence services. The Minister of the Defense Council and the head of the Politburo had saved Czechoslovakia over 300 million korunas of research and development funds by illegally acquiring technology from abroad.

In 1965, Czechoslovakia and other satellite countries analyzed the problem of military technology and weapons. In some areas—computers, for example—they openly admitted that the Warsaw Pact countries were 15 years behind NATO. The Defense Council concluded that if the intelligence services could acquire as much technology as possible, the difference could be reduced to between 7 and 10 years. As a result, it became *official* policy to acquire illegally these various technologies from the West. With regard to getting computers, for example, the Prime Minister himself, Joseph Leonard, was in charge of the operation. Computers acquired illegally from Switzerland were routed through Germany and Austria into Czechoslovakia. Third World and neutral countries—such as Switzerland, Austria, and others—play particularly important roles in acquisition strategies, because in many cases it is easier to buy or steal technology there than in West Germany or the United States.

Where do the intelligence services concentrate their activities? First of all, they are interested in the basic scientific research done by private companies in the West. They follow not only research and development programs, but also the R&D community, the persons involved. Many conferences orchestrated by the Soviet Union and satellite countries are, from the outset, arranged for the sole purpose of inviting Western scientists in order to recruit them, or at least to glean everything possible from them.

Second, Soviet or East European agents conduct close surveillance of Western factory operations, with particular regard to the possibilities for sabotage as well as theft. Indeed, they have instructions not only to steal as much as they can, but also to slow down the research and development process in important areas of technology and scientific development within the United States. I do not believe the United States pays enough attention to KGB and GRU activities in this area. It is interesting to note, moreover, that few officers of the GRU are ever kicked out of Western countries (or arrested). From a strategic point of view, this is very dangerous; the GRU has hundreds of agents, highly trained professionals, operating here in the United States and elsewhere.

A third critical characteristic of a Soviet acquisition policy is the use of deception, which is not adequately understood in the West. The communist system cannot exist without deception. In the present case, the Soviets want the Western nations to believe that they already have certain technologies. Conversely, if the Soviet Union has a particular type of technology, the leadership does everything possible to keep it secret—they are very quiet about it. For example, when Brezhnev said that the Soviet Union would stop production of the neutron bomb if the Americans would do the same, what it really meant was that the Soviets did not have the neutron bomb. We must also recognize that other companies, ministers, and diplomats also participate in Soviet industrial espionage in subtle ways—by tipping off intelligence services or by establishing relationships with Western scientists and engineers, thus helping to pinpoint important scientific work that is being conducted.

In Czechoslovakia, I was aware of three basic methods of technology/technical data acquisition. First, the careful review of open literature from the West, especially since the time of Khrushchev. Thousands of Soviet and East European scientists have been able to study documents and designs that are openly available and easily accessible. They have been kept especially busy surveying the enormous amount of literature openly published in the United States and elsewhere. Second, there is the recruitment of agents on the basis of a shared ideology—an Italian scientist, for example, who belonged to the party. Finally, there is the recruitment of Western agents on the basis of money or blackmail.

Under Gorbachev's leadership, I believe that the pressure on both the KGB and GRU to acquire needed items from the West will be much stronger, because as Khrushchev and Brezhnev both said, "We in the Soviet Union cannot improve technology without access to the West's technology." We must be particularly cautious now. Gorbachev says that he wants to return to détente—not to the "old" détente, but to a "new" détente—which means, I believe, opening our doors much wider and closing those of the Soviet bloc countries much tighter. What is especially important, of course, is whether or not he will be successful in this attempt, which will be measured by how much the Soviet Union ultimately gets from the West.

The need for greater technological progress, and the inability of Soviet industry to make that progress without Western technology, has been a dilemma for Soviet leaders from the beginning. Khrushchev tried, Brezhnev tried, Andropov tried—one hears the same story about centralization having given more power to factories. It never worked before; it will never work in the future. It is as simple as that. I am afraid that in the Soviet Union, where conservatism is the watchword in the party and out of the party, a change in the economic structure is essentially a political problem. Somebody will have to teach Ivan Ivanovich not to drink or be lazy. I once heard an analyst predict that the Soviet Union will collapse tomorrow, that the Soviet Union will soon switch over to capitalism because Gorbachev has allowed millions of small gardens for people to produce their own vegetables. If the Soviet Union did not collapse after World War II, I do not think the introduction of small gardens means it will collapse tomorrow.

I do not believe it is possible, in the short term, for the Soviet Union to achieve needed progress; that is why Gorbachev is so dependent on the KGB. As we see, he has offered more money to people who work hard. But in view of the continued inability of internal policies to produce results, the other avenue—the KGB—will be utilized. They face the same dilemma; so also, to an increasing extent, do the satellites. We should exploit that situation—with our policy and with our counterintelligence.

I think we should make greater use of forums in the West to look more closely at the issues involved in the illegal acquisition of technology by the Soviet Union, and to focus on the specific technologies—robots, for example—that they may want or need. I think our intelligence services must try to find out what these confidential, "secret" plans are that I referred to earlier, from which these directives originate. The Soviet leadership is very closely involved, and ministers have a great deal of power. It is very important for us to know who these heads of departments are in the bureaucracy, because that is where the power lies. And once Gorbachev has the majority of ministers, secretaries, and heads of departments in his camp, he will be very powerful. It makes no difference who is today the Minister of the Chemical Industry, because tomorrow he could be demoted to being head of a gas station. The party is the power, the party *nomenklatura*. It is upon this decisionmaking structure that we must focus our efforts.

7

WESTERN TECHNOLOGY IN THE SOVIET UNION: WHAT HAPPENS TO IT?

Marshall I. Goldman

In studying the effects of East-West trade, I have been struck by a paradox concerning the role of Western technology in the Soviet Union. On the one hand, it is quite true—as the 1985 DOD/CIA report on the subject attests—that the USSR has devoted major efforts to acquiring Western technology, and that this technology has been of considerable importance to the Soviet defense sector. At the same time, I have learned through interviews with American businessmen experienced in trading with the Soviet Union that Western technology—coveted as it is—is not properly assimilated. I have spoken with, or sent out questionnaires to, about 50 different firms in Japan, the United States, and Western Europe, and 90% say without fail that they are disillusioned by what they see in the USSR. Most of the businessmen contacted have seen their products in the Soviet Union, have been on the site of use (or at least have a very good sense of what is going on), and when I ask them how their technology has performed, they uniformly say, "Poorly." The Soviets, they say, are treating their equipment badly.

So here is the paradox: On the one hand, the Soviets are doing brilliantly with what they are stealing; yet on the other hand, what we sell them seems to lead to one economic disaster after another. I am puzzled by this, and it turns out that Soviet authorities are somewhat puzzled as well. In the 1970s, Kosygin and other Soviet leaders lauded Western technology: "We've got to go out and buy complete plants." In 1967, Kosygin gave a talk on the need for Western products, went out and bought a Fiat plant, and seemed to stimulate a whole series of further deals. But the tune seemed to have changed in 1981. In one of Brezhnev's talks, which appeared in *Pravda* in 1981, he said: "We Soviets must examine why we sometimes forget priorities and spend large sums of money to purchase equipment and technology from foreign countries, when we are fully capable of producing them ourselves, and also at a higher quality." This sentiment has been repeated by many other people, including the head of the Academy of Sciences.

I have studied Soviet statistics and machinery imports from the hard currency countries in an effort to see if Brezhnev's argument ever took hold in the form of reduced imports. It can be seen, for example, that there were years—such as 1984—when the imports were pretty meager. An analysis of the grain statistics shows that when the Soviets import significant amounts of grain, their importation of machinery tends to drop. Allowing for inflation, and even discounting the grain factor, you see that they have not been buying increasing quantities of machinery. Indeed, I think a strong case could be made that imports from the West have significantly dropped. The point is that Brezhnev's advice may have been followed. This helps to explain, moreover, why the Japanese, the Italians, the French, the Germans, and the British all complain that the trade balance is so bad, and that the Soviets are not buying enough equipment from them. It explains as well why the West Europeans are now tying strings to Soviet purchases.

Why is the Soviet leadership disillusioned? In part, the problem is rooted in the inefficiencies of the overall Soviet economy. After all, why should their importation of foreign technology be treated that much differently than their handling of domestic technology? In 1981, for example, officials in the Ministry of Foreign Metallurgy were accused of importing—not necessarily from the hard currency world, but from the world in general—$2 billion worth of equipment that simply was not used; it was left to sit out in a field. Similarly, the Ministry of Petroleum Industry bought $52 million worth of recovery enhancement chemicals and never used them. According to one U.S. corporate executive, computers sold to the USSR were reportedly left sitting out in a field with no shelter, apparently because there are no good warehousing facilities in the Soviet Union. Consequently, when the computers were finally installed, they malfunctioned, and it was found that they had been cannibalized. Even when technology is not badly installed, productivity seldom is more than 60 to 75% capacity on the average. There are very few instances in which it is higher, and those instances are remarkable in and of themselves.

How do the Soviets use their technology? On the whole, foreign technology does seem to be better than the domestic technology, but it still is 30 to 40% less productive than similar technology in Western Europe, Japan, or the United States. Why? For one thing, the sales negotiations tend to take two to four times longer than they should. The Soviets have a different conception of time. Consider the following example. The Japanese were interested in drilling oil off Sakhalin, where you must begin outdoor work in the summer or wait an entire year. The Soviets were not that concerned. Why were they not concerned?

Because those doing the negotiating were from the Ministry of Foreign Trade, not the oil sector. The Ministry of Foreign Trade had a particular goal, that being to get a 10% reduction in the price of the contract. The Japanese said, "You are going to lose a whole year if we don't get things done." But the Soviets waited a whole year. Their conception of time is simply very different from that in Japan and the West. Signing the contract, moreover, is like a group exercise. Sometimes as many as 18 signatories are needed, and it seems that nearly every contract must be signed personally by a deputy prime minister. All of this, of course, translates into an enormous logistical backlog.

Beyond this problem, the industrial ministry concerned is always interested in obtaining the fanciest technology possible. They want the most elaborate kind of equipment, so that it will be as independent of the Soviet work force as possible, and as prestigious. This is pure and simple "gigantamania"; Soviet officials all have a "Texas mentality." For example, one of the things that always puzzles me in the Soviet Union (and in Third World countries) is that when you walk into an office, the typewriter always has an extra-large carriage. "Do you ever use it?" I've asked, and they generally respond, "Well, very seldom. But you never know. Some day I might use it." In the meantime, it looks impressive. As one observer put it, "they tend to overspecify and underutilize."

What about "down time"? Down time is terrible, often because there are no tools. If you are outside Moscow, the likelihood of getting adequate spare parts is even lower, and, as a consequence, one of the peculiar habits of Soviet officials is that when they order a piece of equipment, they tend to over-order spare parts. It is not uncommon that 25% of the contract will go for spare parts. And yet they still will run out. If they buy three years' worth of spare parts, they will run out in 18 months. In other words, preventive maintenance is bad, as is storage. Similar to the computer story, some radar equipment was left out in the open for six months.

It is also curious that you rarely see Western-trained Soviet technicians back on the job in the USSR. Why not? Well, it turns out that this training is used as patronage. "You want to see the West? Okay, go off to Pittsburgh and spend the summer." The problem is that the trip just becomes a boondoggle, and trainees are not used to reproduce Western technology back in the USSR. Soviet planners also have the habit of ordering equipment in advance even though the site is not ready. In the case of the Kama River truck plant, an entire shelter built for the foundry had to be torn down, because after it was built they discovered that the new equipment would not fit through the door. The entire structure had to be torn down. Yet, Soviet officials still persist in ordering the equipment the minute a project is approved.

For balance, let me give you some examples where Western technology is put to better use by the Soviets. In the military sector, by and large, equipment is better used, apparently because there is more discipline and more money. So, too, technology is more effectively absorbed in projects where there is a high priority—as, for example, in the gas pipeline, where both the pipeline and the compressors were ordered and delivered on time, and set in operation in comparable or better time than would have been the case in the United States or Western Europe. Computers' subroutines are more elaborate in some cases, and fancier than they are in the United States. There is also the curious case of copying machines: It turns out that Soviet-operated copying machines generate 40 to 50 million copies and are used for what seems an eternity, whereas the same machines in the United States make about two million copies over a lifetime of about four or five years. Similarly, bottling machines are used for a lifetime in the Soviet Union, as opposed to five to ten years in the United States; and a computer would be used 15 to 20 years in the Soviet Union, compared to five to eight years in the United States.

What explains these peculiarities? The bulk of Western technology in the USSR is less productive, and often is not used, yet here we have a few products that are used well and intensely. First of all, the Soviets do not have the concept of "obsolescence." Obsolescence has been legalized, so to speak, but resistance to it still exists. As a result, machines tend to last forever. Of course, that is not always a wise decision. It may be wonderful that the copying machine lasts so long, but why don't we in the West do the same thing? As one American businessman said, "It's like a kid with a 1957 Chevy, who patches it together with a hammer and nail, and keeps repairing it. What happens as a result? Well, the cars are serviceable and 'do their thing,' but they are gas guzzlers. And in today's environment, they would not be considered really productive, because they consume far too much energy." By Soviet standards, however, this approach may make sense, because capital—particularly foreign currency—is in short supply.

Let me return to the example of the copying machine; this continues to fascinate me. I said to the Western manufacturer of the equipment, "Look at how much they're producing. Maybe they are better off." He responded that in the short run they are better off, because they do not need to reduce the copy, enlarge it, turn it upside down, or collate it. They simply need copies. They have the labor force to staple them or do whatever else has to be done. So in the short run at least, they are better off with older technology. In the long run, however, Western businessmen see major problems developing, and this is what I call "the systems gap." The "systems gap" concept argues that, in the long run, Soviet methods are not wise because they discourage familiarity with new techniques and products: As a result, the technological gap between the USSR and the West simply widens. The old-fashioned copiers, for example, are basically electromechanical machines. If they break down, you take a hammer and screwdriver and fix it. The new, more sophisticated machines that we in the West use are electronic, and it takes a different kind of attitude and preparation as far as repair is concerned. In the short run, the Soviets may be all right, because they are getting enough copies made; but in the long run, they are not building up the infrastructure of servicemen, parts, and new equipment necessary to service and repair more sophisticated machines. Hence, there is a real "systems gap": Soviet operators are wedded to the old, outdated system, which makes it very difficult ever to catch up and to move into a more advanced technological era.

What is the underlying problem? To some extent, it is rooted in the fact that when we in the West and Japan sell equipment to the Soviet Union, we are selling products that have been designed and produced in an environment where scarcity is the ruling mentality. That is, after all, what costs and profits mean. In other words, time is money. But Soviet officials do not respond that way. They are buying equipment that is designed according to Western operational principles, which emphasize scarcity, timely repairs, and cost-effective utilization. When shipped to the USSR, however, such technology confronts an environment in which the mentality is one of abundance. Such abundance does not actually exist, but the Soviets operate as if it did. As a result, there is a clash of technology and production style, and the products do not work properly. For the most part, Soviet operators cannot service their equipment, and eventually it falls apart or is locked away.

How do military operations compare? First of all, while the military sector looks quite good technologically (especially for items that are being stolen), there is probably also considerable waste in this sector of the economy—less waste than in the civilian sector, to be sure, but waste nevertheless. The same skewed mentality of presumed abundance prevails.

What should American policy be? After all, despite these production problems, there is no doubt that Western technology has increased Soviet productivity in the military sector (and, indeed, in the civilian sector, although to a lesser extent). But much of it is still used so poorly that I sometimes think we worry too much about the implications of selling technology to the civilian side. I almost have the feeling that there is a mentality in Washington which says, "If it moves, embargo it, because if it moves it must be good." For example, one of my friends is trying to sell food processing equipment to the USSR, which obviously requires, if it is sophisticated today, microprocessors that *could* be used for other purposes (i.e., military programs). But given the poor record of Soviet maintenance, I wonder whether we really have to worry about cannibalism of food processing equipment. In theory, a smart policymaker in the Department of Defense really might conclude that instead of restricting trade, he should instead try to sell the Soviet leaders as much as possible, and flood them with technology since they do so poorly with what they purchase through legitimate channels.

Nevertheless, while Soviet frustration with imported equipment reflects overinflated expectations (what Brezhnev was saying), imports in general are still worth the costs to Moscow. The challenge for Gorbachev is how to use this technology in both the civilian and the military sectors more effectively.

However, in the civilian sector at least (and here I feel on safer ground), as long as scarcity is still a dirty word, I do not see how Gorbachev will be able to use Western technology more effectively, short of a far-reaching economic reform—and *that* is hardly likely.

PART 3

TECHNOLOGY TRANSFER AND SOVIET-AMERICAN RELATIONS

8

TECHNOLOGY TRANSFERS AND U.S. FOREIGN POLICY: CHALLENGES AND OPPORTUNITIES

William Schneider, Jr.

The question of technology transfer was put on a very fast track by the Reagan administration from the beginning. Great efforts were made to formulate a policy with some coherence, and to implement it rapidly—which necessarily left ragged edges in the first year or two of the administration. In a sense, the policy itself got out ahead of the implementation. Nevertheless, I think a significant number of these policy problems have now been largely addressed. We are now in what may generally be characterized as the "implementation phase." As such, we have a little more time to reflect on the character of technology transfer policy, and how that policy might be more permanently institutionalized.

In an examination of U.S. foreign policy generally, and its implementation specifically, I think it is correct to see technology transfer policy—or, considered broadly, export administration policy—as one element of a larger set of foreign policy instruments dealing with resource transfer. The most conspicuous mechanism of resource transfer is, of course, the Foreign Assistance Act, which authorizes foreign appropriations for a variety of different types of resource transfer—security assistance, bilateral economic assistance, and multilateral economic assistance. Because of the fact that only the president can propose this legislation, while only the Congress can enact it, much of U.S. foreign policy is argued out in the context of foreign resource assistance. Arms transfers are another form of resource transfer, albeit one tending toward controversy. Nevertheless, it is safe to say that this form of resource transfer has also assumed a much greater role in the implementation of U.S. foreign policy.

Technology transfer could be characterized as the most subtle and, simultaneously, the most pervasive dimension of resource transfer. I think the reason it has not received much attention is that most of these transfers occur under private auspices, without requiring either an act of the legislative body or intervention by a regulatory mechanism. We have always had legislation on the books that could influence technology flow. Yet it is perhaps only in the past few years that we have clearly identified those policy objectives which must undergird the legislative process. Technology transfer and its control has thus become an important element of our foreign policy.

If it is useful to see technology transfer as part of the larger foreign policy process, it is also fair to say that there are dimensions of this problem which merit—indeed, require—intervention by the Executive branch. Over the past few years, the Reagan administration has attempted to make distinctions as to when it is and is not appropriate for the government to influence the flow of technology. The challenge is to withhold the fruits of Western technological progress from our adversaries without, in so doing, denying the advantages of technology exchange with our allies, which will contribute to the objectives of economic growth and enhanced security.

How do we best implement this policy? In considering this question it is important, first, to distinguish between technology that is "dual-use" technology—that is, technology useful in civilian applications yet controlled because of an inherent potential for military application—and out-and-out military technology, which falls generally under the rubric of "ammunitions technology." Ammunitions technology is controlled by separate legislation and a separate bureaucracy. Nonetheless, the two areas tend to merge, particularly in commercial transactions between ourselves and our allies.

First of all, in implementing the objective of controlling the technological access of adversaries while insuring the same for allies, we must look at what initiatives have been taken by the United States to influence the course of these transactions. Probably the most widely known has been the establishment, and recent renewal, of the Export Administration Act. The Act is intended to assure greater policy coherence and organization within the government as regards the enforcement of its provisions.

A second dimension, not widely known owing to the fact that it is not encompassed by any one policy document, is the reorientation of U.S. policy with respect to technology transfer. Our approach to the question of technology transfer has turned 180 degrees from the policy of the 1970s. Several administrations throughout the 1970s accepted the theory that a substantial transfer of technology to the East would create in the Soviet bloc a stake in continued access to its source. This stake in continued access would be manifested in the willingness of the Soviet bloc to engage in more civilized, less threatening behavior. This did not, however, take place. In fact, the theory has generally been discredited. The basic premise of détente with respect to technology transfer needed to be changed, and, as reflected in a report recently made available by the Secretary of Defense, this change has indeed taken place. Our reorientation is so significant that the allies have to some extent been persuaded by it as well, thus leading to substantial progress in the multilateral arena.

Yet another way to block the flow of sensitive technologies is to encourage a heightened level of public awareness. The report of the Secretary of Defense referred to above is one example of this effort. We have embarked as well on a substantial program with U.S. defense contractors, attempting to acquaint them with the problems associated with technology transfer, in cases of both legal and illegal trade.

Still another important aspect has been the greater attention given to the enforcement side of export control policy. Owing to vague policy guidance during the 1970s, our enforcement apparatus was not well suited to coping with illicit technology transfer. Priorities have now been substantially turned around in the law enforcement community, in accordance with this administration's greater efforts to halt technological theft by the Soviet bloc.

A final point relates to munitions, or technology transfer under munitions licenses. The U.S. nondisclosure policy has been made more rigorous and more responsive to long-term technology transfer concerns. This, of course, deals mainly with West-West technology trade. Nevertheless, it is intended eventually to clarify the issue of what technologies can be transferred in munitions *generally,* as well as the manner in which technology in munitions is to be protected upon transfer.

In looking at the international dimension of policy implementation, the most conspicuous of our efforts have been those to achieve multilateral support for U.S. policy in the realm of technology transfer. I would say that one of the more ragged edges of U.S. policy in the early part of the administration resulted from misjudging the extent to which allied cooperation would be necessary in implementing constraints on the flow of high-technology equipment and knowledge to the East. Over the past several years, this cooperation has begun to take root in the form of a rather revitalized international institution—CoCom. In July 1984, we successfully completed a review that established the current list of controlled technologies, and agreed upon a process by which the list will be reviewed and updated. New technologies will be added and older ones deleted, in a way that will keep the list current, have a minimum effect on legitimate trade, and deny the Soviet bloc access to critical items.

A related issue of concern is the question of commerce with third countries. In response to U.S and allied enforcement procedures, the Soviet Union and Soviet-bloc countries have become more interested in acquiring sensitive technologies from non-CoCom countries. Initial controls in this area are being established through a series of bilateral efforts, which, it is expected, will be expanded to the multilateral arena in due course. We hope this will plug the gaps before they become too difficult to cope with.

Reflecting our interest in controlling the international flow of munitions technology, we also have undertaken efforts to render the transfer of munitions-related information more secure. This has included steps to strengthen security measures relating to military information and data exchange agreements so as to enhance the protection given to technology transfers and to facilitate arms cooperation within the alliance.

The basic premise of export control policy, then, has been clear throughout the Reagan administration. The legacy of statutory inhibitions was rather substantial. The Arms Export Control Act in particular had been a serious inhibition to successful arms cooperation, hence to constructive transfers of arms technologies within the alliance. Over the last two years, however, Congress has moved to support cooperative arms development projects in NATO, most especially via passage of the Nunn and Quayle amendments which set aside specific funding for joint ventures among the allies. Both will contribute substantially to the administration's effort to optimize the balance between denying high-technology access to our adversaries while facilitating exchange within the alliance.

In evaluating the scorecard of policy initiatives, on balance we find a generally good record, though not without failure. In dealing directly with East-West trade, U.S. policy initiatives on the whole have been successful, both in the bilateral and multilateral arenas. Virtually all U.S. technology transfer objectives in the "dual-use" field have been accepted by our CoCom allies. The major outstanding issues relate entirely to enforcement, a problem no easier to solve among our allies than among competing interests within the United States. However, the vigorous efforts made by our allies—for example, in expelling Soviet-bloc diplomats conspicuously identified with illegal technology transfer acquisition—tend to reinforce the intensity with which the matter is being addressed by the alliance as a whole.

With respect to the East-West transfer of munitions-related technology, fairly successful attempts had been made at realizing policy objectives even prior to the Reagan administration. Now that tighter controls over our nondisclosure policy have been established, I think our attempts have been even more successful. The ability of the United States to persuade the CoCom allies to support policy initiatives in that multilateral framework—policy initiatives that are global in scope—is a particularly significant indication of success.

The area in which we have yet to achieve our objectives is that of the transfer of munitions-related technologies, and the associated area of cooperative efforts in arms development. This is beset by a number of problems predating the present administration—problems which nonetheless must be solved—relating to security access for citizens of allied countries, differing personnel security practices among allied countries, and similar matters. I mentioned the NATO cooperative projects legislation. In my opinion, it will remove some of the legal inhibitions to technology transfer in the arms arena. Yet, there still remain nontariff barriers to trade—specifically, attitudes toward cooperation on defense matters, both in industry and government—which will continue undoubtedly to be obstacles in the way of collaborative arms development projects. This is not, moreover, a problem unique to the United States, for in many cases it is difficult for American firms to gain access to European arms markets as well. This is ultimately due to a political requirement in many of these countries that an indigenous production base be maintained in key areas of military technology.

Nevertheless, the heat is on. Budget resources have become so constrained that cooperative arms development in the future is likely to be the rule rather than the exception. Consequently, I am confident that our technology transfer policies can be coordinated so as to allow intra-alliance technology access in a manner that inhibits the potential diversion of key technologies to the Soviet bloc.

9

SOVIET SYSTEMIC CHANGE, TECHNOLOGY TRANSFER, AND U.S.-SOVIET RELATIONS

Victor Basiuk

This paper will discuss the role of technology transfer in U.S.-Soviet relations, with particular attention to systemic change in the Soviet Union. An exploration of this topic is especially relevant at present for at least two reasons.

First, since his selection as the new Party Chairman in March 1985, Mikhail Gorbachev—as well as the Soviet press—has been talking of major changes in the Soviet economy which could have important implications for the Soviet political system.

The second reason is related, yet broader, and not necessarily dependent on what Gorbachev may or may not do in the near future. It stems from the relationship between the Soviet system and U.S. national security.

The Soviets present a threat to the United States because of their ideology and their system. This threat can be neutralized by two means:

1. By maintaining a sufficiently strong military power to deter Soviet aggression or to fight, if necessary. The United States has been supporting a very large peacetime military force for nearly 40 years now.
2. Through systemic change within the Soviet Union, which, in turn, would weaken its ideology and power drive and affect the nature and magnitude of its power. History teaches us that no empire lasts forever. Some decay, others fall apart; still others transform into new political orders. Systemic change in the Soviet Union thus provides us with perhaps the ultimate, if longer-range, solution to the problem of the Soviet threat.

The relevant questions are: What is the outlook for systemic change in the USSR? What kind of systemic change can be expected, if any? What can the

United States do to facilitate a desirable form of systemic change? And finally, in what way, if any, could technology transfer provide us with an instrument for influencing systemic change in the Soviet Union?

THE SOVIET COMMAND ECONOMY AND ITS SHORTFALLS

That aspect of the Soviet system that has been subjected to increasing criticism in the Soviet Union in recent years is the nature of its economy. It thus presents an area of weakness where change is possible. We may recall that, unlike Western economies, the Soviet economy is a command economy.[1] Its cardinal principles are essentially two: (1) It operates by administrative decree—that is, on orders from above—as opposed to the market principles of supply and demand. (2) The success of enterprises is principally measured by the achievement of production objectives (output quotas), not profitability. In pursuing its objectives, a command economy may adhere to certain economic considerations or principles, but this is not an essential characteristic.[2]

One problem with the Soviet economy is that its rate of growth has been continuously declining. In the 1950s, the economy was growing at an average rate of 5.7% annually; it declined to an average of 5.1% in the 1960s, and to 3.4% in the 1970s. For the first four years of the 1980s, it has been growing at an average rate of 2.5%.[3] Not all of this decline can be attributed to systemic factors, but such factors were important.

The Soviet command economy has never been efficient. However, with technological advances, the scale and complexity of its operations have grown; predictably, the inefficiencies of an economy run by orders from above have thus increased, negatively affecting overall growth.[4]

The present rate of economic growth is inadequate to meet the objectives of the Soviet leadership, which call for both guns and butter—a high rate of defense spending as well as improvements in the consumer sector.[5] However, the declining rate of economic growth is not the only—and perhaps not the principal—problem of the Soviet command economy. After all, a rate of growth of some 2 to 2 1/2% is not critical. In fact, it compares favorably with such leading East European countries as Hungary and East Germany. The Soviet command economy, however, displays at least three other major shortfalls.

First, what matters is not only the rate of growth of GNP, but its composition. Soviet economic growth is not primarily in advanced technological products—such as electronics, computers, advanced chemicals—but in products of yesteryear, such as steel, cement, fertilizers, agricultural tractors, and so forth.[6] The Soviet command economy experiences serious problems not only in generating advanced technology, but in absorbing and diffusing it when acquired from the West.

Second, the Soviet economy has difficulties in matching the output of its factories with its users. This phenomenon not only contributes to the inefficiency and slow growth of the economy, but is deleterious to the well-being of Soviet consumers even if adequate supplies of consumer goods are produced. Given the chronic shortage of consumer goods in the Soviet Union, the difficulty of matching supply and demand in the Soviet command economy degrades the quality of consumption to a much greater extent.[7]

Finally, the nature of the Soviet economy has been credited with degrading the very fabric of Soviet society by causing alcoholism, violation of discipline at work, absenteeism, irresponsibility, and dishonesty, thus imposing a brake on both economic and societal growth. A striking feature of this accusation is that it was presented by Academician Tatyana Zaslavskaya to a group of high Gosplan officials and Central Committee members in a closed seminar. Zaslavskaya not only did *not* lose her job, but was reported to be an adviser to Gorbachev.[8]

Most, if not all, of the shortfalls of the economy could be removed by doing away with the command principle and resorting to a market mechanism. However, there is considerable resistance in the Soviet Union to fundamental economic reform. Perhaps the single most important consideration which militates against such a reform is the fact that the command economy is not just another economic system, but a means for controlling Soviet society by the Communist Party. And the Communist Party is concerned about losing its control.

TECHNOLOGY TRANSFER AND SOVIET SYSTEMIC CHANGE

Soviet awareness of systemic shortfalls in the command economy is nothing new; it can be traced to at least the early 1960s. After a wide-ranging debate on this subject, generously aired in the press and professional journals, the Soviet leadership approved in 1965 a series of reforms sponsored by Premier A. N. Kosygin. The reforms preserved the basic principles of the command economy, but also stipulated a number of liberalizing measures.

In spite of official approval of the reforms of 1965, both the Soviet state bureaucracy and the top party leadership began to be concerned about the implications of the reforms for their respective power, and the reforms were watered down in the process of implementation. Inasmuch as there was no hope of reversing or stopping the declining rate of economic growth through the scuttled reforms, in the second half of the 1960s Premier Kosygin began to advocate large-scale imports of technology from the West in the expectation that it would help buttress the economy. By early 1972, he had succeeded in persuading Party Chairman Brezhnev of this necessity. Brezhnev, by that time, had become frustrated by his own inability to improve the economy by various measures short of fundamental reforms.[9]

The Soviet infusion of technology from the West in the 1970s was massive,[10] but, as we saw earlier, it failed to stop the decline in the rate of Soviet economic growth. There is evidence, however, that had it not been for this infusion of technology, Soviet economic growth would have been even slower.[11] Thus, insofar as Soviet imports of Western technology were intended to be a substitute for fundamental economic reforms, they were largely unsuccessful.

Western analyses of Soviet technology acquisition in the 1970s present further evidence of systemic shortfalls in the Soviet economy. In spite of the massive transfer of technology, the USSR has not closed the gap between itself and the West. In nonmilitary technology, the overall technological lag of the Soviet Union behind the United States and the leading industrial nations of the world has not diminished much since 1960.[12]

Moreover, the Soviets have been very slow in assimilating Western technology. Unlike Japan, the upgrading and diffusion of imported technology has been limited. The lack of competition in the Soviet Union has apparently been an important factor in the poor diffusion of technology. By and large, the Soviet Union has failed to integrate imported Western technology with domestic R&D and production. In most instances, "turnkey" plants built in the Soviet Union have continued to depend on spare parts from the West.[13] In the area of computers, the Soviet Union has been faced with a vast variety of rapid innovations in the West which it has not been capable of absorbing, let alone improving upon.[14]

A marked exception to the above was the defense sector. Here the quality of products, the absorption and diffusion of Western technology, and the ability to build on that technology—rather than just imitate it—have been distinctly superior to experiences in the civilian sector. In part, the explanation lies in the priority given to weapons production by the Soviet leadership. However, there is also a more fundamental reason. Unlike the civilian sector, the defense sector operates under conditions resembling those of market systems.[15] A strong element of competition emanates from the existence of U.S. weapons programs. Moreover, the defense industry has a tough and demanding customer—the Soviet Ministry of Defense—which closely looks over the shoulder of defense production, and can reject a substandard product.[16] This is very different from the civilian economy, where shortages of consumer goods are endemic and where customers have very little influence.

THE GORBACHEV REIGN AND THE ECONOMY

When Gorbachev succeeded Chernenko at the helm of the Soviet state, he inherited not only an economy hampered by systemic shortcomings, but one subject to other important constraints and pressures, especially in the areas of manpower and capital availability.

Historically, a large influx of manpower was a very important factor in Soviet economic growth. High population growth, extensive transfer of manpower from farms to industry, and employment of women previously engaged in household work helped fuel the Soviet economy. The last two sources of this manpower have virtually dried up; additionally, demographic data indicate unfavorable trends in population growth. As a result, the net influx of able-bodied manpower into the economy has declined precipitously, from 2,290,000 in 1978 to a projected low of 285,000 only eight years later, in 1986. Moreover, all of this net addition to Soviet manpower in 1986, as well as 237,000 replacements for the dwindling manpower in the European USSR, will come from Soviet Asiatic republics. This population will be predominantly Moslem, most will not speak adequate Russian, will be reluctant to move, and will thus not be readily adaptable to Soviet economic needs. [17]

Of course, there *is* excess manpower in inefficient areas of the Soviet economy, which could go a long way toward compensating for decreasing net additions to the able-bodied age group. However, it is not likely that anything short of fundamental economic reform could effectively tap this resource. The Soviet Union maintains about 5 million men and women in its armed forces (including security troops), which is also an important potential source of manpower for the economy. But the Soviet leadership would be reluctant to resort to this option.

The Soviet Union is entering a period of a capital crunch. The Soviet transportation system needs extensive modernization and expansion, requiring very large capital investments. The USSR is also experiencing skyrocketing raw materials costs. The quality and quantity of easily accessible raw materials have declined, and the Soviets must push further and further into the remote regions of Siberia to extract resources—under unfavorable climatic conditions. Among others, these conditions apply to such vital materials as energy resources. [18] As a system, Soviet agriculture is highly inefficient and is handicapped by a relatively limited amount of rich land and largely unfavorable climate. The Soviet Union, however, has persisted in its efforts to raise agricultural output, which requires in turn an inordinate amount of capital.

In the 1970s the Soviet Union enjoyed the bonanza of skyrocketing prices for oil and gold, both of which it exports. Now, not only is the benefit of high prices gone, but the Soviet Union's output of oil is declining because of production problems.

Considering that Gorbachev's leadership is likely to last for at least 15 years, and that he personally will inherit the consequences of a failure to remedy economic shortcomings in a timely fashion, strong incentives for fundamental change—perhaps the introduction of a market mechanism—exist. They are reinforced by the recent experience with technology transfer from the West: As a substitute for reform, it did not work and instead only highlighted the systemic weaknesses of the Soviet economy.

There are, of course, many hurdles. The communist ideology is one. There is resistance to fundamental economic reform both within the party and state bureaucracy. Soviet managers have had no experience operating in a competitive environment and thus cannot be simply let loose into it. The situation is even more difficult with regard to the international market. Soviet enterprises have been highly protected and are not known for efficiency. As one analyst put it, Soviet managers have no particular desire for "the pleasure of competing with Toyota."[19]

Given the need to revitalize the economy and the very serious difficulties in doing so, where does Gorbachev's leadership stand in this regard? The picture is not entirely clear. The intellectual discussion in Soviet professional literature on this subject is quite broad. It ranges from such unorthodox concepts (by Zaslavskaya) as the emergence of interest groups in the Soviet Union and the need to accommodate them in economic structures, to models not very far from the old Stalinist command economy. But the discussion is still within bounds; suggestions for allowing private property do not go beyond what was permissible under the New Economic Policy (NEP) of the 1920s. Actual reorganization of the central core of the economy, however, has been limited to what was earlier called an "economic experiment" initially confined to five ministries, but now extended to others. The new approach allows more initiative for enterprises and production associations, but does not represent a truly major departure from other tinkerings with the economic structure of recent years.[20]

Of late, however, the official rhetoric dealing with the need to uplift the economy and pursue economic change has been unusually strong. Gorbachev has asserted that economic growth must be accelerated to support both the expansion of Soviet military power and a higher standard of living for the Soviet peoples. He has also gone further to assert that the Soviet Union must set an example for the rest of the world by achieving the highest organizational standards and effectiveness in its economy, since it is precisely in this area that socialism will exert the greatest influence on the world environment.[21]

Gorbachev's emphasis is on an effective exploitation of "the scientific-technological revolution," which requires "a deep restructuring of the system of planning and management of the entire economic mechanism."[22] What that restructuring would entail has not been revealed. The nearest Gorbachev has come to suggesting organizational change was his attack on the power and bureaucratization of the ministries, and a call for a strong Gosplan and more independence for enterprises and production associations.[23]

An even stronger statement on the subject of the economy appeared as the lead editorial in the June 1985 issue of *Kommunist,* the principal organ of the Communist Party of the Soviet Union:

At the meeting of the CC CPSU on the issue of the acceleration of scientific-technological progress, the discussion addressed [the question of] a sharp turn toward intensification of the economy, a reorientation of each enterprise, branch, and of the entire economy toward the intensive path of development. The Soviet Union, which was and remains the embodiment of ages-long social hopes of men, should be the example of highest organization and effectiveness of its economy. The task of accelerating the development of the country has thus attained today first-rate political, economic, and social importance. Its implementation is a matter which cannot be put off; it belongs to the Party as a whole and the people as a whole. To put the issue in this manner is, under the present conditions, the only possible way. We cannot achieve deep transformations, revolutionary in character, by cautious, small improvements. What is needed is a leap forward, a break in continuity.[24]

Gorbachev's statements and the *Kommunist* editorial were part of a widespread discussion in the Soviet Union in preparation for the 27th Congress of the Communist Party, which convened on February 25, 1986. The Congress itself did not shed much new light on the prospect for fundamental reform in the Soviet Union. At the Congress, Gorbachev asserted the necessity for a "radical reform" of the economy.[25] Again, he outlined "the principal directions of the restructuring of the economic mechanism" as including greater independence of enterprises and production associations. Gorbachev went on to say that the ministries should not micromanage enterprises, but concentrate on issues of technological policy instead. The Gosplan mechanism was instructed to concentrate on long-term questions of planning, and become "the truly scientific-economic headquarters of the country, free from day-to-day economic questions."[26]

A great deal of emphasis, however, was placed on investment policy and needed structural changes in the economy. Over 200 billion rubles are to be allocated into what may be termed the "high technology sector," and for modernization of industry in the 1986-1990 Five-Year Plan—more than in the previous ten years. A high rate of investment in modern machinery and equipment—including automation—was singled out as holding great promise for enhancing qualitative growth and effectiveness in the economy.[27] This investment strategy is viewed as the key to capitalizing on scientific-technological progress and bringing about the establishment of a new, technologically advanced economic base.

Since the Party Congress, however, at least three significant steps have been taken with regard to the economy, somewhat reminiscent of the 1920s. In November 1986, the Soviet Union enacted a law which will allow limited private enterprise in a variety of services, such as shoe repair, taxi driving, and small-scale construction and agriculture. Later in the same month, it was revealed that in 1987 individual citizens would be allowed to join together in cooperatives for the purpose of setting up small factories, privately owned. It was envisioned that these cooperatives would comprise between 10 and 20% of the national income within the next decade.[28] In January 1987, the Soviet government undertook to implement its plans for joint business ventures between Soviet and Western firms by setting guidelines for such ventures. The partnerships will be dominated by Soviet firms, which will have no less than 51% of ownership. The firms will be based in the Soviet Union, will have a Soviet chairman of the board and general director, and "mainly" Soviet personnel.[29]

Concurrently with these developments, it was reported that Gorbachev complained about bureaucratic resistance to his reforms. It was also noted that he was wooing writers and intellectuals as a possible countervailing influence against the bureaucrats. Apparently in an effort to shake up government and party bureaucracy, Gorbachev made a series of proposals toward what he called "the democratization of political life." Among other things, these included multiple candidates in local elections and secret-ballot election of local Communist Party officials.

The question arises: How far will this development go? It is noteworthy that Gorbachev is toying with the market principle, but only at the fringes of the economy. To truly revitalize the economy, however, the command economy must be supplanted by a market economy,[30] but there is no indication at this point that Gorbachev is willing to go that far. At the same time, as the inadequacy of present measures becomes apparent, the pressure for a truly fundamental reform is likely to increase.

In particular, China's economic reforms—which expand the application of the market principle in the economy and partially denationalize industrial enterprises—present a threat to the Soviet Union.[31] This threat is perceived in terms of ideology and power. If China's reforms are successful in creating a dynamic economy, the USSR will be affected in at least three ways: (1) the increased growth of China's economic and, potentially, military power would provide an added source of insecurity to the Soviet Union; (2) an economically vital China would present a potentially attractive model for development for the Third World, thus enhancing China's influence in an area highly important to the USSR but for which the Soviets have very little to offer by way of an attractive model; and, (3) finally, Soviet leaders would find it difficult to explain to their people why the Chinese, by deviating from communist orthodoxy, succeeded in creating a vital economy while the Soviet Union had not.

While pronouncements by top party leaders are devoid of references to the notion of adopting market socialism in the Soviet Union (indeed, there have been denials to that effect), there are authoritative voices in Soviet society which explicitly raise this option. B. P. Kurashvili, head of the department of state management theory of the Academy of Sciences, has proposed a restructuring of the organizations governing the Soviet economy which, while resembling Gorbachev's own pronouncements, have strong market overtones as well.

According to Kurashvili, the system of planning by output should "largely give way to a form of planning that would generalize and flexibly channel to society's advantage production-economic activities based on initiatives, activities which would be subordinate to economic laws and the mechanism of economic self-regulation."[32] To this end, enterprises should be given a considerable degree of independence. They themselves "would draw up annual, five-year, and long-term plans, themselves would choose the parties to enter into contracts with, and would themselves determine the content of their contracts. . . . The choice of suppliers and clients and the determination of the content of the negotiations with them would be directed by the regulating force of the market."[33]

The all-Union administrative apparatus for the management of the economy would be drastically consolidated into a single Ministry of the National Economy, embracing industry, construction, and agriculture. At present, no less than 57 separate ministries have responsibilities in these areas. This single ministry would not be involved in the operational management of economic activities. Rather, it would be responsible for the prediction of social requirements and policy in such areas as personnel, science and technology, investment, taxes, credit, and prices.[34] The State Planning Committee (Gosplan) would be relieved of most routine management functions and become an agency for overall social and economic planning. Of course, Kurashvili would not do away altogether with supervision over enterprises and other economic entities. He envisions the existence of appropriate ministries in the constituent republics of the Soviet Union as well as appropriate local authorities. Thus, in addition to the emphasis on economic forces, Kurashvili's approach would entail territorial decentralization.[35]

If adopted, this would be a far-reaching restructuring of the Soviet economy indeed. One recent development which may be a step toward the adoption of a market mechanism is the admission by Soviet sources of the existence of unemployment in the Soviet Union. This significant departure from past rhetoric came with the warning that unemployment will likely reach large numbers as, in response to current party plans, the economy is restructured toward a more advanced technological base.[36] However, as we shall see later, there are less radical options than a market economy, which the Soviet leadership may pursue in the near-term future.

TECHNOLOGICAL IMPACT AND SOVIET SOCIETY

We have pointed out earlier that the systemic difficulties of the Soviet economy find their roots in technological progress, which has introduced high complexity and a much larger scale of operations into the economy. It is thus increasingly difficult to manage the evolving Soviet economy by centralized control from above. But there is another, related impact of technological progress on society, with potentially important *political* consequences: namely, the propensity of technological progress to differentiate and pluralize the interests of a society.

Technological progress promotes specialization and sustained adherence to a particular role or function. As new roles and functions become established, interests related to their survival and the promotion of their well-being crystallize. In highly advanced societies, the impact of technology not only multiplies interests, it makes increasingly difficult the overruling of major interests by the top leadership, due to their highly technical and specialized nature.

The interests developed and/or strengthened by specialization usually have to compete for limited resources, which phenomenon provides an incentive for politicization. As decisionmaking becomes increasingly politicized, the interests that do not have the asset of great technical complexity may nevertheless benefit in terms of power, since they can capitalize on their political skills or other attributes effective in a politicized environment. In short, while the differentiation of interests as a result of technological progress is nothing new, the rise in the importance of these interests, their proliferation, influence, and politicization are a relatively new phenomenon gaining ascendancy in the contemporary governmental process.[37]

Although the above phenomenon is most pronounced in democratic nations, totalitarian and autocratic states—including the Soviet Union—are not immune to the political implications of technology. There is, however, a significant difference in degree.

When the issue of large-scale technology transfer from the West was debated in the USSR during the late 1960s and early 1970s, a clear division emerged along functional lines. Scientists, science administrators, and the Ministry of Foreign Trade were in favor of these transfers. The majority in the military, however, apparently concerned about possible weakening of the priority customarily assigned to military R&D, had reservations about technology transfer. The political police, worried about foreign ties, strongly opposed it. Once the massive technology transfer got underway, issues of *Vneshnyanya Torgovlya* (Foreign Trade), the official organ of the Ministry of Foreign Trade, published an abundance of articles by key ministry officials stressing the benefits of Western technology imports to the fulfillment of the five-year plans, and arguing that the principle of the international division of labor embraced not only COMECON countries, but advanced capitalist nations as well.[38]

Aside from the Communist Party and its primary interest in its own survival, the single most powerful interest group in the Soviet Union is the military-industrial complex. Its influence extends considerably beyond the power of the relevant industries and military organizations. Under Stalin, strong incentives were provided to attract the best talent to heavy industry. Managerial personnel from heavy industry and defense industries were often appointed to the highest political and governmental positions during the Stalin regime and in later years. Thus, initially a product of policy, the military-industrial complex has been increasingly transformed into a powerful interest group with a momentum of its own, enjoying influential supporters in key policymaking bodies of the USSR.

A countervailing interest to the military-industrial complex is that of consumers. Organizationally, this interest is embodied in "Group B" industries (roughly, light industry), which have been known to compete for resources with "Group A" (heavy industry). Consumers as such—that is, in the context of mass consumption—are not organized in the USSR; they lack a focal point and thus do not comprise an interest group in the conventional Western sense. Consumers, however, have several levers of influence which, allowing for the peculiarities of the Soviet political environment, endow them with certain attributes of interest groups. In recent years, Soviet leaders have become concerned with consumers for pragmatic reasons. If workers cannot buy consumer goods of satisfactory quality, productivity suffers. On an ideological level, the Soviet Union is committed to improving the lot of the consumer. Under Brezhnev and his shorter-term successors, supplies of consumer goods were steadily, if not very rapidly, growing in quantity and quality. This tended to fan expectations and make consumers demand more. Finally, the Soviet leadership has also been concerned about potential political implications of consumer-related unrest. The experience of Poland in 1970 and 1980-1981 has not been entirely lost on Soviet leaders.[39] Strikes are illegal and infrequent in the Soviet Union, but they do occur. The largest consumption-related strike in Soviet history thus far occurred in May 1980. Reportedly, more than 200,000 auto workers left work at the Togliatti and Gorki plants, in protest over food supplies. Food was rushed to mollify the strikers.[40]

Other interest groups of note would include scientists, whose role, importance, and relative freedom have increased in recent years. This may be seen as a result of the emphasis placed by the Soviet leadership on science and technology in enhancing Soviet power. Aided by the West, Soviet Jews succeeded in wresting an unprecedented concession from the Soviet government: a fairly sizable rate of emigration from the USSR. Manifestations of local nationalism, tied to economic interests, have been reported in the various constituent republics of the USSR. As the share of Russians in the Soviet population decreases to a minority (a development likely to take place later in this decade), this phenomenon may become more significant.

In short, a change is detectable in the Soviet Union in the post-Stalin era. In Soviet society, various group, institutional, and regional interests—and the balancing process among them—are beginning to play an increasingly greater role. At this point in time, this process is not particularly important politically. However, if fundamental economic reform is introduced in the USSR and the command economy is replaced by a market-oriented system, the political influence of the various interests will significantly grow.[41]

To conclude, given the present level of development in Soviet society and the evolving nature of its economy, it is the economic factors combined with the impact of technological advance (complexity and pluralization) which are becoming the principal vehicles for political change in the USSR. This change will in turn affect the Soviet system and the future of its military might. This represents a major reversal of Soviet history, where traditionally it was the political will which molded the economy, determined the application of technology, and created—from a condition of underdevelopment—the second largest military power on earth.

The ascendancy of the forces of the base (i.e., the economy) over the superstructure (the political system) would bring Soviet society into greater harmony with the original theory of Marxism, which was turned on its head by Lenin and Stalin. It is ironic, however, that Karl Marx has defected from the Soviet Union and is now working for the West. The deterministic influence of the economic base propelled by technological progress has stimulated the rise of market forces, competition, yearning for private ownership, and pluralization of society. It appears that history is on our side. The question remains, however, whether the West will be successful in capitalizing on it by fashioning the right policies.

U.S.-SOVIET RELATIONS, SOVIET SYSTEMIC EVOLUTION, AND TECHNOLOGY TRANSFER

It must be emphasized at the outset that Soviet systemic change cannot be steered from the outside; it must be a product of the internal dynamics of Soviet society. Influence from the outside, if any, can produce only limited results, and only then if exerted in response to, and in support of, forces and developments already taking place in the Soviet Union.

As we have seen, there are forces in the USSR which exert powerful pressures for systemic change, and such change is likely to take place. It is therefore important for the United States to be alert to systemic evolution in the USSR, and watch it closely. In the process of systemic change, the Soviet leadership will face more than one option; depending on the development of events, the choice could be close. The United States, perhaps in cooperation with its allies, may find itself in a position to influence developments just enough to lead the USSR away from an undesirable option—undesirable, that is, from the point of view of the West—and toward a more desirable one. Because of the Soviet weakness in so critical an aspect of economic growth as technological progress, technology transfer could be an important instrument for influencing Soviet systemic evolution.

Actually, a U.S. policy to influence Soviet societal or systemic change in the interest of national security is nothing new. It might be useful to review briefly such policies of the past, which would give us a clearer perspective on present opportunities and potential pitfalls.

Although the policy of containment was principally aimed at opposing Soviet military expansionism, it also had an "internal" dimension directed at Soviet societal and systemic change. It consisted of the expectation that once the Soviet external drive was contained and the Kremlin's messianic movement frustrated, "pluralizing tendencies" would develop in the USSR and Soviet power would "mellow."[42] As can be seen, this dimension of policy was basically passive.

Under the policy of détente, the "internal" or "systemic change" dimension was stronger and more active. It was believed that the exposure of Soviet citizens to the West through trade, cultural and scientific exchanges, and other contacts would modify their value system and foster the mellowing process. Therefore, such exposure was to be actively promoted. The massive technology transfer of the 1970s was viewed as being in harmony with the rationale of détente. The problem was that, on balance, the technology transfer contributed more to the enhancement of Soviet power than to its mellowing.

Under earlier policies, the target of societal and systemic change was the ideology, value system, and cohesiveness of the Soviet Union. Given the strong controlling influence of the party apparatus and the highly centralized command economy, progress was slow and the policy was viewed in the long term, taking many decades to achieve its goals. The second half of the 1980s and the early 1990s open up new opportunities, with targets emerging out of developments within the Soviet Union itself. These targets are the command economy itself and its close ally, the military-industrial complex.

A reform which would discard the command economy in favor of a variant of market socialism would significantly accelerate the pluralization of Soviet society, the erosion of communist ideology, and the modification of values among the Soviet population. In market socialism, priorities in the civilian sector would be largely decided by the consumers as they spend their rubles. The Soviet military-industrial complex would be sustained by governmental appropriations, but it would be increasingly placed on the defensive as the society pluralized and countervailing interests gained in influence.

The liberalization of the Soviet economy would also be advantageous to the United States economically, inasmuch as it would likely open up more opportunities for trade with and investment in the USSR. Under these circumstances, U.S. political and economic interests would more likely than not be mutually reinforcing—which has not been necessarily so in recent years.

Strong rhetoric by the top Soviet leadership about radical departures from the past notwithstanding, the Soviet Union might not resort to a fundamental reform abandoning the command economy for a number of years. The Soviets may—indeed, they are likely to—try some other options first in the hope that they might prove sufficiently effective.

One such option would be to continue "muddling through" with the command structure, opting for some radical change within it—such as significantly curtailing the power of the ministries, giving more freedom to the enterprises and production associations, and making the lower-level party organs principally responsible for seeing to it that the enterprises' planned production targets are achieved. Such "reforms" are not likely to solve the problems of the Soviet economy.

Another option would be to resort to sectoral reforms, of which agriculture is a prime candidate. The abolition of the collective farm system would boost production of food and release substantial investment resources for industrial needs. Gorbachev could go a step further. In addition to the agricultural reform, he could introduce an NEP-like economy, which would allow private ownership of smaller enterprises. As we have seen, steps in this direction have already been made. Both of these options would stimulate value change and pluralization in Soviet society, but certainly not to the extent that the abolition of the command economy would. They would not solve the problem of the Soviets' inability to move to the forefront of technological advance. They could eventually turn out to be a step toward a market economy.

The Soviets could resort to an export-oriented strategy,[43] either as a core option or, perhaps more likely, pursued in conjunction with some of the aforementioned options. This would entail: (1) the selective introduction of foreign competition into the Soviet market so as to put pressure on domestic producers to improve their products; and (2) the promotion of exports, at reduced prices. This would be a difficult option to carry out; its systemic ramifications would depend on its specific form and on its relation to other options which might be pursued concurrently.

What role could technology transfer from the West play in influencing systemic change in the USSR? Even under the best of circumstances, the Soviet Union would continue to depend on advanced technology from the West for a number of years. Given economic reforms, the need for Western equipment and technology is likely to increase, since major reforms initially introduce instability and do not immediately lead to an increase in productivity. Western technology would thus continue to provide a potential leverage for the United States and its allies with regard to the USSR.

Unlike the case of détente (which requires a benign international climate to promote its objectives of societal change), a technology transfer policy to influence systemic change in the USSR does not depend on the nature of the international climate. It could be used in a spectrum of relationships ranging from quite benign to very tense. In fact, for certain kinds of systemic change it could be more effectively used under less-than-benign conditions. When it came to power, the Reagan administration undertook to impose restrictions on technology transfer to the Soviet Union for national security reasons other than systemic change. There is evidence, however, that this policy influenced the Soviet leadership toward systemic change; it highlighted to them the shortfalls of their system and strengthened their determination to make that system capable of generating advanced technology on its own, and incorporating it within the economy as well.[44]

Using technology transfer to influence Soviet systemic evolution does not consist of simply imposing restrictions on the availability of advanced technology to the USSR. From the point of view of U.S. national security and Soviet systemic change, transfers of technology to the Soviet Union could be divided into two broad categories: "power-augmenting" and "power-detracting." The former would include military technology, certain categories of "dual-use" technology especially useful for augmenting Soviet military capability, and certain technologies whose availability from the West would be especially important in assisting the Soviet economy to continue functioning short of resorting to fundamental reforms. These technologies are likely to be in the dual-use category, but restrictions on their transfer should be given consideration not solely on the strength of their contribution to Soviet military power, but their relevance to systemic change as well.[45]

"Power-detracting" technology is mostly consumer-oriented, which tends to "pluralize" Soviet society or generate a resource demand that competes with the military-industrial complex. One example is that of automobile technology, whose utilization requires not only major resources for plant and equipment, but also a network of related structures and services: roads, garages, and service stations.[46] Other technologies in the "power-detracting" category would include those applicable to home entertainment centers (pluralizing values, stimulating consumerism), single-chip computer technology for personal computers, and advanced programmable pocket calculators (potentially pluralizing business activity).

It must be understood that the line between "power-augmenting" and "power-detracting" technology can never be finely drawn. Some technologies will be more "power-augmenting" than "power-detracting," and vice versa. Tradeoffs will inevitably exist, and decisions will have to be made on the merits of the tradeoffs involved. Moreover, the components of the two categories will change, depending on developments in the Soviet Union. Thus, the category of "power-augmenting" technology would significantly narrow if the Soviet Union were to shift to a market economy; this category would then be more closely confined to militarily relevant technology.

Obtaining the cooperation of U.S. allies will be essential for influencing Soviet systemic evolution in a desirable direction. This will not be an easy task where restrictions are involved, mainly because the economies of Western Europe and Japan are much more dependent on the trade of technology than is that of the United States. It therefore will be important to emphasize that the United States does not intend to conduct economic warfare with the Soviet Union, and that the transfer of "power-detracting" technologies should be encouraged. Within the framework of the agreed-upon objective of fostering Soviet systemic evolution, restrictions on technology transfer should be minimal and low-key. It should be pointed out to the allies also that attention to systemic change in connection with technology transfer carries potentially significant security and economic payoffs in the not-so-distant future. In the economic sphere, these include considerably expanded trade with, and investments in, a Soviet economy free of the shackles of the command structure. Finally, because of its geographic proximity to the Soviet Union, it would be of particular interest to Western Europe to assist the Soviet Union in the transition toward a market-oriented economy, since the failure to carry out economic reforms in a timely fashion could be destabilizing domestically and internationally. It is possible that the new Soviet leadership might find the Polish case instructive.

Technology transfer is not the only avenue for influencing systemic change in the USSR; there are others. As pointed out earlier, the success of economic reforms in China is likely to have an important impact on developments in the Soviet Union. Indeed, it was reported that Gorbachev established a special committee to monitor the Chinese economic reforms. It therefore would be in the interest of the United States to explore how, through an appropriate policy with regard to China's economic reforms, the United States could influence Soviet systemic change in a desirable direction. Here again, a technology transfer policy with regard to China oriented toward systemic change might be conducive to desirable systemic change in the USSR.

Targets of opportunity should also not be overlooked. Such events as the accident at the Chernobyl nuclear power plant in the Ukraine in April 1986 could have ramifications with exploitable potential for desirable systemic change.

A period of systemic change in the Soviet Union will not be devoid of dangers as well as opportunities, and a U.S. policy attempting to influence its direction cannot be devoid of risks. Facing actual or potentially destabilizing consequences of reform at home, the Soviet government may choose to take a tough stance or an adventurous move abroad. On the other hand, increased pressures on resources as a result of the restructuring of the Soviet economy may incline Soviet leaders toward a more amenable stance on arms reductions. As the United States attempts to facilitate Soviet systemic evolution toward a freer society unencumbered by an oppressive command economy, it may run the risk of eventually facing a militarily powerful Soviet Union and a vital Soviet economy presenting us with a challenge similar to that of Japan. In constructing such a policy for systemic change, tradeoffs are inevitable. Policymakers must be careful to ensure that miscalculations or mishandling of policy do not magnify the risks.

At a minimum, it will be essential for the U.S. government to pay close attention to the potential of Soviet systemic change, and the challenges and opportunities it presents for U.S. security policy. At present, this subject is not receiving sufficiently close attention.

NOTES

1. Considering that the Soviets have been tinkering incrementally with their economy in recent decades, one could—if one wanted to be a purist—describe the Soviet economy more precisely as a "predominantly command economy, marginally modified by other characteristics." In this paper, the term "command economy" will be used as a stylistically more convenient description of the Soviet economic system.

2. For a more extensive discussion of the command economy, see Gregory Grossman, "Notes for a Theory of the Command Economy," *Soviet Studies,* Vol. XV (October 1963), pp. 101-123.

3. For the period from 1950 to 1980, the percentages were computed from John Pitzer, "Gross National Product of the USSR, 1950-1980," in U.S. Congress, Joint Economic Committee, *USSR: Measures of Economic Growth and Development, 1950-1980* (Washington, D.C.: U.S. Government Printing Office, 1982), p. 15. For the 1980s, they were computed from CIA figures.

4. This is recognized in Soviet professional literature. See, for example, G. Popov, "O sovershenstvovanii tsentralizovannogo khozyaystvennogo rukovodstva" (On Improvement in Centralized Economic Management), *Voprosy Ekonomiki,* No. 5 (May) 1985, pp. 88-89.

5. See M. S. Gorbachev, "Korennoy vopros ekonomicheskiy politiki partii" (The Key Issue of Economic Policy of the Party). Report at the meeting of the CC of the CPSU on the Issues of the Acceleration of Scientific and Technological Progress, June 11, 1985. *Kommunist,* No. 9 (June) 1985, pp. 14-15.

6. Soviet economic literature, although it realizes the deficiency of the Soviet economy in failing to move adequately into technologically advanced products, nevertheless takes pride in the sheer quantitative achievement of Soviet production. Thus, L. Albakin writes, "Indeed, today Soviet industry produces more output than all the countries in the world put together in 1950. In the output of certain, quite important types of production (steel, fertilizers, tractors, combines, and cotton and wool fabrics), the Soviet output exceeds the total output of the U.S., the United Kingdom, West Germany and France put together." "Vzaimodeystviye proizvoditelnykh sil i proizvodstvennykh otnosheniy" (Interaction Between Productive Forces and Production Relationships), *Voprosy Ekonomiki,* No. 6 (June) 1985, p. 12.

7. See, for example, Ya. Orlov, "Spros naseleniya i zadachi proizvodstva i torgovli" (Consumer Demand and the Tasks of Production and Trade), *Voprosy Ekonomiki,* No. 9 (September) 1983, pp. 100-109. Orlov cites numerous examples where the system encounters difficulties in matching supply and demand. Oversupply of useless goods in some regions coexists with severe shortages of other goods in the same or other regions. To give one example of the shortfalls of the Soviet system: The planned production objectives for enameled household pots were expressed in weight. Factory managers, eager to fulfill the plan, rose to the occasion and undertook to produce pots of the capacity of seven liters and above. The result was a vast oversupply of very large pots and shortages of small and medium sizes (see p. 102). Similar and costly problems exist in the distribution of consumer goods.

8. For the text of Zaslavskaya's paper, see "The Novosibirsk Report," *Soviet Studies,* Vol. 28 (Spring 1984), pp. 88-107.

9. For details, see Victor Basiuk, "Implications of Differential Transfer of Technology to the USSR and Resultant Options for U.S. Technology Transfer Policy," Report to the Office of the Deputy Under Secretary of Defense for Research and Engineering (International Programs and Technology), McLean, Virginia, March 1981, pp. 16-29. See also, Bruce Parrott, *Politics and Technology in the Soviet Union* (Cambridge, Mass.: The MIT Press, 1983), pp. 239-255.

10. No comprehensive statistics on Soviet imports of technology in the 1970s are available, but some indication of their scope can be provided. Between 1970 and 1979, Soviet imports of "high technology products" (a category developed by U.S. Department of Commerce analysts) increased from $402.9 million annually to $2.37 billion, or by 489%; those of "manufactured products" (which can be considered "advanced technology products" by Soviet standards) increased from $2.2 billion to $13.6 billion, or 518%. These figures do not include the transfer of unembodied technology. Derived and/or computed from John A. Martens, "Quantification of Western Exports of High Technology Products to Communist Countries," East-West Trade Policy Staff Paper, Office of East-West Policy and Planning, International Trade Administration, U.S. Department of Commerce, January 1981, p. 14.

11. Philip Hanson estimates that Western equipment imports contributed about 0.5% per year to the rate of growth of Soviet output in the industrial sector. See his *Trade and Technology in Soviet-Western Relations* (New York: Columbia University Press, 1981), p. 211.

12. Bruce Parrott, "Conclusion," in Bruce Parrott, editor, *Trade, Technology, and Soviet-American Relations* (Bloomington: Indiana University Press, 1985), p. 354.

13. Philip Hanson, "Soviet Assimilation of Western Technology," in ibid., pp. 67-69.

14. See S. E. Goodman, "Technology Transfer and the Development of the Soviet Computer Industry," in ibid., pp. 117-136.

15. One must recognize, of course, that the distinction between the "civilian" and the "defense" sector is blurred in a number of products in the USSR as elsewhere. Here the term "defense sector" refers to those industries specifically producing in response to orders from the Ministry of Defense.

16. See John W. Kiser, "How the Arms Race Really Helps Moscow," *Foreign Policy*, No. 60 (Fall 1985), pp. 42-47, and Julian Cooper, "Western Technology and the Soviet Defense Industry," in Parrott, editor, op. cit., pp. 181-182.

17. Murray Feshbach, "Population and Labor Force," in Abram Bergson and Herbert S. Levine, *The Soviet Economy: Toward the Year 2000* (London: George Allen and Unwin, 1983), pp. 101-104, and personal communication with Feshbach. According to Feshbach's projections and estimates, between January 1980 and January 1990, the net increase in the Soviet labor force will reach only 5,990,000 persons, while during the preceding ten years the increase was 24,217,000, or four times greater (p. 96).

18. See L. Voronin, "Sovershenstvovaniye khozyaystvennogo mekha nizma— nepremennoye usloviye perevoda ekonomiki na intensivnyy put' razvitiya" (Improvement of the Economic Mechanism is an Essential Condition of the Transformation of the Economy Toward the Intensive Path of Development), *Planovoye Khozyaystvo*, No. 8 (August) 1985, pp. 9-10.

19. Jerry F. Hough, "Gorbachev's Strategy," *Foreign Affairs*, Vol. 64 (Fall 1985), p. 42.

20. For a Soviet assessment of the experiment, see "Ekonomicheskiy eksperiment: itogi pervogo goda i puti dal'neyshego sovershenstvovaniya" (The Economic Experiment: Results of the First Year and the Paths for Further Improvement), *Planovoye Khozyaystvo*, No. 4 (April) 1985, pp. 59-73.

21. Gorbachev, in *Kommunist*, No. 9 (June) 1985, p. 15. To buttress his position on this subject, he cited no less an authority than Lenin.

22. Ibid., p. 26. See, M. S. Gorbachev, "O sozyve ocherednogo XXVII S'yezda KPSS i zadachakh svyazannykh s ego podgotovkoy i provedeniyem" (On the Convening of the Next 27th Congress of the CPSU and the Tasks Related to its Preparation and Conduct), *Kommunist*, No. 7 (May) 1985, pp. 6-7, and passim.

23. This particular organizational approach can be traced to Zazlavskaya (op. cit.) and to other influential Soviet economists. See, for example, G. Popov, "O sovershenstvovanii tsentralizirovannogo khozyaystvennogo rukovodstva" (On Improvement of the Centralized Economic Management), *Voprosy Ekonomiki*, No. 5 (May) 1985, pp. 87-92.

24. "Gotovnost' vzyat' otvetstvennost' na sebya" (Readiness to Take Responsibility on Oneself), *Kommunist*, No. 9 (June) 1985, p. 5.

25. M. S. Gorbachev, "Politicheskii doklad Tsentral'nogo Komiteta KPSS XXVII S'ezdu Kommunisticheskoy Partii Sovetskogo Soyuza" (Political Report of the Central Committee of the CPSU to the 27th Congress of the Communist Party of the Soviet Union), *Kommunist*, No. 4 (March) 1986, p. 29. It is noteworthy that Gorbachev actually used the term "reform" (*reforma*). His previous avoidance of this term, and the use of such words as "transformation," "restructuring," and so forth, were interpreted by Western analysts as an indication of the intent to resort to something less than fundamental reform. Of course, the use of the term "reform" does not necessarily mean that Gorbachev will undertake fundamental reforms.

26. Ibid., pp. 29-30.

27. Ibid., pp. 23-24. The resolution of the Party Congress (March 12, 1986) unanimously approved Gorbachev's report and its specific provisions. For the text of the resolution, see "Rezolyutsia XXVII s'yezda Kommunisticheskoy partii Sovetskogo Soyuza po Politicheskomu dokladu Tsentral'nogo Komiteta KPSS," *Kommunist,* No. 4 (March) 1986, pp. 81-98.

28. See Selestine Bohlen, "Soviets Enact Law Allowing Limited Private Enterprise—But Call It Socialism," *Washington Post,* November 20, 1986, p. A41, and Selestine Bohlen, "Major New Soviet Reforms to Allow Private Factories," *Washington Post,* November 28, 1986, p. A7.

29. Gary Lee, "Moscow Woos Westerners for Joint Ventures," *Washington Post,* January 28, 1987, p. F1.

30. See V. Basiuk, op. cit., pp. 17-28. These pages analyze the various remedial measures introduced by the USSR (the Shchekino method, mathematical models, etc.) and the reasons for their very limited success. It appears that the Soviet economy cannot effectively assimilate certain minimal autonomous measures intended to provide incentives and stimulate the economy: in operation, they continuously conflict with, or are otherwise handicapped by, the overall highly centralized and bureaucratized structure. Perhaps in theory it is possible to design a hybrid command economy which would provide a successful fusion between control at the top and an effective functioning of autonomous incentives at the lower levels, incentives of the type which would not threaten the survival of the command economy. However, considering the complexity of modern economies, it is extremely unlikely that such a hybrid command economy could effectively operate in practice.

31. For a more extensive discussion of China's economic reforms, see Jan S. Prybyla, "China's Economic Experiment: From Mao to Market," *Problems of Communism,* Vol. XXXV (January-February) 1986, pp. 21-38.

32. B. P. Kurashvili, "Sovershenstvovaniye khozyaystvennogo mekhanizma: Kontury vozmozhnoy perestroyki" (Improving the Economic Mechanism: The Outlines of a Possible Restructuring), *Ekonomika i Organizatsia Promyslennogo Proizvodstva,* No. 5 (May) 1985, p. 64.

33. Ibid., p. 65.

34. Kurashvili makes some concessions to planning by output by saying that it could be preserved in the area of fuel and energy. Accordingly, he allows for the establishment of a separate Ministry of the Fuel and Power Industry.

35. See ibid., pp. 76-77.

36. See V. Kostakov, "Odin, kak semevo" (One as Seven), *Sovetskaya Kul'tura,* January 4, 1986, p. 3; and Philip Taubman, "Soviet Aides Get Jobless Benefits if Displaced by Agency Cutbacks," *New York Times,* January 9, 1986, p. A1. Professor V. Kostakov, a deputy director of Gosplan's Institute of Economic Research, projects that, in response to the Party's guidelines to improve productivity through organizational restructuring and the introduction of more advanced technology, the number of employed in the manufacturing sector will be reduced by 13 to 19 million workers. He notes: "It may appear new and unaccustomed to all of us to face the necessity to look for work, which, to be sure, many of those in both the manufacturing and service sectors will have to do. We are used to just the opposite—to jobs looking for people."

37. See Victor Basiuk, *Technology, World Politics, and American Policy* (New York: Columbia University Press, 1977), pp. 2-3, 80, 98, 266-267.

38. See, for example, N. Patolichev, Minister of Foreign Trade of the USSR, "K 60-letiyu leninskogo dekreta o natsionalizatsii vneshney torgovli" (On the 60th Anniversary of Lenin's Decree Regarding the Nationalization of Foreign Trade),

an annex to the journal, *Vneshnyaya Torgovlya,* No. 5 (May) 1978; N. Tret'ukhin, "Uluchsheniyu planirovaniya vneshney torgovli—postoyannoye vnimaniye" (Constant Attention Must be Paid to the Improvement of the Planning of Foreign Trade), *Vneshnyaya Torgovlya,* No. 12 (December) 1979, pp. 2-5; P. Mikheyev, "Rol' i znacheniye importa mashin i oborudovaniya v narodnom khozyaystve SSSR" (The Role and Significance of Imports of Machinery and Equipment in the National Economy of the USSR), *Vneshnyaya Torgovlya,* No. 11 (November) 1978, pp. 22-28.

39. In an oblique reference to consumer interests, L. I. Brezhnev stated, in the Report of the Central Committee to the 26th Congress of the CPSU (February 23, 1981): "Events in Poland convince us again how important it is for the Party and its leadership role to pay careful attention to the voice of the masses, to fight decisively various manifestations of bureaucratism and arbitrariness, to develop actively the democracy of socialism, and to conduct a measured, realistic policy in external economic relations." L. I. Brezhnev, "Otchetnyy doklad Tsentral'nogo Komiteta KPSS XXVI S'yezdu Kommunisticheskiy Partii Sovetskogo Soyuza," *Voprosy Ekonomiki,* No. 3 (March) 1981, p. 8.

40. Kevin Klose, "Massive Walkouts Reported at Two Main Soviet Auto Plants," *Washington Post,* June 14, 1980, p. A15.

41. For a more extensive discussion of the rise of interests in the Soviet Union, see Basiuk, "Implications of Differential Transfer of Technology to the USSR and Resultant Options for U.S. Technology Transfer Policy," op. cit., pp. 6-14.

42. "X" [George F. Kennan], "The Sources of Soviet Conduct," *Foreign Affairs,* Vol. 25 (July 1947), p. 582, and Harold Lasswell, "'Inevitable' War: A Problem in the Control of Long-Range Expectations," *World Politics,* Vol. 2 (October 1949), pp. 15-17, 35-39. Lasswell, whose article appeared two years after the much better known article by "X" (Kennan) and presented a considerably more elaborate and systematic theory of containment, made a distinction between three principal types of pluralization: ethnic, functional, and territorial (p. 16).

43. I am indebted to Jerry F. Hough of Duke University for the suggestion of an export-oriented strategy as a possible Soviet option.

44. See, for example, "V chem otvetstvennost' nauki?" (What is the Responsibility of Science?), an interview with Academician A. P. Aleksandrov, President of the Academy of Sciences of the USSR, conducted by Kim Smirnov, *Izvestiya,* June 10, 1985, p. 2. To quote Aleksandrov: "The United States of America is severely aggravating the international situation. All sorts of embargoes, restrictions on the many purchases of many types of technology and the means of production, and, under pressure from the United States, curtailment of scientific ties with Western countries—all this is aimed at a single goal: to slow down the pace of development of the Soviet Union.

But when we ensure the introduction of the latest generations of technology and, with the aid of science, bring our economy to the technological forefront of the world—that will be our principal answer to all and any aggressive efforts. This being so, our entire country, science, and industry must immediately generate great creative efforts toward correcting what is in some instances an excessive orientation toward foreign technologies and supplies [of equipment], toward a sharp acceleration of our own research and development."

See also Gorbachev's speech before the Central Committee of the CPSU of June 11, 1985 (*Kommunist,* No. 9, 1985, op. cit., pp. 13-33). To quote from Gorbachev, "We are not advocating self-sufficiency. But we cannot permit our country to be dependent upon deliveries from the West. The experience of recent years has taught us a great deal. Therefore, in both the domestic and the international aspect, the task of accelerating the country's development has acquired today prime political, economic, and social significance. Before us lies the implementation of the new and technological restructuring of the national economy and the qualitative transformation of the material-technological basis of society." (p. 15).

45.   The technologies in this category might include those: (1) essential to the USSR to eliminate bottlenecks in its industry and technological processes; (2) particularly expensive to develop internally; and (3) which make an especially high contribution to the productivity of Soviet labor.

46.   Western analysts noted that construction of automobile plants in the USSR with Western technology and equipment was not a net addition to the Soviet economy. It required substantial diversion (about two-thirds of total costs) of scarce materials and skilled personnel from related domestic economic sectors, including those militarily relevant. See George D. Holliday, "The Role of Western Technology in the Soviet Economy," in U.S. Congress, Joint Economic Committee, *Issues in East-West Commercial Relations* (Washington, D.C.: U.S. Government Printing Office, 1979), p. 58.

10

U.S.-SOVIET SCIENCE AND TECHNOLOGY EXCHANGES AS AN ASPECT OF EAST-WEST TECHNOLOGY TRANSFER: REVIEW AND LESSONS OF EXPERIENCE IN THE 1970s

John R. Thomas

Any examination of East-West technology transfer must take into account science and technology (S&T) exchanges between the United States and the USSR.[1] In particular, this pertains to the bilateral S&T exchanges of the 1970s, which involved hundreds of scientists on both sides. This paper summarizes the experience of that era as a basis for drawing conclusions about how the United States should conduct S&T exchanges with the Soviet Union in order to maximize the benefits for the United States, while minimizing undesired technology transfer losses. In this connection, special note is made of systemic, cultural/historical, organizational, and other related factors that limit the USSR's ability to engage in mutually beneficial technology exchanges with the West. The study goes on to examine how these constraints on Soviet behavior affected the conduct of exchanges under the 1972 U.S.-Soviet Agreement on Cooperation in Science and Technology, and how this experience should guide U.S. actions under any resumption of large-scale S&T exchanges with the USSR.

SOVIET MOTIVATION FOR S&T EXCHANGES

The Soviet need for Western science and technology developed (and continues to exist) against a specific background. Massive Soviet investment in science and technology since the 1920s has not been matched by a proportionate *qualitative* payoff except in a very few select areas, such as theoretical physics, mathematics and metallurgy. The Soviet S&T community and the economy have, on the whole, met in *quantitative* terms the high-priority military and heavy industry requirements set by the Soviet leadership. Yet when Soviet scientists have momentarily forged ahead in an S&T area, as in nuclear fusion research (*Tokamak*), they soon fall behind and thereafter remain unable to keep up with the West and the United States, particularly in the application of basic research. Similarly, while the USSR launched the first satellite (*Sputnik*) in 1957 and the first manned orbital flight in 1961, it was the United States that landed men on the moon in 1969—a feat Soviet scientists tried to emulate and then abandoned. In fact, some in the West maintain that the overall scientific-technological "gap" between the United States (and the industrially advanced Free World in general, including Japan) and the USSR is growing, especially with regard to information processing and advanced communication systems. Hence, even when Soviet scientists score theoretical and experimental breakthroughs before their counterparts in the West, they often fail to translate these achievements into an Eastern lead in application and production.

This Soviet deficiency is not, and never has been, a question of individual capabilities. On visiting Soviet research institutes and industrial enterprises, and on meeting Soviet scientists and technologists, one is impressed by their knowledge and individual abilities. (This point is underscored by international recognition of their work, most recently by the Nobel Prize in Physics awarded to Peter Kapitsa in 1978.) Nor are lagging achievements by the Soviet S&T community the result of insufficient resource allocations. The communist regime has made a massive investment in physical plants, scientific education, and training. For example, the Soviet Union currently has close to 1.5 million scientists, over a fourth of whom have advanced doctorate and *kandidat* degrees. The USSR also has over 5,000 research institutes performing work across the widest S&T spectrum in the world. Indeed, in some categories, the Soviet regime's investment in science equals or surpasses that of the United States. Soviet leaders have been investing over 3% of the Soviet gross national product in research and development (the heart of any S&T effort), compared to a U.S. investment level that normally ranges below 3%.

Moreover, the sizeable Soviet investment has been made on a continuing basis, and not erratically, as in the United States (where, for example, it took events such as the Soviet space *Sputnik* breakthrough in 1957, or the first manned orbital flight in 1961, to galvanize major scientific efforts). Therefore, the real reasons behind the lackluster Soviet *qualitative* performance in S&T, and the resultant need for foreign technology, must and do lie elsewhere—for example, in the negative impact of systemic, organizational, historical, and cultural factors. I would argue that the Soviet need for Western technology and bilateral exchanges arising from these shortcomings are magnified as well by the larger Soviet goals to modernize the USSR's economy and complete its vast military buildup in support of an expansive post-World War II foreign policy.

FACTORS AFFECTING SOVIET S&T PERFORMANCE

Systemic

The most basic factor affecting Soviet S&T performance is inherent to the Soviet system: the pervasive party control over all elite groups, including the military, the governmental bureaucracy, industrial production managers, the arts and literary community and, finally, but not least, the S&T community. The party's perseverance and overall inflexibility in exercising such control is heavily reinforced by a selection process—through the *nomenklatura* system—that assures continuity in office of an elite tenaciously bent on preserving its rule, even at the expense of failing to modernize the economy and the S&T community in order to increase overall efficiency. This situation exists because the party itself was not modernized after Stalin's death. Khrushchev tried unsuccessfully to do so with his proposed party reforms in the 1960s; even though designed to affect only the middle and lower levels of the party *apparat*, and not the very top, for example, the Politburo, Khrushchev's proposals aroused such widespread opposition that they were largely responsible for his downfall in 1964. This raises the fundamental question of whether the Soviet system can, without being modernized and reformed at the highest policy command levels, provide the proper political setting for S&T achievements that match the material and human investment in S&T made by the Soviet regime. It remains to be seen whether Gorbachev truly desires, and is able, to carry out the needed political reform, or whether he will instead effect a *generational* change without the necessary *structural* and *attitudinal* reforms—reforms which include the cultivation of greater tolerance for alternative views and approaches.

Organizational

Organizational factors also heavily affect the USSR's ability to engage in mutually beneficial East-West S&T transactions. The Soviet S&T community suffers from organizational deficiencies that affect its ability to perform productively. Ironically, in a highly centralized political system, the Soviet S&T community is severely affected by the fact that it does *not* have a "command center" for coordinating efficient R&D and production. On the contrary, duplication and counterproductive rivalries exist among, and are fostered by, the major S&T agencies—namely, the USSR and the Republic academies of sciences, the 50-odd production ministries, and the State Committee for Science and Technology (GKNT).

The fragmented Soviet S&T community is plagued in particular by three major problems. First, there are jurisdictional disputes between the Academy of Sciences and the GKNT, which arose as a result of the academy's loss of monopoly over (a) establishing and maintaining contacts with foreign science communities, and (b) providing the main guidance for the development of Soviet science. (The academy lost this monopoly after the forerunner to the GKNT was formed in 1961, due to Khrushchev's dissatisfaction with the academy's performance.)

Second, there are problems between the academy and some 50 Soviet production ministries over the issue of basic versus applied science. Traditionally, the academy has wanted to engage in basic research; the ministries, however, want the academy's help on the applied end, in order to meet production goals. Since the mid-1970s, frictions have increased, since the academy no longer gets all of its funds from the state budget, as had been the case earlier. At present, academy research institutes must make up funding shortfalls by obtaining contract work from production ministries, which allows the latter to exert pressure on the academy to work on applied problems. This, in turn, creates still another negative reaction: many academy scientists on assignment (*kommandirovka*) to ministry enterprise are extremely unhappy, because they have to be away from their prestigious academy institutes to work on what is often considered less challenging and interesting "nuts-and-bolts" production tasks.

Finally, there are problems between the State Committee for Science and Technology and the production ministries. The GKNT is charged with identifying foreign technology and guiding its introduction into the ministry production process. But the ministries resist GKNT's effort to impose new technology on them, because no allowance is made for the downtime involved in installing new equipment and retraining workers. Yet, the interruption of production for such downtime may reduce the ability of manufacturing enterprises to meet their annual production goals, and this would affect bonuses and promotion. Consequently, the ministries resist innovation, even though over the long run it would lead to greater output.

Thus, it is ironic that, in a system touted for its rationality and planning, the establishment of the GKNT and the subsequent reorganization of the USSR Academy of Sciences—including the transfer of some academy research institutes to the jurisdiction of production ministries—have led to greater inefficiency and organizational problems, instead of the intended streamlining and responsiveness to Soviet economic needs. The shortcomings of Soviet S&T planning are most graphically reflected in the gap between research and application. Since Gorbachev's accession to power in 1985, new proposals for the formation of integrated science-production complexes have been made to address these problems (as reported in *Izvestiya,* the Soviet government's central press organ, in mid-December 1985). Whether these measures will prove more successful than similar initiatives enacted in the past—especially the comparably labeled NPOs (scientific production complexes)—remains to be seen. In any case, these "new" proposals do not address the continuing and intruding bureaucratic problems between the academy, the GKNT, and the ministries.

Cultural/Historical Factors

Cultural and historical factors also play a role in the quality of Soviet science and technology performance. The organization of Russian science, represented at the leading edge by the Russian Academy of Sciences (founded in 1725 under Peter the Great), was originally based on West European models, which were highly academic with little effort addressed to scientific application and virtually none to production. A heavy residue of this academic approach remains in the USSR Academy of Sciences, the successor to the Russian Academy, despite the Soviet regime's efforts since the 1920s to bring the academy's research institutes closer to application and production.[2] Moreover, even though statistically the Soviet population is heavily urban, in reality it still retains an essentially rural mentality, particularly with regard to time and labor discipline. This can be seen most prominently among Soviet workers outside the main population centers, where many workers, though called on to run modern machinery or work in advanced laboratories, still have the outlook of the *derevnya* (i.e., relaxed rural attitude) toward industrial production and discipline. This cultural/technological lag affects both Soviet manufacturing enterprise and S&T performance.

Other Relevant Factors

Other factors bearing adversely on Soviet S&T performance and creating a need for Western technology include the ongoing absence of the necessary *supporting infrastructure* for efficient S&T development. The USSR simply does not have any counterpart to the many small supply companies that exist in the United States to provide instrumentation, Bunsen burners and test tubes, chemicals, and other common supplies needed to conduct experiments and testing. As a result, many Soviet scientific institutes must divert personnel and time to obtaining or actually making such equipment and supplies. This grossly inefficient situation is due mainly to the traditional Soviet priority placed on military and heavy industry production, at the expense of balanced economic development. This imbalance ultimately affects adversely the development of an appropriate supporting infrastructure to meet the needs of the civilian economy and the S&T community.

THE EFFECT OF DIFFERING U.S. AND SOVIET S&T APPROACHES

For all these reasons, the Soviet S&T approach (in philosophy, organization, and policy) differs significantly from that of the United States. This, in turn, tends to limit the possibility for mutual benefit in U.S.-Soviet S&T exchanges and in the larger arena of technology transfer interaction. As an illustration of Soviet-American differences, Soviet S&T policy frequently tackles problems in a narrow context, which often leads, for example, to the establishment of separate institutes with massive funds and personnel focused narrowly on specialized S&T tasks. U.S. research and development programs, on the other hand, seem to address questions over a broader scientific range. Then, too, Soviet S&T funding plans are laid out for a number of years, which can be a strength in terms of providing continuity in efforts to score breakthroughs, but a weakness in terms of continuing to expend funding on work that may be irrelevant to current needs.

Similarly, the Soviet educational system controls where its S&T graduates will work on completion of their education. This is a strength in terms of meeting the Soviet economy's needs, as *perceived* by the Soviet leaders. It may be a weakness, however, in that it encourages allocation of critical manpower resources on the basis of political, instead of scientific-technical, judgments at top levels. These judgments may not be alert to, or comprehend the significance of, the latest S&T trends, and therefore may lock Soviet S&T manpower into areas no longer on the leading edge of S&T development. In effect, this misdirection of manpower wastes skills, dampens enthusiasm, and discourages initiative.

The Soviet party control structure, embedded in the Soviet S&T community (similar to the parallel party structure in the Soviet military, the Main Political Administration), can be a strength in terms of imposing the party's will on the S&T community to meet the leadership's priorities. But the situation also constitutes a weakness when it results in political hacks substituting ill-informed judgment for the informed views of experts who are more familiar with S&T trends, who could anticipate and meet Soviet requirements more productively.

The Soviet S&T community is politicized (and thereby rendered less effective) not only because of the party's pervasive controls, but also because it is subjected to an organizational straitjacket: It is entirely a part of the state framework. (This contrasts with the U.S. S&T community, which is divided among government, academia, and private industry.) As a result, the "all-state" context frequently does not allow for alternative or creative exploration of S&T problems. Yet, such exploration is more likely to produce better results—as it has in the United States—than a monopolistic, state-directed S&T effort, afflicted by indifferent, insensitive, or illiterate judgments of the governmental bureaucracy, comparable to those of the party *apparat*.

Moreover, as part of the party and state control over the travel and contacts of Soviet citizens, the access of Soviet scientists and technologists to foreign S&T communities is highly controlled and limited. This prevents greater and freer interaction between foreign and Soviet S&T communities that could serve as a stimulus to better Soviet S&T results. It contrasts as well with the untrammeled access enjoyed by U.S. scientists and technologists to their counterparts abroad.

So, too, the Soviet S&T community itself, like the system as a whole, is highly centralized within each of the major components that make up that community, namely, the USSR Academy of Sciences, the GKNT, and the production ministries. This creates the problem of "the Center" versus *mestnikh* ("the locals"), leading to strains between the scientific-technological hierarchy and facilities in Moscow on the one side, and the S&T communities elsewhere in the 15 Soviet Republics on the other. The regional communities consider the "Muscovites" to be overbearing in their direction and oversight of local S&T work. In the 1970s, for example, Moscow research institutes took over cooperative activities with U.S. scientists, arrangements for which were worked out originally by local institutes outside the Soviet capital. Again, this overcentralized Soviet approach contrasts with the relatively decentralized science policy process in the United States.

Finally, a related problem affecting U.S.-Soviet S&T cooperation stems from the domination of the Soviet S&T community by those of Russian stock, as opposed to the many other nationalities that make up the USSR. Russian scientists have monopolized joint activities with the United States, as they have the Soviet S&T community's hierarchy and activities in general. Again, this situation parallels the Great Russian domination of the political system, and contrasts with the U.S. "melting pot" approach that reduces majority versus minority strains.

U.S.-SOVIET S&T COOPERATION IN THE 1970s

The Eleven S&T Agreements

The factors noted above affect the ability of the Soviet S&T community to interact with foreign counterparts on the basis of mutual benefit, particularly with advanced communities such as that in the United States. This observation is borne out by the experience of S&T exchanges and joint activities conducted in the 1970s under the eleven bilateral U.S.-Soviet agreements concluded in 1972-1974. These agreements, slated to remain in force for an initial period of five years, included the "umbrella" Agreement on U.S.-Soviet Cooperation in Science and Technology and ten other specialized agreements in areas such as space, ocean research, energy, public health and medicine, agriculture, and transportation. Many were renewed upon the expiration of the initial operating period.[3]

In promoting cooperative projects and joint activities with Soviet scientists and technologists at the height of détente in the mid-1970s, the United States was guided by one major consideration: to support exchanges in areas where the USSR had done advanced work or had invested resources and manpower in solving S&T problems that could save U.S. scientists time and duplication of effort. This was the case, for example, in theoretical physics, in some areas of energy (e.g., magnetohydrodynamics), in material sciences (particularly metallurgy), and in metal work (e.g., welding). The United States also sought to benefit from access to unique Soviet data, such as the large-scale records on heart and other diseases gathered by the state-directed Soviet medical apparatus, records not maintained as widely and systematically in the West.

In connection with these goals, the United States promoted joint activities which had—or were likely to generate—some or all of the following features, intended to maximize successful interaction between U.S. and Soviet scientists and technologists:

1. Availability of cooperative projects in both basic and applied sciences
2. Indication on both sides of substantial interest in cooperation

3. Evidence of significant Soviet scientific capability or achievement
4. Prior familiarity of U.S. scientists with their Soviet counterparts and their work
5. Evidence of Soviet willingness to contribute to mutually beneficial interaction, for example, allowing their first-rate scientists to travel to the United States for joint scientific meetings
6. Appropriate arrangements for long-term cooperation, for example, continuing joint projects and seminars.

The United States used the following criteria to assess the success of the joint activities that it eventually supported:

1. Did the interaction provide access to first-rate Soviet scientific and technological personnel and facilities?
2. Did the interaction contribute to our knowledge of the work of Soviet scientists and technologists?
3. Did the interaction produce concrete results—such as publications—which permitted dissemination of newly gained information or knowledge to the U.S. scientific and industrial community at large?

From the U.S. viewpoint, the results of the U.S.-Soviet S&T interaction overall were mixed. Mutual benefit obtained clearly in a few areas; less-than-hoped-for results in others. While the United States gained significant intangible results (e.g., information about Soviet S&T policy and organization, personal contacts with Soviet scientists, etc.), the scope and quality of the joint activities—and the resultant S&T benefits to the United States—were limited by many detrimental Soviet policies and practices.

Problems Affecting U.S.-Soviet S&T Cooperation in the 1970s

In general, S&T exchanges pose a special problem for the USSR. Unlike transfer of equipment, machinery, or blueprints, S&T exchanges involve human interaction. This means the personnel involved can look, talk, and listen—and, most importantly, be influenced by person-to-person contact. For a regime that tries to shield its people from association with the outside world (except for those cleared for such contacts), exchanges mean exposing the Soviet S&T community—a key group—to foreign influence in a most intimate, one-on-one context. This is even more sensitive than visits by performing theater and music groups, which are on stage for only a few hours and have little chance for the personal, individual, and continuing contact enjoyed on a daily basis by a scientist in the lab of a host country. Such contact is of great concern to a Soviet regime bent on minimizing, if not preventing, contact between its citizens and foreigners.

Thus, the scope and quality of S&T interactions conducted during the 1970s were affected by the following illustrative problems:

1. There were frequent (and often lengthy) Soviet delays in answering communications and queries from the United States. In some cases, the lack of a timely response to a scheduled and agreed action resulted in postponement or abandonment of a joint activity, with detrimental consequences for the pace and scope of the intended cooperation.

2. Soviet participants frequently deferred or canceled project meetings and other joint activities at the last minute. In the Soviet Union such action extended to eliminating research institutes and other facilities from itineraries after site visits had been worked out with, and agreed to by, the Soviet side in advance.

3. The Soviet regime maintained extensive limits on access to its scientists and technologies, and to relevant information required by U.S. scientists in order to promote meaningful cooperation. For example, progress was delayed or reduced when the U.S. side did not receive timely data needed for project definition and implementation, or, on completion of an activity, was supplied with Soviet reports containing inadequate information. In still other instances, the USSR would not allow many of its first-rate scientists and technologists to travel abroad to participate in joint activities.

4. The political limits on foreign travel by Soviet citizens were exacerbated by the USSR's funding problems. Thus, the Soviet shortage of hard currency affected the duration of visits and reduced the number of Soviet scientists and technologists who could travel to and work in the United States.

5. Internal jurisdictional problems among major Soviet science and technology agencies or ministries involved in U.S.-Soviet cooperation were responsible for a lack of progress in some instances. As long as these problems remained unsolved, they caused delays in project implementation, which led U.S. scientists to drop out of a cooperative effort because of other professional commitments.

6. Soviet authorities occasionally attempted to dictate the choice of U.S. participants. They did so by trying outright to bar the entry of American scientists and technologists into the USSR, or by raising trivial issues that had no bearing on the scientific capabilities of the U.S. participants. On other occasions, the Soviet side attempted to achieve the same effect of discouraging "undesired" U.S. participants by delaying the issuance of visas until those scientists and technologists themselves changed their travel plans and canceled their visits to the USSR. This effort was abetted by the fact that Soviet issuance of visas was, more often than not, a last minute action.

7. Cooperative scientific-technological activities were affected by the science and, particularly, the technology gap between the United States and the USSR. Because the USSR lags behind the United States in many areas, the interest of U.S. scientists and technologists in cooperating with the Soviet Union (particularly in long-term joint research projects as opposed to brief visits and exchanges) was small when considered against the size and the potential of the two scientific-technological communities involved. The situation was compounded by the problem of identifying and gaining access to advanced Soviet theoretical work, greater experimental data, or unique facilities, as compensation for Soviet interest in, and benefit from, the generally superior U.S. applied science and technology. The enthusiasm of U.S. scientists and technologists for participating in joint projects was further affected by cumbersome administrative procedures and constraints. The latter were not offset for U.S. scientists by looking forward to professionally rewarding substantive work, given the gap between the USSR and the United States in many S&T areas. Indeed, some participating U.S. scientists experienced difficulties in demonstrating to themselves and others the scientific worth of joint projects; this affected the willingness of others on the U.S. side to participate in subsequent joint projects.

8. Many actual and potential U.S. participants reacted negatively to the USSR's harsh treatment of its dissident scientists and technologists. This attitude developed in some instances after U.S. participants were personally confronted by the dilemma of how to respond to invitations to meet with Soviet scientists and technologists out of favor with their regime and barred from work at their former research institutes. Some of these alienated Soviet scientists tried to maintain their professional skills by holding seminars in their apartments and inviting visiting U.S. scientists to share their latest work at these so-called "Sunday seminars"; other dissident scientists tried to make individual contacts with U.S. participants, confronting the latter with the possibility of being charged by the Soviet regime with "engaging in activities incompatible with U.S.-Soviet scientific and technological cooperation." But avoiding interaction with their alienated Soviet counterparts was against the normal instincts of our scientists and technologists, particularly because many dissidents had done first-rate work for which they were known through their earlier published work. (Apparently as punishment by the Soviet regime, references to and citations of the dissidents' scientific work were eliminated from Soviet bibliographic documents.)

9. U.S.-Soviet science and technology cooperation was also affected by an overriding internal Soviet precept: precedence of party and government control over efficiency. Because U.S.-Soviet S&T cooperation had the potential for indirectly infringing on such control—by opening up the system to U.S. influence and thereby leading to an imagined or real loosening of the Soviet regime's hold over its people—some cooperation was not allowed and most was

tightly circumscribed. In these circumstances, fruitful interactions resulting from normal and direct contacts between U.S. and Soviet institutes and individual scientists and technologists were not possible. In fact, the Soviet regime monitored and oversaw all contacts between Soviet and U.S. scientific-technological personnel, even at the height of U.S.-Soviet bilateral cooperation in the mid-1970s. This approach affected the ability of Soviet scientists and technologists, whether at home or abroad, to share research results with their U.S. counterparts. For example, Soviet scientists could not give drafts of working papers to their counterparts without specific permission and lengthy delays, even when these papers arose out of collaborative effort. The attitude of U.S. participants was further affected by the inability of Soviet scientists and technologists to engage in other, normally accepted activities, such as open and unfettered contacts outside official meetings (e.g., visits to homes). In sum, Soviet procedures affected the quality of exchanges and the willingness of U.S. scientists and technologists to participate in U.S.-Soviet S&T cooperation.

10. Finally, another key asymmetry between U.S. and Soviet systems affected bilateral S&T cooperation. All Soviet scientists are state employees and therefore can be ordered by their government to engage in joint activities with the United States. By contrast, U.S. scientists work primarily in industry and universities and cannot be similarly ordered to engage in such interaction. This asymmetry puzzled many Soviet officials and affected U.S.-Soviet cooperation accordingly. Some U.S. scientists, in protest of the Soviet regime's treatment of its dissidents, or on the basis of individual judgments about the small benefit to be derived from cooperation, refused to participate in joint activities. Soviet authorities then ascribed such refusal to behind-the-scenes discouragement by the U.S. government, since it was unthinkable to them that any Soviet scientist would refuse to participate if ordered to do so by the government. (Such a refusal by Soviet scientists was unlikely in any case for other reasons; more than their U.S. counterparts, they were, and are, eager for joint work with the generally more advanced U.S. S&T community.)

THE ACADEMY'S ROLE AND IMPLICATIONS FOR U.S.-SOVIET EXCHANGES

The USSR Academy of Sciences is the most creative part of the Soviet S&T network and works at the leading edge of those developments that could be of greatest benefit to the United States. Yet, against the background of organizational fragmentation and given the lack of a unifying, coordinating entity—a role once entrusted to the academy, which as noted earlier has lost its decisive role and accompanying political influence—effective, meaningful cooperation has been difficult to achieve. In this connection, an overriding political fact should be noted: As an institution, the academy has never contributed a genuine scientist-member to the Politburo. (By contrast, the military, the KGB, and even the Foreign Ministry have been represented in this top ruling body.) Then, too, the GKNT has moved from an initial role in the 1960s of overseeing technology to the concurrent role of monitoring applied science. Since the line between basic and applied science is already fuzzy in many areas, the academy is suffering erosion of its position by the GKNT, even in the area of its supposed jurisdiction—that is, basic science.

The academy's position in the recent past was weakened further by the party's increasing unhappiness with academy performance on several counts. The academy is the last, if not the only, major institution with some autonomy in the Soviet Union: It elects its members by a secret vote. The academy provoked the party's ire, particularly among the old ideologues such as Suslov, when it resisted the election of party hacks (e.g., S.P. Trapeznikov) as academy members, very prestigious titles even if less significant politically. The party's negative attitude was further heightened by growing dissidence in the Soviet science ranks, which in the academy context is symbolized by Sakharov and by the academy's refusal to date to expel him from its ranks. This show of independence only increases the pressure within the leadership to bring the academy to heel. Such pressure has already been underway, highlighted by Secretary Suslov's several unprecedented appearances at the academy in the early 1980s to deliver personally the party's stern message on toeing the line. (The erosion of the academy's freedom was best illustrated earlier by the Soviet regime's abrupt deferral of the academy's 250th anniversary celebration from 1974 to 1975; this caused much embarrassment to the Soviet science community, since it had issued invitations to foreign guests and arranged elaborate commemorative ceremonies and events.) Then, too, party membership has become almost *sine qua non* for academy membership and advance in the S&T hierarchy. Such party membership subjects an academy member not only to normal administrative control, but also to party discipline.

Equally important, the Soviet leadership's growing stress on applied science in order to improve and increase production has further decreased the academy's influence. In the face of current and projected poor Soviet economic performance, manpower shortages, systemic problems (e.g., party control at the expense of efficiency), and other difficulties, the academy stands to lose even more of its influence, particularly if it continues to advocate work on basic research as its prime interest.[4]

But any decrease in the academy's role and capabilities has a direct bearing on long-term development of Soviet science, and on the potential for U.S.-Soviet S&T cooperation that benefits the United States. Diminishing academy capabilities would negatively affect the health of Soviet science, since the academy represents the most vital and creative part of the Soviet S&T

community. Moreover, because the academy has been oriented heavily toward fundamental research, reducing its role in this area would affect the quality of basic research in the USSR, with ensuing implications for future U.S.-Soviet cooperation. In the 1970s, U.S. cooperation benefited from the academy's advanced fundamental research in areas such as theoretical physics and mathematics. Consequently, any marked shift by the academy to applied research, where Soviet achievements on the whole have been meager, would reduce the benefits to the United States of any extensive cooperation with the academy.

STRUCTURING S&T EXCHANGES WITH THE USSR TO INSURE U.S. BENEFIT

Despite substantive Soviet shortcomings and the procedural obstacles to normal exchanges, the United States can benefit from S&T interactions with the USSR. But for this to happen in a format that still minimizes unwanted technology transfer, bilateral exchanges should meet the following four general requirements. First, they must be properly *arranged*. For example, the United States should: (1) identify and select for exchanges S&T areas of Soviet strength and avoid areas of known Soviet weakness; (2) avoid loopholes such as Article IV of the 1972 Agreement which may give unwanted wide-ranging Soviet access to U.S. industry; (3) provide for direct access by U.S. scientists to the best Soviet scientists and to first-rate Soviet research facilities, such as the advanced institutes of the USSR Academy of Sciences; (4) minimize the need to deal with intruding bureaucratic layers of the GKNT or the ministries; (5) provide for equal and reciprocal exchange of data and working drafts; and (6) obtain for U.S. scientists the same freedom to travel within the USSR as enjoyed by Soviet scientists in the United States, including attendance at internal workshops and professional meetings, and travel from host campuses to other universities, laboratories, and facilities.

Second, bilateral exchanges must be properly *administered* and *implemented*. For example, mid-level U.S. administrators should be qualified to negotiate, have in-field experience in the USSR, and have Russian language capabilities to avoid overdependence on Soviet interpreters and veteran "tech transfer gamesters." Participating U.S. scientists should be obligated to provide results of their joint work with Soviet counterparts to the U.S. government, so that it can build a record of experience, and an information base to draw on, for historic comparison and comprehensive evaluation of gains and losses to the United States. This would complement the individual benefits derived by participating U.S. scientists and institutions.

Third, given the intensive efforts of the Soviet regime to acquire military and dual-use technology from the West, S&T exchanges should be properly *monitored*. For example, the relevant U.S. national security agencies should have adequate resources to monitor the movements and activities of participating Soviet S&T personnel in the United States. U.S. host institutions and scientists also should be obligated to cooperate by reporting any inappropriate activities of Soviet personnel on American campuses or elsewhere.

Finally, the exchanges should be properly *assessed*. For example, after the scientific results of joint work are made available by participating U.S. scientists and institutions, qualified analysts should evaluate these results on a continuing basis, and make available gains-and-losses summaries in a timely fashion to U.S. administrators and policy offices. In this connection, U.S. "self-assessments" of joint activities should *not* be carried out by scientists who participated in exchanges, though they can and should contribute their views on the benefits and losses of their specific projects.

In specific procedural terms, any proposed large-scale joint activity with the USSR should first be pretested for likely U.S. benefits, and only then implemented along the lines of the following illustrative steps. First, survey visits should be arranged initially, with U.S. scientists going to the USSR first, to ascertain in advance of project work how much they will be shown and how far the Soviets intend to cooperate, *before* we open up our laboratories and expose our best people to Soviet "brain-picking."

The initial survey visits should be followed up by long-term, in-field visits of individual scientists for three months or longer. Only then should these initial steps be capped by joint, multistage research projects that might involve U.S. and Soviet teams at work for extended periods, alternatively in the United States and in the USSR. Periodic assessments in the course of the joint work would allow judgments to be made about the desirability, in terms of U.S. interests, of continuing the projects to conclusion.

The foregoing U.S. policy approach and implementation procedures would minimize the intrusion of larger Soviet political-military policies and procedures on U.S.-Soviet scientific exchanges, to the detriment of U.S. interests. Comparable U.S. approaches and procedures applied to broader East-West technology interactions could similarly protect the United States against a "one-way flow" in the Soviets' favor.

BENEFITS OF U.S.-SOVIET EXCHANGES
TO THE UNITED STATES

If the experience of the 1970s is taken into account and the above requirements for proper arrangement, administration/implementation, monitoring, and assessment of exchanges are met, the United States can maximize benefits from S&T exchanges and minimize technology transfer losses. It can capitalize on the breadth and specific strengths of Soviet S&T research and development work noted earlier, even as it pursues the exchanges fully aware of Soviet political and military goals. In the process, the United States can improve its understanding of Soviet S&T policy, organization, and cadres, and thereby better assess Soviet S&T weaknesses and strengths. To attain such an improvement is indeed a desirable goal for the United States: As Soviet leaders know much more about U.S. science due to the openness of our society, increased U.S. knowledge would, conversely, help close the information gap and improve the quality of future exchanges, with resulting benefit to the United States. Improved knowledge of Soviet S&T operations would also help us better answer why the massive input and high political priority given its S&T community by the Soviet regime have not been matched by the output of that community. (This deficiency is freely admitted by the Soviet leaders themselves.)

Finally, the interaction of U.S. scientists with Soviet scientists can favorably influence the Soviet S&T community. The asymmetry between the Soviet regime's investment in S&T and the output achieved suggests that Soviet scientists "vote" their unhappiness via low productivity. Their unenthusiastic attitude is undoubtedly heightened by their contacts with Western scientists, who teach them about freedom in general, and scientific freedom in particular, outside Soviet borders. At the extreme, the unhappiness of Soviet scientific and technical experts is reflected in the significant fact that many of the Soviet dissidents are scientists. The continuing low morale and productivity of such a key Soviet group ultimately could force alteration of the USSR's policy toward the West. To make up for their own S&T deficiencies, Soviet leaders might then have to pursue a more conciliatory policy toward the West in an effort to gain wider access to Western scientific and technological achievements. As in the past, such an approach by Moscow could turn out to be a tactical, short-run move. Whether it could be transformed into a permanent change would depend on larger factors, such as the overall strategic balance between the USSR and the West, as well as the relative success of the West in containing an expansive Soviet foreign policy.

SUMMARY AND CONCLUSIONS

This study has assessed scientific-technological exchanges as a unique form of technology transfer that entails two-way, human interactions. U.S. experience in bilateral exchanges with the USSR during the 1970s was reviewed and analyzed, and both procedural and substantive requirements for future exchanges ensuring benefits to the United States—and minimizing undesired technology transfer—have been identified. From these observations, it can be concluded that the Soviet drive for technology transfer damaging to U.S. interests can be transformed, in the context of S&T exchanges, into U.S. benefit by properly fashioned joint activities. Moreover, Soviet scientists' low productivity to date, despite massive material infusion and high political priority, can doubtless be further affected by contacts with their Western counterparts. Since the Soviet leaders must rely on the S&T community to modernize the USSR's economy and develop its weapons systems, they may eventually be forced to respond to the attitudes underlying the low productivity of their scientists—attitudes based in part on the impact of their interaction with U.S. scientists, who enjoy the fruits of free scientific inquiry. One accumulating impact relates to the desire of Soviet scientists to participate in normal international S&T activities, including the freedom to travel abroad and to have less restricted contacts with Western scientists at home, as well as reduced Soviet constraints on the exchange of research results.

If the pressure of Soviet scientists for such freedom produces a more open relationship between the USSR and the outside world, it could help reduce U.S. concern over technology transfer damaging to Western and, specifically, American interests. Such a relationship could make it more difficult for the Soviet regime to hide any S&T effort devoted to military purposes, as it has done in the past and still can do under the tight restrictions applied to interactions with the West. Indeed, a more open S&T relationship with the West could serve as a significant step toward opening up the USSR in other key areas such as arms control (for example, on-site inspection), and thereby relieve still further the current concern over East-West technology transfer in the United States. In turn, such developments could serve as long-run steps toward improving the larger U.S.-Soviet relationship.

In sum, broader and more open U.S.-Soviet S&T relations could not only lessen technology transfer concerns, but could also make a major contribution toward the reduction of tension in the strategic arms relationship, of vital importance to the very existence of both nations. Whether such openness in S&T exchanges develops will depend, of course, on whether the Soviet regime, partially in response to its S&T community's desire for greater freedom to interact with the West, makes fundamental systemic changes that open up Soviet society to normal intercourse with the outside world—for example, lifting censorship and travel restrictions, and easing the current compartmentalization of Soviet people, including scientists, from each other, as well as from foreigners. Such societal openness has not been traditional either in Tsarist Russia or the USSR. Yet, since it is at the heart of international S&T life, if introduced to the Soviet Union it would relieve some immediate Western concerns related to undesired technology transfer that may add to Soviet military strength at U.S. expense. In the long run, such Soviet societal openness—forced in part by S&T developments that erode secrecy and the control of data by a few—could also affect the USSR's goal of undermining the Western world, which has been at the core of Soviet policy since 1917. Properly arranged and monitored U.S.-Soviet S&T exchanges could contribute to such a "subversion" of the Soviet system and its expansive policy abroad.

NOTES

1. In addressing issues related to East-West technology transfer, this paper broadly defines the process to include not only the transfer of products (equipment, instrumentation, etc.) but also of knowledge that can be applied in research, development, and production. Under this definition, technology transfer covers not only commercial/trade transactions, but also scientific-technological exchanges and joint projects.
2. A significant exception to this is the academy's heavy and increasing involvement in military research and development. For detailed discussion, see John R. Thomas, "Militarization of the Soviet Academy of Sciences," *Survey* (London), Spring 1985.
3. However, most activities under these agreements were halted or reduced by the United States in reprisal for the Soviet invasion of Afghanistan in 1979, the imposition of martial law in Poland in 1981, and the Soviet shootdown of Korean Airlines flight 007 in 1983. But the pace picked up again after President Reagan expressed his support for expanding exchanges and contacts with the Soviet people at a meeting with U.S. administrators and coordinators of science exchanges on June 27, 1984, and at the Geneva Summit Meeting in November 1985.
4. It remains to be seen if Gorbachev will have a different attitude from his predecessors. It should be noted that the closest academician to him is Velikhov, who is known for weapons research work and may or may not stand up for retaining the academy's autonomy and basic research. In any case, Gorbachev has already said that he expects the application of S&T to production to be the primary goal of Soviet science. This means that the academy will have to adjust to Gorbachev's (and the party's) views of priority for applied science and not vice versa.

PART 4

TECHNOLOGY TRANSFER AND SINO-AMERICAN RELATIONS

11

TECHNOLOGY TRANSFER TO CHINA: WHERE IS THE UNITED STATES HEADED?

Denis Fred Simon

Sino-U.S. relations have grown steadily since the establishment of formal diplomatic relations in 1979. Interactions between both countries have included expanded cultural and educational exchanges as well as increased trade and cooperation in science and technology. Reciprocal visits of military delegations have also taken place as Beijing and Washington have considered various forms of defense-related collaboration. Yet, as the Sino-U.S. relationship has evolved over the last several years, there has continued to be a lack of consensus in Washington about the principal aims and objectives of its growing ties with Beijing. More often than not, the United States has assumed a compatibility or complementarity of interests and goals, and has proceeded in its policies on technology transfer and proposals for military cooperation without a very precise or coherent sense of how or to what extent an expanded Sino-American relationship actually can or will serve U.S. interests. While the prospects for U.S. business in China have loomed large as one of the major attractions, history has shown that it is by no means clear that the needs and desires of the American business community should be the primary factor guiding Washington's policies toward the PRC (or, for that matter, other nations). As the PRC has moved toward a more "independent" foreign policy stance in world affairs, questions remain about what benefits technology transfers to China will yield as far as U.S. global interests are concerned.

Gabriel Almond, in his seminal work entitled *The American People and Foreign Policy,* argues that in the realm of foreign policy, the U.S. populace tends to react more on the basis of mood or disposition than on factual information or the analytic process. This chapter argues that, more often than not, this is exactly what has transpired in the case of Sino-U.S. relations. We are now in a "pro-China" mode, with each successive administration feeling obliged to do more with China than its predecessors. As a result, we have tended to make policy and operate on the basis of wishful thinking rather than careful analysis. From the perspective of our long-term foreign policy interests, there are a number of potential risks in moving ahead with the Sino-U.S. relationship, especially with respect to expanded technology sales, without greater clarity of purpose and a set of more realistic expectations. The principal issue is not whether we should sell equipment and technology to China; it is rather what expectations we have and what goals we hope to achieve by expanding economic ties and commercial science and technology (S&T) relations with China. In order to preserve the longevity and strength of the Sino-U.S. relationship, both sides need jointly to identify and agree upon a more explicit set of common interests that will carry them forward into the 21st century.

CHINA'S GOALS FOR TECHNOLOGICAL MODERNIZATION

In March 1985, China's Central Committee announced the "Decision on the Reform of the Science and Technology Management System." This reform statement, which followed the October 1984 Central Committee decision on reform of the national economy, contains eight major provisions regarding the country's S&T structure and operation. The basic thrust of the reforms in S&T is to promote greater financial accountability within research units by reducing the amount of direct funding provided by the central government. In doing so, Chinese leaders hope to stimulate improved links between research and production, thereby increasing interest in the application and more effective use of technology.

Among the eight provisions are reaffirmation of the "open door policy" and the critical role of foreign technology. The document states that "the important role of importing technology should be recognized for developing production and upgrading existing enterprises." And, in keeping with the trend in PRC technology import policy away from whole-plant acquisitions, it states that "importance should be attached to importing patents, technical know-how, and software, and to expanding various forms of international cooperation in development."

In many respects, the reform document is merely a reflection of policies toward science and technology that have been in existence in various sections of the country since 1981. For the most part, these policies are aimed at promoting indigenous technological advance to support both civilian and military modernization *and* to close the "gap" between China and the industrialized world. Chinese leaders from Deng Xiaoping on down realize that without appreciable advances in science and technology, it will be difficult to attain and sustain desired levels of growth in agriculture, industry, and national defense. In fact, the PRC leadership has specifically linked the goal of quadrupling the gross value of industrial and agricultural output by the year 2000 with expanded application of science and technology. As much as 50% of the gains toward this goal will have to come from technology-related improvements in efficiency and productivity.

Foreign technology is viewed as a catalyst in China's modernization program. China's seventh Five-Year Plan contains provision for the import of 3,000 key technologies and related items during the 1986-1988 period.[1] The desire for expanded access to foreign technology, however, should not lead one to suggest that China has abandoned its goal of greater national technological self-reliance. To the contrary: Foreign technology is viewed as a complement to, not a substitute for, progress in domestic S&T programs. Chinese concerns regarding excessive reliance on outsiders for needed technology inputs remain quite extensive. These concerns were most clearly articulated by Zhang Aiping, Minister of National Defense in mid-1983, when he cautioned the country's defense industry and R&D organizations to recognize that foreign nations would continue to be unwilling to provide China with the most advanced technology.

Chinese technological priorities include the areas of microelectronics and computers, telecommunications, energy, transportation, and agriculture. In many respects, China has become enthralled with what Toffler has called "third wave" technologies: biotechnology, informatics, new materials, and microelectronics. Microelectronics appears to have become China's number one technological priority for a number of reasons. First, it remains a key technology for advances in new industries such as computers and telecommunications. Second, advances in microelectronics are needed to support military modernization, particularly in areas such as command and control, avionics, radar, and missile guidance. And third, microelectronics can be used as a key technology for upgrading traditional industries. Accordingly, China's goals for electronics advance have been made more ambitious than its general aims for other technology. While in most other fields China hopes to attain the 1970s and 1980s levels of the West by the year 2000, it hopes to achieve those levels in electronics by the year 1990.

The most outstanding aspect of China's program for promoting technological advance has been the relative progress made over the last several years. Of course, substantial problems remain with respect to both domestic R&D programs and the assimilation of foreign technology. These problems include lack of adequate planning, a shortage of competent technical and managerial personnel, and a poor infrastructure to support technological progress. Nonetheless, acknowledging these continued shortcomings should not lead us to ignore the major changes that have occurred since the S&T modernization was formally announced at the March 1978 national S&T conference. The implementation of the reforms in S&T has taken on additional importance because of the "hothouse" economic environment in which new S&T policies have been introduced. This environment is one in which the role of technically qualified persons has been enhanced and technical innovation has assumed a priority position on the agenda of both factory and R&D managers.[2] As Lu Dong, Minister-in-Charge of the State Economic Commission, recently remarked, "Technical advance is of strategic significance to the development of [our] national economy and will remain [our] chief task for years to come."[3]

DEFINING U.S. GOALS VIS-A-VIS THE PRC

Numerous studies of American foreign policy behavior have been produced over the last several decades, each one trying to discern what the appropriate objectives of U.S. foreign policy should be. In most of these studies, there is general agreement that any evolving relationship—whether it be in the form of an economic treaty or an explicit military alliance—must be a function of our political, military, and economic interests. Arnold Wolfers, author of *Discord and Collaboration,* has suggested that foreign policy goals fall into two basic categories: *possession goals* and *milieu goals.* The former refers to those values, rights, and interests particular to a specific nation-state; the latter is concerned with the environment in which a specific nation-state operates, including such factors as regional alignments and the economic development of other states. Similarly, Robert Osgood, in an article entitled "Ideals and Self-Interest in American Foreign Relations," suggests that foreign policy goals can be thought of in terms of *self-interest* versus *national idealism.* Whereas self-interest is concerned with the welfare of one's own nation-state, national idealism deals with those moral values and aims that transcend self-interest, such as peace, justice, freedom, human rights, and so forth.

The Sino-U.S. relationship, especially in the technology transfer area, can be viewed as a product of the interplay of several of these factors. First, our relationship with China seems motivated by pure *self-interest.* For obvious reasons, we are concerned with Chinese behavior toward the United States, and how our involvement with China might promote our own economic prosperity (through trade), enhance our national capabilities (through access to critical raw materials or energy resources), support our ideological preferences (free markets, open political system, religious freedom), and protect our political-military interests in East Asia and other parts of the globe (controlling Soviet expansion, tying down more than 50 Soviet divisions on the northern border, containing Vietnamese aggression, restraining support for revolutionary movements in Asia, etc.).

Second, our relationship with China also is informed by a series of *milieu goals*. China's growing participation in East Asia and the world precludes, to some extent, a return to the simple bipolar politics of the Cold War. Whether we like it or not, we are enmeshed in a complex web of relationships with China, involving the Japanese, the West Europeans, the Soviet Union and the Eastern bloc, and parts of the Third World, for example, the ASEAN nations.[4] And, while John Copper has argued in *China's Global Role* that the PRC may not yet be a world power in the traditional sense, it is certainly becoming an important regional actor in East and Southeast Asia. Over the next decade, we can expect that its foreign policy initiatives and economic activities will increasingly affect (in a positive or negative fashion) regional political, industrial, employment, and trade patterns as well as investment and lending practices. Thus, while PRC modernization does not portend a direct clash with the United States, it could have a significant impact on one of the most economically and technologically dynamic regions in the world.

Third, our relationship with China also has been a product of our penchant for *national idealism*. In many ways, our attitudes toward China are conditioned by a sense of "developmentalism"; we feel obligated to assist a billion people overcome their poverty—even if it involves our making a profit along the way. Assuming a high degree of malleability on the part of Chinese society, the methodology preferred by some is to pursue a form of "social engineering" in China—through educational and cultural exchanges—in order to usher in a series of Chinese leaders and institutional structures supportive of the traditional Western system of international law and organizations, and therefore committed to behaving in accordance with accepted norms of international behavior. In other words, we want China to join the community of nations as an upstanding citizen, and to behave in a way consistent with our own values and norms.

Of course, our idealistic notions about what we want for China should not blind us to the rhetoric that frequently informs our own foreign policy. Paul Seabury, in *The United States in World Affairs,* cautions that we must be careful to distinguish our declaratory policy (what we say) from our action policy (what we actually do).[5] From a long-term economic and strategic perspective, there are high stakes involved in Sino-U.S. relations. We want to be certain that we do not act prematurely or upon everything in equal measure that we profess, either willingly or not, to be part of our policy. We want to *sequence* our policy toward China so that as our relations develop we still have something to offer to promote future growth. Robert Johansen, in a book entitled *The National Interest and the Human Interest,* argues that more often than not we in the United States tend to confuse, or assume compatibility between, our self-interest and our more broadly defined global concerns. Our sense of idealism often leads us to see a mirage when we look at China, ignoring the pendulum-like political swings of the past and the great uncertainties of the post-Deng Xiaoping era as we work toward devising a new, more moderate political future for the Chinese. We tend to be emotionally taken by historical ties, the mystery of the Orient and similar sentiments, assuming that we can somehow foster China's constructive involvement in world affairs in a way that will also be conducive to our own vital interests.[6] While the goal may be legitimate, we need to think more about the constraints incumbent upon us and the array of diplomatic tools we have at our disposal for actually achieving this goal.

Obviously, various groups within the United States have different expectations regarding the evolving Sino-U.S. relationship. We must better identify and articulate what our goals are and whether they can be achieved, separating out particularistic interests from broader national interests. Japan appears to have a national "China strategy," and China appears to have such a strategy regarding its relations with the United States, with technology transfer and securing foreign investment being two priority goals.[7] As a highly pluralistic nation, the United States contains various groups that tend to act out their own versions of "foreign policy"; it is by no means certain that the aggregation of individual interests adds up to an appropriate set of overarching national goals. Moreover, at a time when military and financial resources are constrained, we must be prepared and able to spell out whether—and if so, how—our orientation toward China in general, and our policies regarding technology transfer in particular, fit into the complex network of our larger global interests.

THE OBJECTIVES OF TECHNOLOGY TRANSFER TO CHINA

The question posed by the sale of advanced equipment and technology to China captures, to a large degree, the issue of whether U.S. economic or commercial relations contribute to the achievement of all or any of the three types of goals specified above, that is, possession or self-interest, milieu, and national idealism. Taking economic aid as a focus, Klaus Knorr in *Power and Wealth* suggests that we can divide the potential or actual benefits from aid into three categories: short-term economic payoffs, short-term political and military payoffs, and long-term payoffs. In the Chinese case, even though we have yet to make available formal aid to China, it is clear that there are direct economic benefits to reap from expanded technology-related ties—even if the grandiose notions of the "market of one billion" are not realized. Economic gains are likely to come from expanded exports of U.S. equipment and manufactured products, from the import of strategic metals and energy, and from our ability to decrease inventory surpluses through sales to China.

The extent to which we are able to extract political and military payoffs from these economic and technology ties, however, is uncertain. On the one hand, our denial of technology to China to influence its behavior may seriously alienate Chinese leaders who, after almost a century of foreign domination, would strongly resent any purposeful American effort to constrain Chinese modernization. Though the Chinese need foreign technology for all aspects of their modernization program, the United States can probably do very little to "control" the overall course of that program. An explicit attempt by the United States to restrict technology flows further would be viewed in some Chinese political circles as evidence of the lack of reliability of the United States as an "associate" of the PRC. On the other hand, however, our growing involvement with China should not lead us to believe that the opposite holds true, namely, that by selling technology and trading with China, we have somehow fostered a "pro-U.S." China. While Beijing continues to see Washington's policies on technology transfer as symbolic of the U.S. commitment to the overall Sino-American relationship, we have not yet been willing to seek out a similar yardstick by which we can judge China's level of commitment.

As suggested earlier, several recent analyses of Chinese foreign policy by Harry Harding (*China's Foreign Relations in the 1980s*) and defense policy by Gerald Segal and William Tow (*Chinese Defense Policy*) indicate that China intends to pursue an *independent* foreign policy. As one Chinese scholar has stated, "We will never yield to any external position, will never attach ourselves to any big power or group of powers, and will never enter into an alliance with any big power or establish strategic relations with any big power."[9] In the September 16, 1984, issue of *Liaowang,* a similar declaration was made in reference to China's evolving relations with the United States and the Soviet Union: "Between the United States and the Soviet Union, we will neither take the so-called "equal distance" stand nor "play cards."[10] As Beijing has sought to moderate tensions with the USSR and as lingering doubts about the credibility of the United States have once again emerged, the necessity and value of a "lean-to-one-side" policy have dissipated.[11]

In this context, we must ascertain what we can realistically hope to achieve in an explicit political sense from our relations with China. The possibilities fall into several categories: Do we want to expand our overall political influence in China? Do we merely want to preserve and maintain the present state of relations? Do we want to play a role in helping to consolidate the position of the present government or its successor? Do we want to enhance our prestige in China? Or do we want to use the relationship as a signaling device to others regarding our attitudes toward their behavior or policies?

Three basic goals have been articulated as specific benefits that could accrue to the United States as a result of expanded technology transfers: (1) U.S. sales of technology to the PRC will give China a vested interest in maintaining a close relationship with the United States and the West. As a result, Beijing will have to think twice about taking actions that could upset the United States or its allies. (2) Increased transfers of technology will help support current modernization efforts, thereby consolidating the position of the present pragmatic leadership. (3) Finally, selected technology transfers will help advance China's economic and defense modernization in ways that could offset, in part, the growth of Soviet and/or Vietnamese power in the region. So far, however, in all three cases the evidence to justify a complete relaxation of existing controls remains mixed.

Knorr admonishes his reader to distinguish between economic relations and aid programs that are designed to obtain influence or shape events in the target country and those relations that are driven by a desire to support the recipient on its own terms. China's penchant for wanting more advanced levels of technology raises the possibility of undesired military advances. It also raises the more fundamental question of how effectively the Chinese can use this technology on the civilian side where it is needed the most. Past evidence of absorption problems, in projects ranging from the Spey engine to the Wuhan steel mill, suggest that in providing the PRC with too advanced technology, we may be contributing to future problems rather than solutions. Given the difficulties inherent in trying directly to shape developments in China, we must ask whether we are comfortable with accepting Beijing's choices and stated goals. Modernization failures related to foreign technology imports could be a source of backlash against the open door and further foreign involvement in China. Moreover, as Lee Chae-jin notes in his recent book *(China and Japan: New Economic Diplomacy),* which examines Sino-Japanese problems regarding the now infamous Baoshan steel complex, there are no guarantees over time that either side's expectations of the other will be partially or completely fulfilled.

Thus far, perhaps the most serious problem that has emerged in our dealings with China is our fear of confronting some of the possibly undesirable results of our growing technological and economic ties. Our policies have been based on *justification* rather than on *evaluation.* This is true in several areas. First, we have tended to ignore Beijing's constant clamoring about its intention to pursue an independent foreign policy. Whether it be continued criticism of U.S. policy in the Third World, support for the PLO, or Beijing's decision to sell arms to Iran and/or Iraq, Chinese leaders have indicated that they will pursue what they deem to be their own interests. In a world of sovereign nation-states, there is nothing wrong with this. But, in contrast to those who see a modernizing China as necessarily having a more moderate foreign posture, Segal and Tow suggest that an economically developed China is likely to be more self-confident and independent—and therefore possibly more assertive in international affairs. Moreover, Samuel Kim has suggested that China continues to maintain a high degree of ambivalence regarding its new international entanglements. Rather than adjusting to its growing interdependence with the rest of the world, China's tendency will be to thwart the constraints of interdependence in order to maintain as much independence of action as possible.

Second, the main form of leverage that the United States has over China is its possession of and control over technology. Beijing clearly resents this situation as it limits China's freedom of action and makes it vulnerable to external forces outside its direct control—whether they be U.S. export regulations or the multilateral CoCom restrictions. In this regard, Beijing has not waned in its commitment to greater technological self-reliance—even as the open door remains "open." One of China's principal aims is to make significant progress in its science and technology modernization program in order to reduce its technological dependence. Even though the Chinese claim to prefer U.S. technology and have expressed strong interest in a variety of U.S.-manufactured items, China will continue to diversify its international S&T relations. In doing so, it seeks to minimize the extent to which it is too closely tied to any one nation, and to assure itself the ability to play off other nations (and their firms) against each other, thus improving its commercial negotiating position. This effort to diversify will include the expansion, albeit gradual, of contacts with the USSR and Eastern Europe.

Third, we have tended to ignore the extent to which China has maintained its commitment to national defense modernization, especially in the strategic weapons area.[12] China's strategy for military modernization has been: (1) to strengthen advanced R&D programs; (2) to develop (or gain access to) advanced know-how and technology to support strategic weapons; (3) to streamline production facilities, especially where poor quality or obsolete weapons were being produced; and (4) to target funding better by reducing financial disbursements to those units that have been inefficient or ineffective producers. Pronouncements by Zhang Aiping (Minister of Defense) and Chen Bin (former Director, National Defense Science, Technology and Industry Commission—NDSTIC) have outlined this approach in discussions about the purposes behind the current campaign to have military industry assist the civilian sector. Under the present situation, it is likely that the defense sector will have access to and will benefit from the advanced technology and equipment flowing into China even though most of it is ostensibly for civilian purposes.[13]

Fourth, we have tended to be overly optimistic regarding Beijing's ability to implement its modernization and reform policies. Numerous problems remain in terms of political disagreements regarding the pace and direction of reform.

In late 1983, this resulted in the campaign against spiritual pollution in which the notion of "the open door being open too far" was raised. Even though the campaign did not get out of hand, the fact is that many Chinese scientists and intellectuals were anxious for several months about another possible policy reversal. Other problems, such as resistance to the reforms, corruption, bribery, inefficiency, and so forth, also plague the modernization program. Moreover, there are questions regarding whether or not the introduction of market forces into the economy can be maintained without a similar opening up of the political system. While we clearly should not mistake increasing "pluralism" among the leadership as a sign of pending instability, we should be just as careful not to ignore signs of fragmentation and existing problems as seen in light of policy implementation.

In effect, because we tend to approve of the general direction of Chinese modernization policy, that is, of the tacit movement toward a "mixed economy"—we tend to overestimate the overall stability of Chinese society. Our assessments about a growing market for U.S. equipment and technology and other products are based, for the most part, on the successful emergence of this mixed economy. Yet we must also consider the fact that current policies run counter to most of the policy doctrines that were in force for three decades. Inequality is growing in terms of both actual wealth and status. Any society undergoing the massive changes underway in China is prone to various forms of internal tensions. These cannot be dismissed—even though Deng is making a monumental effort to ensure the continuity of his policies as well as overall stability.

Aside from obstructionism and bureaucratic inertia, there are massive shortages of energy, uncertainty of supply regarding various factory inputs, an inadequate transportation and communications system, and limited numbers of qualified personnel in both managerial and technical positions. As suggested earlier, these constraints, combined with several others, are likely to limit the immediate contribution of foreign technology in most civilian areas.[14] Moreover, as many of the foreign firms involved in joint ventures and the offshore petroleum industry report, foreigners are frequently viewed with suspicion and mistrust—often making it difficult to work side by side in a number of work settings.

In order to assess the risks of current technology transfer policy to China, we must have a better idea about the potential benefits that we can hope to realize. The benefits to the United States in broad political or strategic terms can only be analyzed in relation to a clearly stated set or list of American objectives.[15] At times, we have tended to operate according to a rather unclear, ambiguous definition of U.S. interests regarding China and its modernization effort. The notion of playing the "China card" in our dealings with the USSR, which had been a major driving factor in the normalization of relations and relaxation of technology-related export controls, has proven to be unrealistic at best. Once defined, some of our goals can be achieved through indirect means while others will be achievable only with purposeful and deliberate cooperation on the part of China. Where the United States might want to influence developments in China or Chinese external behavior, however, excessively close business ties might hinder government flexibility. Such was the case during the period of U.S.-Soviet détente when the growing involvement of U.S. business in the USSR eventually became a mechanism for reverse leverage by Moscow on the United States.

U.S. CONTROLS ON TECHNOLOGY TRANSFER TO CHINA

China regards the technology transfer question as an issue of national sovereignty. In principle, and in spite of some exceptions, it rejects all notions about end-use requirements and has viewed the existence of "export controls" as a form of discrimination against China. Chinese leaders have placed steady pressure on U.S. officials and businessmen to relax remaining controls, even though the period since 1980 has seen substantial easing of restrictions on the export of advanced technology to China.

Relaxation of restrictions on technology exports to the PRC has occurred at a fairly rapid pace, if one considers that as late as 1978 the United States placed China and the USSR basically in the same country category under the export control regime. The process by which controls have been liberalized actually began as a consequence of the visit to China of former Secretary of Defense Harold Brown in 1979. By January 1980, U.S. officials were sending signals to Beijing that export controls would be eased and that serious consideration would be given to Chinese requests for nonlethal defense-related items. As a result, China eventually was moved into a "P" category, a special grouping created by Washington for the PRC in part to symbolize that China was distinguished from the USSR in the review of proposed technology transfers. The Soviet invasion of Afghanistan helped justify differential treatment for the PRC.

The emerging "China differential" was manifested in the so-called "two times" rule. Under this formula, technology transfers to China were set at "two times the level that would have been approved to the USSR prior to the invasion of Afghanistan." U.S. policy regarding China was also made more explicit, that is, the U.S. government publicly declared that it considered China's successful economic modernization to be in the American national interest. By mid-1982, however, Beijing had grown increasingly frustrated with Washington, feeling that somehow the further relaxation that it claimed to have been promised had not occurred and that delays continued to limit technology acquisition by various Chinese organizations. The fact that the Taiwan issue also became a major point of disagreement between the two countries helped to exacerbate the severity of the technology question.

In response to extreme Chinese pressures, the Reagan administration announced a major liberalization toward China in May 1983, though it took until November 1983 to work out the actual implementation provisions. Under the new policy guidelines, China was moved into the "V" classification category, along with those countries friendly to the United States. Unlike many of these other nations, however, several special mission areas were designated as "off limits" as far as technology transfer was concerned. Technology transfers making a demonstrable contribution to the following areas could be denied: nuclear weapons, nuclear weapons delivery systems, antisubmarine warfare, electronic warfare, intelligence gathering systems, and air power projection capabilities. In order to facilitate the review of China cases, a new system of classification was set up; the system contained a green, yellow, and red zone—each designating certain technology levels for approval or denial to the PRC. Seven key technologies were cited: computers, computerized instruments, microelectronics, semiconductor production equipment, recording equipment, and oscilloscopes.

As of late 1985, the liberalization process has continued to move forward. Within CoCom, a major relaxation has just been instituted. Similarly, a new review of the technology thresholds identified in the original U.S. green zone has also been carried out. Twenty-seven technology categories have been loosened up for sale to the PRC. The cumulative effort of such actions is likely to be the expansion of the types and level of technology and equipment eligible for export to China.

Interestingly, the present level of controls has been further relaxed without the existence of a strong consensus that provisions for the post-Deng succession have been completed, or that a long-term commitment to the policies of the present regime will remain in force. Momentum also seems to be gaining for direct military sales to China, including items such as the TOW missile, avionics, and ammunition production equipment. Under present circumstances, however, it is not yet in the U.S. interest to sell advanced military technologies to China. First, there are more important development needs in China to address, ones that ultimately pose less of a potential risk to the United States. Second, U.S. allies in East and Southeast Asia remain apprehensive about a possible improvement in PRC defense capabilities, particularly since the situation vis-à-vis Vietnam remains so volatile. Third, China has placed strategic weapons development as its number one military priority, and if past practice is any guide, it is likely that advanced, dual-use technologies will end up being made available to these programs. Under such circumstances, the present controls, limiting transfers which support the six so-called "special mission areas," should not be reduced.

U.S. technology sales to China also must be viewed within the context of the technology and equipment being supplied by other nations to China. Attempts by the United States to limit technology transfers to China are meaningless without multilateral support from CoCom. Indications are that, in some cases, Japan and/or West European firms are either bypassing CoCom or are offering a level of technology below the critical thresholds identified in the CoCom control lists. Moreover, in spite of the continued loosening of controls, there are indications that China has secured advanced foreign technology through clandestine means. The September 1984 issue of *China Trade Report* (published in Hong Kong) has noted that some equipment continues to be smuggled into China through Hong Kong. Western visitors report seeing computers and other equipment, clearly not yet approved for export, in Chinese factories and research institutes. Chinese investment in the United States has also begun to grow, some of which is clearly oriented toward gaining access to advanced technologies in American industrial circles.

In order for technology controls to be implemented more effectively and exports to be facilitated more efficiently, the president or the State Department must come out with a comprehensive statement about U.S. objectives and expectations regarding China. With respect to export controls, there is presently a disjunction in the U.S. bureaucracy between the policy formulators and the policy implementors. It is ironic to find the joint chiefs of staff and high-level U.S. officials from various branches of the U.S. military traveling to China offering various weapons systems and related equipment while at the same time other parts of the Defense Department have taken a hard line in trying to prevent technologies related to these items from being sold to the PRC. Most important, it makes little sense for the Commerce Department to oversee the control of trade when its primary function is the promotion of trade. Export controls should be the purview of an interagency government group involving permanent representatives from Commerce, Defense, Treasury, and the intelligence community.

It is very likely that Beijing will continue to complain about existing controls, especially if the momentum for further relaxation appears to be slowing down. Yet, in the view of this analysis, the answer is not to turn the clock back and reintroduce previous limits. Rather, the answer is to make more effective use of export controls as an instrument of foreign policy and diplomacy in Sino-U.S. relations, and to ensure that they can be employed as a signaling device in both a positive and a negative fashion. This can best be done by viewing export controls as part of a broader spectrum of policy instruments, including technical assistance packages, trade preferences, scientific cooperation, cultural exchanges, and so forth. Controls should be responsive and provide flexibility, not rigidity. We are so concerned with the fragility of the Sino-U.S. relationship that we are afraid to confront Beijing with any evidence of its malfeasance or to express strongly our concerns about outstanding issues.

China must be made to realize that greater trust and stronger political relations must accompany, if not precede, the open door on technology transfers and not vice versa.

RISKS TO THE UNITED STATES

Overall, the risks to the United States of becoming deeply involved in China's civilian and military development programs vary according to one's initial assumptions. If one believes that a rapidly modernizing China will be conducive to peace and stability in East Asia, then the risks of not becoming involved might be greater than the risks of direct involvement. According to this line of thinking, by entangling China in a web of commercial agreements, cooperative exchanges, and technology transfer contracts, it will be difficult, if not impossible (or at least very costly), for China to extricate itself from these relationships without doing direct and extensive harm to its modernization drive.

If one starts off with a somewhat different assumption—namely, that China will seek to minimize external constraints on its behavior—then the logic of the argument provides a different set of possible outcomes. Under this alternative scenario, as China achieves gains in its economic and technological capabilities, it will reduce, wherever possible, entanglements that constrict its behavior. In fields such as energy development, this could mean that, given present training and technology practices, by the late 1990s China will begin to push foreigners out of the industry at a sustained, albeit gradual, pace. Depending upon the nature of the domestic political scene, this could be done amicably or in a rather abrupt way. In either case, the possibility of "forced" foreign departures from the energy industry and others could occur under circumstances other than replacement of the present leadership by a more radical set of leaders.

Similarly, by further providing China with unencumbered access to U.S. technology, Washington would effectively remove some of the leverage it now has over Beijing. In spite of Beijing's complaints, it seems reasonable for the United States, wherever appropriate, to impose conditions on the transference of its technology, for example, nonmilitary end-use, nondiversion to third countries, and so forth. U.S. officials should continue to make our concerns regarding technology transfer explicitly known to their Chinese counterparts. China is not a unique case; it always has the option of rejecting American know-how if it does not like the terms. Without such stipulations and guarantees about end-use from China, it remains certain that the United States cannot prevent unauthorized use of its technology.[16] Of course, even with such stipulations, clandestine use is possible. But once it is revealed that China has broken its pledges, international public opinion would lead other countries to question Beijing's credibility.

By offering China vast amounts of technology, we will be reducing the technological and economic constraints on its modernization program substantially. In general, this would be a valuable achievement. At the same time, however, we will inevitably be releasing certain resources for further defense modernization. Jiang Xixiong, Minister of Nuclear Industry, in suggesting that China's civilian nuclear program should be given strong support by the military, has noted that "it will be easier to build up the national defense once the country's economy is in full swing and the country is more powerful economically."[17] In remarks before the NDSTIC, Chen Bin has said that "a strong country with good prospects will surely strengthen the construction of the national defense and help the development of weaponry."[18] These general views reflect China's strategy, which is to establish a military-industrial complex more closely resembling that of the United States than the highly compartmentalized system that had been adapted from the Soviet Union in the 1950s. Chinese leaders believe that the U.S. economic and technological advances in the 1950s and 1960s were based on close cooperation and sharing between civilian and military organizations. Rather than pursuing the past policy of fostering such cooperation on an ad hoc basis, China wants to institutionalize cooperation and interaction through exchanges of personnel and sharing of data.

If it is possible that the Chinese military will gain access to various dual-use technologies, then it must also be asked whether China will transfer U.S. technology to unauthorized third parties—such as the Soviet Union. While there has been some growth in Sino-Soviet trade over the last two years, it seems likely that political relations between the two countries will continue to proceed slowly over the next several years. Little progress has been made on resolving the three main issues that continue to divide the two countries: Soviet troops on the Chinese border, Soviet presence in Afghanistan, and Soviet support for Vietnam and its policy in Kampuchea. At the same time, however, a new five-year trade pact and an S&T cooperation agreement were signed in 1984, suggesting that the Chinese have not totally lost interest in Soviet technology and equipment. It is unlikely, however, that China would risk losing the political leverage vis-à-vis the USSR, which it derives from technology transfers from the United States by providing open access to American technology—unless relations between Beijing and Washington were somehow to sour suddenly.

Whether or not a serious downturn in Sino-U.S. relations occurs will depend, to a great extent, on each other's expectations for the relationship as well as on the disposition of the Taiwan issue. In recent years, relations have begun to mature, meaning that both sides recognize that disputes will occur and that they will not see eye-to-eye on all issues. Serious, though manageable, disagreements have arisen over China's failure to honor its grain agreement with the United States, the issue of American textile quotas, U.S. criticism of China's population control policies, technology transfer, China's Vietnam policy, and the delays introduced by the United States regarding implementation of the Sino-U.S. nuclear cooperation agreement. The dissatisfaction engendered by each of these disagreements, however, has been outweighed by the apparent benefits accruing from purported cooperative intelligence gathering efforts targeted against the USSR, and potential Chinese assistance in relaxing tensions in areas such as the Korean peninsula. Talk about a formal security relationship has largely disappeared—which has probably been of benefit to both sides in terms of reducing the potential negative impact of such an "alliance" on the prospects for improving their respective relations with the USSR.

Unlike the above issues, however, the issue of Taiwan could single-handedly derail significant parts of the relationship. After the "success" of the Deng regime in the Hong Kong issue, there appears to be a growing sense of concern attached to the resolution of the Taiwan issue. Deng's age, combined with the fact that time is working against Beijing's attempts at reunification, apparently has made some Chinese leaders anxious about reaching a preliminary accommodation on the issue over the next few years. Any action by the United States toward Taiwan that could be construed as antithetical to the reunification goal would be poorly received in Beijing and thus could affect the forward momentum of Sino-American relations. This message, which was highlighted in the October 14, 1985, issue of *Beijing Review,* was also clearly conveyed to Vice President Bush during his visit to China in the autumn of 1985.

Should Sino-U.S. relations experience a serious downturn, it is also possible that China would take its newly acquired technology and know-how and use it in ways inconsistent with U.S. interests. For example, in the energy field, Beijing might decide to explore or exploit oil reserves in presently contested areas, such as those adjoining Taiwan. It might also move into other areas in the South China Sea, thereby provoking potential conflicts with other countries such as Vietnam and the Philippines. In a similar vein, China might also copy some of the technology acquired from the United States—ignoring its patent protection commitments—and manufacture the equipment on its own. Similar attempts were made to copy some of the fertilizer and petrochemical plants imported in the mid-1970s. While China did not have a patent law at that time, there are many in China today who are not convinced of the utility of the patent law, and feel that it was adopted merely to placate foreign firms.

Any serious downturn in Sino-U.S. relations could have a negative impact on China's relations with Japan, especially if the focus of the problem were Taiwan. Given the extensive amount of financial assistance already made available by Japan to China, a sudden policy reversal or retreat from the open door could seriously hurt Japanese commercial interests. It must also be acknowledged that there is an element of fragility inherent in the Sino-Japanese relationship itself. This fragility, which appeared during the "textbook crisis" in the early 1980s and again in the anti-Japanese student riots in Beijing during the last quarter of 1985, is a reflection of historical animosity, jealousy, and national pride. Should China feel that Japan was gaining undue advantage, it might rethink its decision to permit extensive Japanese participation in its overall development.

PRC MODERNIZATION AND U.S. INTERESTS IN THE INTERNATIONAL CONTEXT

Current U.S. policy toward China is designed to support PRC modernization. We must recognize, however, that we have very little ability to set limits upon how strong China becomes. If we want a China capable of resisting Soviet power, we must also realize that possession of such enhanced capabilities will give China the ability to intervene in other spheres of regional and global affairs. As a result, it is important to gain insight into China's intentions as well as its capabilities. Unfortunately, we have little to go on except statements of Chinese leaders and limited examples of Chinese behavior under current circumstances.

Yet, several trends may be identified on the basis of these statements and past history—both of which have been somewhat reliable indicators. First, China will continue to pursue an independent foreign policy, not joining either superpower or leaning to one side. The once provocative possibility of the United States developing a formal security agreement with the PRC has grown more remote. Defense-related cooperation with the United States will be limited to a small number of select areas. For the most part, China will attempt to identify with the Third World, and as such pursue policies that seek to reform aspects of the present international system—leading it to clash at times with U.S. interests in this area. These clashes could occur over policy in the Middle East, events in Southeast Asia, and China's support for various communist movements in Asia and other parts of the Third World. In addition, the issue of Taiwan remains volatile from the PRC's perspective, especially given the U.S. commitments undertaken in the Taiwan Relations Act.

Second, in spite of the open-door policy, China will maintain its uneasiness about integration into the world political economy. It wants technology and capital from the West and Japan, but is still unwilling to accept many of the values and ideas that accompany these items. Accordingly, control will continue to be an important Chinese objective, especially when more narrow, local interests begin to come into conflict with centrally derived objectives.

Third, China's once holistic view of the world is now breaking down, and its appreciation for the complexity of the international system is increasing. This makes management of foreign affairs more difficult and problematic as China has to assess its own interests and goals regarding a multitude of issues that vary in intensity, scope, and implication.

A fourth trend is that the commitment to modernization will be maintained. Nonetheless, even taking into account the extent of this commitment, greater realism remains warranted due to an increasing number of factors that could upset the course of modernization. These factors include unfulfilled rising expectations, problems with political succession, overambitiousness, continued reliance on sloganeering, and a growing divergence among local and central interests. China will seek greater clarity of purpose and direction, but it will be increasingly difficult to determine who will actually provide the definition and guidance for action. Accordingly, we must carefully monitor the emerging domestic situation, recognizing that the evolving triangular relationship among the party, state, and military will be the critical determinant of China's political future.

Under this scenario, one should be cautious about the immediate gains from developing an extensive network of commercial technology relations with China. This is not meant to suggest that the United States should not actively support China's modernization. Nonetheless, we should realize that extensive foreign involvement in China's modernization program could become problematic, especially if serious difficulties started to emerge. Foreign participation is part of a fair-weather system; foreigners will be associated with the problems, but receive little credit for the successes. Should substantial cracks appear in China's modernization monolith, foreign firms will need to be in a position where they can extricate themselves quickly and with only moderate costs.

Over the next five to seven years, the emergence of several pockets of excellence in the Chinese economy is more likely than drastic failure or radical success in the modernization program. These pockets will result from a combination of government nurturing, foreign technology, and managerial expertise. Electronics, textiles, and machine tools are candidates for such attention. In many cases, however, Chinese efforts to market these types of products will likely encounter stiff competition from other Asian nations as well as possible protectionism in the United States and other industrialized nations. Trade frictions could very well occur, especially if several of the Asian nations are unable to restructure their own economies as rapidly as planned.

In order to support modernization, China will continue to seek out assistance and investment from foreign firms as well as concessionary funding from various international sources.[19] Even though China has formulated new policies to promote foreign involvement, designing policy is not in itself equivalent to coming to grips with the problems. Foreign firms continue to report difficulties in doing business in China; some report being squeezed by Chinese firms and local authorities. Pressures during negotiations are intense, and as one lawyer has indicated to the author, many fall apart precisely because Chinese technology demands are too high and the price they are willing to pay is too low.[20] As decentralization increases and local areas become more concerned with their own profit-making potential, it is likely that various demands on foreign firms will increase, as will frustration. According to one Chinese official, those firms supplying more technology will be given preferential treatment and increased access to the domestic market. The costs of doing business in China, in terms of both time and money, will remain high.

In the final analysis, once the United States identifies more clearly its political and economic interests regarding the outcome of the modernization program, it should devise an appropriate strategy for responding to Chinese needs through technology transfer. Becoming more responsive, for example, to China's program for the technical transformation of enterprises would be one positive step. This strategy should be complemented by an appropriate mix of financial supports, trade incentives, and so forth. At the same time, however, the United States also must maintain some form of "influence" over China that extends beyond our decision to include it in the triangular politics of Sino-Soviet-U.S. relations. There must be an integrity to the Sino-U.S. relationship that stands on its own. For this purpose, our only real instrument of leverage remains technology. Our intention should not be to withhold technology in an excessively unequivocal fashion; it would not do us any good to retreat from our present level of technology transfer to China. Rather, our objective should be to show Beijing that U.S. technology flows quite smoothly when the dynamics of the relationship are on an upward trend. China will most likely perceive continued U.S. efforts to use technology as an instrument of foreign policy in a negative fashion, but that only reinforces its importance to both the United States and China. If we are able to plug many of the holes in our multilateral control system, we can use technology effectively in this bilateral context to serve our stated objectives.

Whether or not the Chinese will choose to forgo U.S. technology because of our stubbornness or refusal to change remains to be seen. Beijing's constant criticisms of Japan for its failure to transfer technology, and its recognition that Western Europe does not have the technological dynamism of the United States or Japan, may leave it with no alternative but to deal with the United States on our terms. It makes a difference whether the U.S. government becomes active in supporting such transfers or whether it assumes a passive role. China would do well to experience both sides of the coin and to choose the option it prefers. Its choice will be reflected in its moderation of criticism of the

United States, its willingness to expand cooperation on global issues, and its integrity with respect to the use of technology.

NOTES

1. *China Daily,* November 25, 1985. A similar set of technology import requirements was also established during the sixth Five-Year Plan. See *China's Foreign Trade,* No. 8, 1985.
2. A series of regulations and institutional mechanisms have been put in place in order to facilitate the domestic transfer of technology. In essence, these changes are aimed at the creation of an internal technology market. See *China Daily,* November 30, 1985.
3. Lu's remarks were made at a 10-day national conference in Beijing focused on the role of imported technology in speeding up industrial technology development. *China Daily,* November 25, 1985.
4. One of the things that the United States has learned in its use of export controls and its policies toward CoCom is that the successful enforcement of controls on technology exports must be a multilateral effort. As cases such as the gas pipeline have indicated, without a political consensus and cooperation among allies and friendly nations, controls on the flow of technology will have little, if any, impact.
5. Paul Seabury, *The United States in World Affairs* (New York: McGraw Hill, 1973).
6. This is precisely what happened in the late 1960s and early 1970s in the aftermath of the Cultural Revolution. We tended to believe that everything in the PRC was rosy and therefore accepted a picture of China that was a far cry from the reality—thus leaving us almost totally surprised by events such as the anti-Confucius campaign, the rise and fall of the Gang of Four, and so forth.
7. China also has benefited from its expanded relations with the United States as a result of the deterrent effect that Beijing-Washington ties have had on Moscow. In addition, relations with the United States and the countries of the Western alliance have given China the ability to avoid drastic increases in defense expenditures and utilize scarce financial and manpower resources in areas vital to overall economic modernization.
8. The key issue is not that we should somehow expect China to follow our lead in all matters of international relations. Rather, it is that we need to understand better how our interests might diverge as China acts upon its own national and political, military, and economic interests in the context of various regional and global settings.
9. Li Dai, "Our Country Has Opened a New Situation in Foreign Affairs," *Shijie Zhishi* (World Affairs), January 1, 1985, pp. 6-7, in *FBIS,* PRC, February 5, 1985, pp. A1-A3.
10. *FBIS,* PRC, September 13, 1984, pp. K1-K2.
11. According to Wu Xueqian, China's Foreign Minister, the basic elements of the PRC's independent foreign policy include: (a) fighting hegemonism and safeguarding world peace; (b) developing relations with all countries on the basis of the five principles of peaceful coexistence; and (c) firmly supporting Third

World countries in their struggle to defend national independence and develop their national economies. See *China Daily,* May 18, 1984. The five principles referred to by Wu are: mutual respect for sovereignty and territorial integrity, mutual nonaggression, noninterference in each other's internal affairs, equality and mutual benefit, and peaceful coexistence.

12. Chinese leaders look fondly upon their successful efforts to develop nuclear weapons. For some, the "big push" approach that was used to develop these weapons represents a viable model for achieving present and future priority goals, both inside and outside the defense area. See "China's Atomic Weapons Story Told," *New York Times,* May 5, 1985, p. 34.

13. Since 1981, some of the Chinese pressures for a more forthcoming U.S. policy on technology transfer appear to have come from the PRC defense sector, which apparently went along with Sino-U.S. normalization, in large part because of the potential technology transfer benefits. For example, the Chinese military is in great need of advanced microelectronics design and production know-how, and has thus been quite active in seeking out these items from West European as well as U.S. firms.

14. The key exceptions will be in those areas, such as electronics and computers, where the Beijing government, for defense as well as civilian reasons, has adopted a policy of nurturing from the center while at the same time allowing enough market to stimulate improved productivity and technical advance.

15. It is clear that U.S. goals may shift over time as the bilateral relationship evolves or as regional and international alignments shift. Nonetheless, this does not preclude policymakers from addressing the question of goals, especially since the often temporal nature of these goals requires constant reassessment and reformulation in order to remain relevant and useful as guidelines for behavior.

16. One way to further reduce unauthorized use is to require U.S. firms periodically to visit project sites to inspect equipment and/or to compartmentalize, through various physical security measures, sensitive aspects of the equipment and technology sold to the Chinese. Also, leasing of equipment with provision for purchase after X years may be another way to buy time in the face of present uncertainties.

17. *China Daily,* December 29, 1984, p. 1.

18. *FBIS,* PRC, February 28, 1985, pp. K3-K4.

19. Even though there has been some concern that China might draw financial resources away from other LDCs, the lobbying power of countries such as India has prevented such a trend from occurring. Nonetheless, as monies for international assistance become tighter, it is likely that competition for funds will become stiffer, thereby creating tensions among countries as they vie for concessionary monies. While private capital will still be readily available, China will exploit public sources to the fullest possible extent because of lower interest rates.

20. During negotiations, China tends to overstate its capabilities in order to attract a foreign firm, but once the agreement has been concluded, it tends to understate its capabilities in order to secure additional technical assistance. In many cases, China seeks this additional assistance free of charge because it suggests that the rendering of such assistance is in keeping with the spirit of cooperation implied in the agreement.

21. As negotiations over the nuclear energy cooperation pact indicate, if China seriously wants a technology, it will compromise what it often contends are "nonnegotiable" principles.

PART 5

RECENT DEVELOPMENTS IN U.S. EXPORT CONTROL POLICY

12

NATIONAL SECURITY EXPORT CONTROLS IN THE REAGAN ADMINISTRATION

Lionel H. Olmer

Few policies of the Reagan administration were more carefully considered prior to the first term, or adhered to in principle with such consistency, than that regarding export controls relating to national security. Neither an aroused business community complaining bitterly about the loss of competitiveness due to meaningless restraints unilaterally imposed by the U.S. government, nor a Congress confronting enormous trade deficits (at least in part due to export controls), nor even friendly foreign governments made antagonistic by the extraterritorial reach of U.S. regulations seem to have deterred the administration in any significant way from trying to do what it said it would.

Now, some five years later, it is appropriate to examine the results, for two reasons. First, there is a new Export Administration Act in place, which reflects (at least theoretically) the experience of the past. Second, the government has just published an updated and far more complete report on Soviet efforts to obtain Western technology, revealing the massive nature of the problem and some of the limits inherent in any control effort.

What were the objectives of the Reagan administration's export control policy relating to national security? How well were they, and are they, being achieved? Were they appropriate and relevant policies? What considerations should apply now and in the future in recognition of what has or should have been learned?

THE ADMINISTRATION'S OBJECTIVES

From the earliest days of 1981, there were four policy objectives, which represented a consensus among all agencies involved in export controls, and which remain the fundamental basis for the development and implementation of specific regulations and negotiations with our allies.

1. The definition of "strategic, dual-use technology" needed to be expanded, because the era of détente had spawned laxness, which had contributed greatly to the development by the Soviet Union of military capabilities based in part on dual-use, Western technologies that otherwise might not have been available. Insofar as export control was concerned, the overused expression held that we should "tighten up at the top and clear out at the bottom" of the technology control list.

2. The mess left behind by 10 years of neglect in the management of the system needed to be cleaned up. In other words, we needed to eliminate backlogs of license applications and get more serious about enforcing export control laws. (When the administration took office in January 1981, there were more than 2,200 backlogged license applications. This was reduced to about 200 within five months.)

3. The multilateral mechanism of export controls—specifically, the CoCom (Coordinating Committee for Multilateral Export Controls) process—needed to be strengthened by means of (a) gaining a consensus on a more restrictive multilateral trade policy; (b) harmonizing licensing procedures among CoCom members so that the business community in each country is subject to roughly the same kind of treatment; and (c) improving and toughening enforcement laws and procedures.

4. The business community (in the United States in particular) needed to understand that these are the Reagan administration's policies; that the administration is committed to them; that although they will impose a cost, that cost is a necessary one; and that implementation will lead to greater efficiency, predictability, and consistency. In other words, no more "whipsaw" treatment, no suddenly changing "light-switch" diplomacy, and no meaningless unilateral controls.

At times, one or another of these objectives has been pursued more aggressively, and at times subsidiary objectives, which had a major impact on the entire program, were added. In this latter regard, President Reagan's decision to forge a new relationship with the People's Republic of China necessitated a liberalization of technology transfer policies with the PRC, and this is causing fundamental changes to take place within CoCom. Second, negotiations aimed at bilateral understandings with non-CoCom countries have been initiated, since the availability of technology around the world in places *not* subject to CoCom control dramatically increases the risk of diversion to the Soviet Union. This policy response to real-world conditions is still in its infancy, but there is an awareness that unless pursued vigorously and effectively, the CoCom system could itself become irrelevant.

HOW WELL WERE AND ARE THE POLICIES BEING CARRIED OUT?

If progress toward these objectives is examined as a whole, and in not too clinical a manner, the administration is seen to have done quite well. In the first place, the technology control list has been tightened at the top, and there has been some "cleaning out" of less sensitive technologies at the bottom. In the judgment of many, not enough has been accomplished, but a start has been made. For example, controls on personal computers and embedded microprocessors have either been eliminated or loosened considerably. On the other hand, sophisticated digital telephone switching equipment has been added to the list of critical technologies, and there has been some movement toward gaining allied agreement to control "disembodied" technology (that technology which is transferred independently from a product). Heretofore, and even today, it has only been the United States, for the most part, which controls disembodied technology. Nevertheless, this process of tightening at the top and loosening at the bottom has taken far too long, and it has been far too acrimonious. In the process, Congress has been alienated, along with the business community and many of our allies. Moreover, this halting progress has not paid sufficient attention to the fantastic and dynamic spread of sophisticated technology around the world.

As a second broad achievement, backlogs in the export control system have been virtually eliminated. Statutory deadlines are being met, the system is better organized, and the various governmental agencies responsible for this area of policy are cooperating more fully at technical levels. Substantial additional government resources have been committed to the enforcement process, where a far better job is also being done.

Third, CoCom does indeed work better. There is substantive political commitment at high levels; there has been some improved harmonization of licensing procedures; and a few countries have gotten tougher on enforcement. Moreover, some progress has been made in forging new bilateral relationships with non-CoCom countries, thus widening the control network. However, a number of problems remain to be overcome: (1) Our CoCom allies do not want to make CoCom a formal or treaty mechanism having policy responsibilities. Moreover, they do not want the organization to become too efficient, because if it had more than a marginal technical competence, it might take the place of national-level authorities. (2) Our allies have come to believe that U.S. policy is largely contrived for the benefit of American business (an observation that would amuse many in the American business community if the thought were not so painful). (3) The export control system remains terribly inefficient at its roots, with little prospect for any major improvement to a degree that businessmen would find reassuring.

Fourth, and finally, the business community has certainly been educated. It believes that export controls are here to stay. From its viewpoint, is the system now more predictable? For the most part, yes, but it is still a morass of regulations bedeviling many a U.S. company (particularly small- and medium-sized firms). In addition, serious internal dissension still plagues the administration, and this puts a heavy burden on decisionmaking and delays the licensing process. There is a great deal of evidence that not enough decontrol is taking place, and there continues to be widespread unevenness in the application of CoCom controls by member states.

IMPORTANT CONSIDERATIONS FOR THE FUTURE

In considering future policy, I fear there are more questions than answers.

1. What should be the philosophic underpinning of the export control system? The philosophy generally embraced in recent years was first articulated some 10 years ago by J. Fred Bucy, then president of Texas Instruments. It was based on ideas introduced in a report produced in 1975 by a Defense Department panel headed by Bucy, and in essence it argued that it was more important to control know-how than products. However, a recent unclassified report by the CIA says, in effect, that products are as important as, or more important than, technology inasmuch as "batch acquisitions and samples which are reverse-engineered outstrip the acquisition of technology and are of more immediate value to the Soviets." We need to ask, therefore, whether or not to downplay the concept of controlling "arrays of know-how" in export control policy. Where in the manufacturing process, it must be asked, can we best and most effectively intervene with minimum disruption to trading interests, and yet still prevent development of Soviet military capabilities? Should the "Militarily Critical Technologies List" (MCTL) be deemphasized in favor of trying to stop products from being diverted to the USSR? Given the volume of production of semiconductors worldwide (in excess of 60 billion annually), what would be the implications for a system emphasizing hardware control?

2. Can we clearly distinguish between preventing acquisition of "strategic" technology of military value and the desire by some (in the administration) to

use the export control system to impede Soviet industrial development? If we do subscribe to the latter approach as a policy objective (and the administration proclaims that this is *not* its policy), we can forget about allied cooperation in the control of dual-use technology, and we can be assured of galvanizing the entire business community in opposition to U.S. policy.

3. Can the system be made more efficient or is it hopeless? I think there should be concern about the possibility of constructing an irrelevant control system. If the Soviet authorities continue to acquire technology and develop their military capability despite the fact that the export control system works perfectly (and at substantial cost to U.S. industrial competitiveness), will the existence of such a system have made any difference?

4. Can we develop better measures to judge whether, in particular cases, the costs of export control are worth it? The same CIA report mentioned earlier says that "in the armor area, the Soviets are using Western technology not to catch up, but to enhance a capability that is already equal to or better than that of the West."

5. Can U.S., CoCom, and bilateral control arrangements ever hope to keep up with the pace of technological change?

6. Can Congress be an effective watchdog or will it merely rise to complain every few years only in the context of renewing legislation?

7. Will the administration develop a better capability to deal with the flow of unclassified data that has been enormously useful, and of military significance, to the USSR?

It will not be easy to come up with answers to these questions. However, the fundamental precept to guide inquiry should be that, first and foremost, U.S. and Western technological preeminence must be maintained. Given that leading-edge technology today derives from the private sector, and not from military-related procurement (and has done so for at least the past 15 years), it is necessary that our companies compete successfully in the world arena. If they fail to generate profits that can be converted to research and development, innovation, productivity growth, and new products eagerly sought after by the public, we truly will lose the ability to structure and maintain an effective export control system.

Virtually everyone would agree that however well constructed, an export control system can be only partially successful in preventing the Soviet Union from acquiring Western technology and products. The margin of possible success, therefore, should not be pressed at the cost of losing the very edge we believe is essential to our security.

13

CONGRESSIONAL CONCERNS AND INITIATIVES: A VIEW FROM THE SENATE

Paul Freedenberg

Five years ago, I served as International Finance Economist for the Subcommittee on International Finance and Monetary Policy of the Senate Banking, Housing, and Urban Affairs Committee, which had primary jurisdiction in the Senate for the renewal of the Export Administration Act (EAA). At that time, I wrote an article for the *National Journal,* in which I concluded:

The fact that the Export Administration Act of 1983 will have a profound effect on our nation's security and economic well-being in the balance of the decade *promises to make the debate lively and contentious and the final product impossible to predict.*

Little could I or anyone else have then known just how lively, contentious, and difficult to predict the legislative process for the renewal of the EAA would prove. Most pieces of legislation that need to have policy differences resolved by a House-Senate conference committee reach final form after two or three conference sessions. The conference on the Export Administration Act went on, by contrast, for more than a year through 15 conference sessions spanning the 98th and 99th Congresses (and hundreds of hours of staff meetings) before a compromise agreement finally could be reached.

Indeed, the severity of disagreement over the Act within and between the legislative and executive branches led Congress to allow expiration on two separate occasions of the statutory authority for the control of exports—that is, the Export Administration Act of 1979. As a result, the executive branch was forced to administer export control, export enforcement, and antiboycott compliance programs under the emergency powers of the president, as specified in the International Emergency Economic Powers Act (IEEPA).

How could we reach a situation where there was no underlying statutory authority in place, in so important an area, for one and one-half years? How did export controls become the subject of one of the most heated debates in Congress in the last decade? These are but two of the questions that I wish to address in this chapter.

THE LEGISLATIVE DEBATE OVER EXPORT CONTROLS

The Question of National Security Controls

The legislative process began as early as mid-1983. In their original form, the House and Senate bills presented a fairly clear dichotomy of views. The House bill, introduced by Congressman Don Bonker (D-Washington) and supported by most sectors of the business community, was premised upon the belief that the government could do a far better job of preventing the illegal diversion of high technology to U.S. adversaries if controls were reduced, thereby allowing trade authorities to focus their limited resources on control of only "the most significant technologies." In contrast, the Senate bill, with principal input from Senators Jake Garn (R-Utah) and John Heinz (R-Pennsylvania), focused on two problems: on the one hand providing for greater "contract sanctity" by raising the threshold for the imposition of foreign policy controls, while on the other hand, expanding the scope of national security export controls, and tightening up the mechanisms by which the executive branch administers and enforces these controls. This reflected a compromise struck between the two senators early in the drafting process.

Unlike their House counterparts, who seemed most concerned with the ability of American business to compete worldwide for high technology markets, the Senate was chiefly concerned with the political and military competition with the Soviet Union. In general, the Senate was skeptical that any lasting positive gains could be achieved from increased trade with the USSR, and much more concerned about the dangers of technology transfers that might enhance the military capabilities of the Soviet Union and its allies. A majority in the Senate believed that what the business sector really wanted was predictability and efficiency in U.S. export control policy, the reduction of license processing time, and the decreased probability that foreign policy controls would be imposed on normal trade flows.

In an effort to expand the scope of national security controls and to tighten up the mechanisms of enforcement, the Senate bill provided for:

1. the increased involvement of the Department of Defense (DOD) in the review of certain Free World export license applications, and a greatly increased role for the U.S. Customs Service in the enforcement of the Export Administration Act
2. the inclusion of new areas of technology on the militarily critical technologies list (MCTL), including goods which would augment a production line used in the application of militarily critical technology, or aid in the analysis of a U.S. military system (thereby revealing the design of that system, and making the development of countermeasures to it easier)
3. the imposition of import sanctions on foreign companies that violate U.S. national security or CoCom controls, a wider assertion of extraterritoriality
4. an increase in the use of "foreign availability" criteria in licensing and commodity control list formation and
5. the strengthening and upgrading of CoCom as an organization.

House leaders argued, however, that the export licensing process was already a cumbersome bureaucratic nightmare, and that the Senate's desire to expand the scope of national security controls—by, among other things, giving the Defense Department a role in reviewing Free World license applications—would exacerbate the situation. Nevertheless, the House bill also sought to limit customs authority in the enforcement of EAA regulations. In an effort to "streamline" controls and focus on the most critical strategic technologies, the House bill provided for:

1. the removal of any licensing requirements on exports to CoCom countries—that is, the West European allies and Japan
2. the decontrol of microprocessors that are embedded in militarily insignificant commodities that cannot be transferred from those commodities to other uses and
3. an annual review of unilateral U.S. controls and the termination of those controls directed to destinations consistently approved to receive U.S. exports.

The Question of Foreign Policy Controls

In addition to their concern over the breadth of national security controls, the American exporting community sought some sort of restraint on executive discretion to use trade sanctions in pursuit of foreign policy objectives, especially in the wake of sanctions imposed following the Soviet invasion of

Afghanistan and the military crackdown in Poland. From the business community's perspective, foreign policy controls often led to an unpredictable trade environment that called into question the reliability of U.S. exporters and their overseas subsidiaries. Hence, another area of debate became the extent to which Congress would:

1. protect foreign companies—including U.S. subsidiaries, affiliates, and the like—from the extraterritorial application of U.S. export controls and
2. support commercial contracts already entered into at the time the president imposed foreign policy controls—the so-called "contract sanctity" issue.

As one might expect, the House EAA renewal bill stipulated that controls imposed after the date of enactment could not have extraterritorial application without the specific authorization of Congress. The Senate bill contained no such provision. Indeed, both the Senate and the Reagan administration expressed a preference for maintaining then-current law, which provided for the extraterritorial extension of U.S. export controls to cover (1) reexports of U.S. products, (2) exports by U.S. overseas subsidiaries, and (3) exports of foreign products containing U.S. technology. In Senate-House conference negotiations, the Senate position prevailed, and current law was left intact. In point of fact, extraterritorial assertions were expanded through the import controls clause.

The Issue of "Contract Sanctity"

Perhaps the most hotly contested issue in the debate over extension of the Export Administration Act of 1979 was the question of the extent to which Congress would authorize the president to break or otherwise affect commercial contracts already entered into when imposing foreign policy controls. Prior to the passage of the new act, the law in effect placed *no* restrictions on the president's power to affect contracts in existence at the time he imposed foreign policy controls. As a result, there were several occasions in which contracts of U.S. companies were broken up upon imposition of such controls.

As part of the Garn-Heinz compromise noted earlier, the Senate bill effectively precluded the president from breaking or otherwise affecting contracts in existence at the time foreign policy controls are imposed. This position came to be known as "absolute" contract sanctity. The House bill, on the other hand, called for contract sanctity, but identified specific circumstances under which the president explicitly was permitted to break contracts. Those circumstances included acts of aggression or international terrorism, gross violations of internationally recognized human rights, or the conduct of nuclear weapons tests. In the Senate-House conference during the 98th Congress, however, members of the House ultimately agreed to the Senate position.

Subsequently, in the interest of achieving a more balanced posture, Senators Garn and Heinz offered yet another "compromise" bill in the Senate during the closing days of the session, which contained language somewhat different from that agreed to by the conferees. That compromise language became the contract sanctity provision adopted in the 1985 Export Administration Act. The provision ultimately enacted precludes the breaking of contracts, except in those situations where a "breach of the peace" poses a serious and direct threat to the strategic interests of the United States, and where the prohibition or curtailment of such contracts, agreements, licenses, or authorizations would be instrumental in remedying the situation posing the direct threat. The provision also specifies that the controls shall continue only as long as the direct threat persists.

While not defining the term "breach of the peace," it is clear that Congress, in enacting this particular version of contract sanctity, tried to narrow, but not eliminate, the authority of the president to impose controls on trade agreements. Congress expects that the president will break contracts only in the gravest of circumstances.

Perhaps the most significant piece of legislative history on this matter is the statement made by Senator Garn on the floor of the Senate during consideration of the compromise package on the next-to-last day of the 98th Congress. At that time, Garn indicated that "breach of the peace" meant only an armed attack by one nation against another which threatened the very survival of the United States as a nation. The U.S. exporting community hoped that such a narrowly crafted contract sanctity provision would be helpful in reestablishing their credibility, without sacrificing vital U.S. strategic interests.

Yet even with the achievement of this compromise on the contract sanctity question, a number of outstanding issues remained in the area of foreign policy controls. These issues continued to be characterized by a divergence of perspective between House and Senate. Specifically, Senators on the conference committee sought two additional restrictions on the president's latitude in imposing such controls:

1. The requirement that certain criteria be "determined" rather than merely considered before foreign policy export controls can be imposed and,

2. The stipulation that no foreign policy controls could enter into effect until the president reported certain information to the Congress and the General Accounting Office.

House members also sought additional qualifications on presidential discretion, specifically:

1. Providing for the reimposition of certain foreign controls on Iraq and South Africa that were lifted by the president in 1982 and 1983; it was the Senate's inability to reach agreements with the House on what were acceptable sanctions on South Africa that doomed the Export Administration Act in the House of the 98th Congress and,
2. An amendment to provide that a country may not be removed from the list of terrorist countries unless the president certifies that such country has not provided support for terrorist activities during the preceding 12-month period.

Other Factors Contributing to the Heated Debates over Export Controls

In addition to the foregoing dichotomy of views between the Senate and the House, a variety of other factors helped produce two years of heated debate over export controls. The fact that the House bill tended toward an easing of export controls and the Senate bill toward restricting the president's power and discretion in the imposition and administration of export controls meant that the Reagan administration often found itself involved in a case of "strange bedfellows": frequently supporting and being supported by liberal House Democrats, and frequently opposing and being opposed by conservative Senate Republicans. There were also the "turf battles" within the executive branch that were fueled by the legislative process:

*   between the Departments of Commerce and Defense over the extent to which the Department of Defense should be given statutory authority to become involved in the review of Free World license applications and
*   between the Department of Commerce and the U.S. Customs Service over the extent to which Customs should be given statutory authority to enforce the Export Administration Act. Once it became apparent that Customs would have *some* authority, the question became which of the two agencies should be given the lead in overseas investigations of possible EAA violations.

There were also controversial provisions that had to be dealt with regarding the ratification of nuclear nonproliferation treaties. Certain jurisdictional claims over the bill by the House Judiciary Committee and by the House Energy and Commerce Committee had to be resolved. And, finally, the business community itself was split on several issues as to both substance and priority. Those companies most hurt by foreign policy controls, represented by the Business Round Table (BRT), placed emphasis on "contract sanctity." Those most affected by delays arising from national security concerns—for example, the Computer and Business Equipment Manufacturing Association (CBEMA), the American Electronics Association (AEA), and the Electronics Industry Association (EIA)—emphasized the need to keep the Department of Defense out of Free World licensing.

In the end, the resulting piece of legislation contained some pluses and some minuses for all parties concerned. As a spokesman for the electronic industries recently put it:

After a detailed review of the 1985 amendments, I would have to say that our industry has been successful in accomplishing many of the objectives outlined in our 1983 testimony. Of course, not all of our suggestions have been adopted. However, on balance, we feel that the new legislation contains many significant improvements over current law and only a few troublesome provisions.[1]

THE EXPORT ADMINISTRATION AMENDMENTS ACT OF 1985

We now turn to a consideration of the major changes wrought by the new amendments to the Export Administration Act in the two major areas of national security controls and foreign policy controls.

National Security Controls

In this area, neither the Senate nor the House walked away with its top priority intact; however, each was able to achieve that priority in large measure.

The Senate wanted codified into statute a role for the Department of Defense in the review of Free World license applications. In the end, this was done administratively rather than by statute, with the president ordering the Departments of Commerce and Defense to work out an arrangement for the joint review of certain Free World applications. Pursuant to this presidential mandate, the Department of Defense was given the right to review Free World license applications submitted to Commerce for the export of a commodity to any one of 15 designated Free World countries, if the commodity concerned falls within one of seven designated commodity classifications.

The identities of the 15 countries remain classified—largely because of the diplomatic sensitivities in making public the suspicion that a given country's export control system makes it particularly vulnerable to exploitation by the Soviet bloc as a point of illegal diversion.

The seven commodity classifications can be made public:

Commodity Control List (CCL) Numbers

1355A	Electronics and semiconductor manufacturing equipment
1529A	Measuring/calibration equipment
1564A	Microcircuits and integrated circuits
1565A	Computers (including new items created after July 15, 1984)
1757A	Silicon and other components
1357A	Carbon-carbon technology and manufacturing
1763A	Nonferrous composite materials

DOD's participation began February 15, 1985, and it was projected that upwards of 20,000 license applications would fall within the 15 country classification matrix during the first year. Commerce electronically transmits to DOD the data that appear on the face of all applications falling within the matrix. DOD has seven days in which to advise Commerce if it wants to see hard-copy of the application. If DOD requests to see hard-copy, it has 15 working days in which either to pass on the application or to recommend denial on the grounds that it presents a risk of diversion. At present, DOD requests hard-copy in approximately 40% of the cases.

The Senate also achieved the statutory role it desired for the U.S. Customs Service in the enforcement of the act. The enforcement and investigatory role that Commerce will play domestically and overseas was also spelled out. Commerce enforcement agents were also given broad police powers.

The top priority for the House in the national security area was the decontrol of all exports between the United States and its CoCom allies. In the end, the House was able to obtain passage of a provision that decontrolled only exports of low-level technology between the United States and its CoCom allies.

Nonetheless, it is still expected that this decontrol provision will diminish the annual licensing load by 10 to 15%.

With regard to the implementation of this decontrol provision, let me underscore two points. First, even though the provision is often referred to as the "CoCom decontrol" provision, it has nothing to do with multilateral control by the United States and other CoCom members of exports to the Soviet bloc and the PRC. Rather, it relates solely to trade from the United States to its 14 CoCom partners. Second, the CoCom decontrol provision applies only to exports made by individual validated license. It does not affect exports made by multiple license.

Additionally, it must be determined whether or not the item to be exported qualifies as "low-level" technology—that is, whether the item falls at or below the Administrative Exception Note (AEN) level as defined by CoCom. This level is essentially a means of determining the sensitivity of traded technologies with reference to the Soviet Union. It means that the performance characteristics of the commodity in question would not, if exported directly to the Soviet Union, require the review of all CoCom members. In such a case, the CoCom AEN definition requires only the notification of all CoCom members that the export has taken place. If the technology in question satisfies this definition, it also falls in the category of "low-level" technology as set down in the Export Administration Act amendments.

It turned out that 47 of the Commodity Control List (CCL) entries contain such AEN-type provisions. Therefore, Commerce published in the *Federal Register* a list of these 47 entries affected, and spelled out the levels of technology in each that fall at or below the AEN level. Thus, if the commodity to be exported to one of the 14 designated allies is at or below one of these AENs, no validated license or other form of permission from the U.S. government is required.

A second aspect to the so-called CoCom decontrol provision deals with exports of items *above* the AEN level in trade between the United States and its CoCom allies. For these, an individual validated license will continue to be required, but Commerce's processing deadlines will be greatly shortened. The process will work as follows:

1. A license application is filed.
2. From the moment it is registered, Commerce has 15 working days (i.e., three weeks) to approve it, deny it, or advise the exporter that 15 more working days are needed to complete the licensing process.
3. At the time Commerce registers the application, it will notify the applicant that the application has been received, and provide the applicant with a license number. This procedure will allow the applicant to export on or after the 16th working day, if the applicant has not heard back from

Commerce to the contrary by the end of the 15th working day. That is, without action by Commerce to deny the license or to request 15 more days, the license automatically becomes valid and effective. At that time, the exporter may ship without having to wait to receive a formal license to export. Instead, the exporter can indicate on the Shipper's Export Declaration (SED) and on other required documents the license number provided by Commerce upon registration of the application.
4. If Commerce requests an additional 15 days, the same procedure follows if Commerce has not notified the applicant on or before the 30th working day that the application is denied.
5. The procedure was to go into effect 120 days after enactment of the Export Administration Act, that is, on or about November 12, 1985.

Note here that as a practical matter, 30 working days may not be enough in those cases where Commerce has to conduct a prelicense check of the end-user. Rather than for Commerce to deny the application—which would result in the applicant having to start the licensing process over again from scratch—it might well make more sense for the applicant and Commerce to agree to waive the 30-day rule, and allow Commerce the extra days it needs to complete the prelicense check and, thereby, the licensing process.

The Export Administration Act of 1985 also shortens the processing deadlines for exports to destinations other than CoCom countries. For example, whereas the 1979 EAA required Commerce to issue or deny a license within 90 days if outside referral is not required, the new Act requires Commerce action within 60 days. Yet another important change in terms of processing time is that requests to Commerce for commodity classifications will have to be completed within 10 working days.

Other national security control changes in the new Act include:

1. A requirement that the Commodity Control List be reviewed annually with a view toward eliminating from the list those items that no longer need to be controlled for national security purposes.
2. A provision that authorizes the Secretary of Defense to add to the Militarily Critical Technologies List (MCTL) certain "keystone" equipment that would give insight into the design and manufacture of a U.S. military system.
3. A provision which mandates that a validated license cannot be required for replacement parts which are expected to replace on a one-for-one basis parts that were in goods lawfully exported from the United States.
4. A provision that prohibits the imposition of export controls on a good solely on the basis that the good contains an embedded microprocessor. Controls may be imposed on the good only if the function of the good itself would

make a significant contribution to the military potential of a controlled country.

5. A provision that specifies the Department of Defense as an agency that should be consulted when foreign availability determinations are made concerning items controlled for national security purposes.

6. A provision that, once a foreign availability determination has been made, negotiations will take place with the foreign sources of the item in question. If the negotiations do not result in elimination of the availability within 18 months (six months plus 12 additional months if the president certifies to Congress that negotiations are progressing), the act mandates the decontrol of the item.

7. A provision authorizing import sanctions not only for violations of U.S. national security controls, but also for violations of foreign laws or regulations that implement multilateral agreements in cases where the foreign country in question does not enforce such laws or regulations. The majority of CoCom members agree that such controls are appropriate.

8. Finally, a provision that countries which enter into agreements on export restrictions comparable in practice to those of CoCom are to be treated like CoCom members for purposes of export controls (including comparable treatment on multiple as well as individual licenses).

Foreign Policy Controls

In addition to the strongly contested "contract sanctity" issue discussed earlier, the new amendments contain a variety of provisions requiring the Department of Commerce to consult, in varying degrees, with Congress, certain other agencies, and affected U.S. industries when imposing foreign policy controls, and to make certain determinations when imposing them. Additionally, the above-noted concern of some House members that certain controls be reimposed on South Africa resulted in a restriction on the export of nonsensitive items for the use of that nation's police or military forces.

The requirement that foreign availability be taken into account when extending foreign policy controls, and the further requirement that, if negotiations cannot eliminate foreign availability within six months, an export license for the "available" commodity be issued, also brought significant changes in the area of foreign policy controls. Note, however, that export licenses may be denied if the secretary of state determines that foreign policy control would continue to be effective in achieving its intended purpose despite the existence of foreign availability. Moreover, controls imposed to meet international obligations, to combat acts of international terrorism, or to prevent human rights violations are exempt from this new foreign availability requirement.

Also of importance is a requirement that a country cannot be removed from the list of terrorist-supporting countries until the president certifies to Congress that the country in question has not provided support for terrorist groups during the preceding six months and has provided assurances that it will not support acts of terrorism in the future. A provision that redesignated Iraq as a country that supports international terrorism was deleted in Conference Committee.

CONCLUSION

The new legislation amends and extends the Export Administration Act through September 30, 1989. In the interim, one can expect to see Senators Garn and Heinz, Congressman Bonker, and other interested parties on the Hill and in the private sector engaging in vigorous oversight activities, and seeking to take some kind of remedial action where it is perceived that the executive branch is not carrying out the mandates and meeting the time constraints of the Export Administration Act as Congress intended. Yet the likelihood of these efforts in no way detracts from the tremendous program embodied in the new amendments. In the two most difficult issue areas—national security controls and foreign policy controls—compromises have been achieved which command broad consensus in the executive and legislative branches as well as in the business community.

This consensus will be strenuously challenged as the implications of technology transfer for both the interests of national security and the objectives of foreign policy increase, as they surely will. It remains to be seen whether the consensus will prove sufficiently resilient in the face of these as yet unknown challenges.

NOTES

1. Allen Frischkorn, GTE Service Corporation, in a speech before the U.S. Chamber of Commerce, July 18, 1985.

14

U.S. EXPORT CONTROLS: THE LIMITS OF PRACTICALITY

R. Roger Majak

In 1985, the U.S. export control program survived its most severe test: It was renewed by Congress at a time when the United States was experiencing its highest trade deficit in history ($130 billion), becoming in the process a net debtor nation for the first time in more than 75 years. It is estimated, moreover, that export controls cost the United States $12 to $16 billion in lost foreign trade. For Congress to renew a program that seems to pose a major obstacle to exports in the face of high trade deficits—deficits that it regards as unsustainable and of top political priority—suggests a strong congressional consensus in support of export controls.

In my view, however, this consensus is shallow. It does not extend much beyond the simple proposition that controls are preferable to unrestricted technology transfer. Nor does it reflect congressional agreement on the appropriate scope and methods of control. On these issues, equally crucial for those administering the controls and for those affected by them, as well as for the ultimate effectiveness of export control policy, there is little consensus. In fact, congressional views remain sharply polarized, with the voting power of each faction roughly equivalent. Indeed, pressures to reduce controls substantially in view of the trade deficit are countered by equally strong pressures to increase controls, based on contentions that technology transfer increases U.S. defense spending requirements by improving Soviet military capabilities.

In short, the export control program is a low-consensus program based upon a political stalemate between those who would tighten controls and those who would relax them. Empirical evidence of this standoff can be found in the relatively close votes by which amendments to the Export Administration Act (EAA) have typically been decided. The 1985 renewal legislation passed both houses of Congress by wide margins, but only after two years of behind-the-scenes bargaining and compromising, in which each provision to ease controls was either modified or traded away for a provision strengthening controls, and vice versa.

I begin with these observations because the lack of political consensus on technology transfer issues, generally, and export controls, specifically, are at the heart of the challenges we face in this particular dimension of U.S. foreign and national security policy. Consider, for example, the question of administrative discretion. U.S. export controls are subject to enormous executive discretion, far more than is accorded under such programs as foreign aid and military sales. Key aspects of the program—such as the specific technologies subject to control, ways and means of decontrol, the controls applicable to particular countries and groups of countries, the extent of coordination with allies—are subject to constant change in accordance with day-to-day executive decisions and bureaucratic pressures. Since many of the differences of opinion found in the legislative branch occur also within the executive branch, the relatively high degree of discretion enjoyed by program administrators can, and often does, lead to unpredictability and inconsistency in the implementation of export controls.

There is also the problem of procedural complexity. The "law" that institutions will focus on procedural issues when they cannot agree on substance was not written by the U.S. Congress, but it certainly applies there, particularly in the technology transfer area. Indeed, the new act is liberally sprinkled with listings of sometimes contradictory policy criteria, demands for reports to Congress, and requirements for consultation among executive departments. Many of these represent procedural compromises to avoid unresolved policy disagreements.

The executive branch also contributes new layers of procedure. For example, when the Commerce and Defense Departments could not agree on interagency review of licenses to Free World destinations, the White House finally resolved the issue by establishing an interagency committee chaired by the National Security Council both to oversee the processing of Free World licenses and to allocate interagency license review powers in the future. Hence, so long as political consensus remains low, the procedural complexity of U.S. export controls is likely to remain high, and perhaps even increase.

Clearly, more effective technology transfer control at less direct and indirect cost is the fundamental challenge facing the United States in its endeavor to maximize the national security benefits of U.S. technological innovation. Impossible as it is to measure cost-effectiveness precisely, let alone agree on an acceptable cost-benefit ratio, three facts suggest that current controls are not likely to be highly successful.

First, more than 99% of all individual licenses submitted for Free World destinations are approved, as are more than 80% of all individual licenses submitted for controlled destinations. Second, while the number of licenses reviewed by the Defense Department has increased more than fivefold since 1981, there has been no increase in license denials. Third, recent time studies by the Department of Commerce indicate that in the 30 to 180 days required to process individual export licenses, an average of less than 20 minutes is devoted to the actual analysis of pertinent facts and a final decision on the case. Even conceding that many license requests that probably would be denied are simply never submitted, it seems that any regulatory system that devotes such high percentages of its attention and energy to processing ultimately acceptable exports, simply in order to identify the few that are unacceptable, is at best unnecessarily costly—and probably relatively ineffective. This seems true if for no other reason than the fact that current procedures leave few resources available to help identify new and emerging technologies of potential military use, and to bring them under timely control.

These problems, it must be stressed, are not of recent origin. Successive administrations have failed to find the means and political will to narrow the focus of controls, and have yielded instead to the inertia of broad controls left over from the deepest Cold War period, when virtually nothing was approved for sale to the communist world. Complex procedures tend to substitute for effective communication among agencies and specialized bureaucratic units involved in license investigation and analysis. The problem of slow processing is compounded by the fact that an export license delayed often becomes an export denied in today's fast-moving, competitive international trading environment. In fact, more technology transfers may be "denied" simply by delay than deliberately for reasonable cause.

Our broad approach to technology containment reduces the effectiveness of controls in another major way. Effective export controls are heavily dependent upon the existence of multilateral cooperation with our principal allies and trading partners. While we have a low level of political consensus in support of broad controls, most of our allies have just the opposite—broad political consensus for narrow controls. Because many allied technologies have U.S. origins or components, this contrast in approach can cause difficulties. The possibility that access to technologies of U.S. origin could be cut off if the allies fail to cooperate fully in controlling the export and reexport of sensitive technologies assures a degree of cooperation—but such cooperation is not without substantial political costs. The effectiveness of U.S. controls is further reduced by the subtle means that many CoCom nations have found to reduce the constraints of multilateral technology transfer controls, short of outright evasion or noncompliance.

Nevertheless, even the cooperation of our CoCom allies would not be enough to stem inappropriate technology transfers. For a truly effective control system, we must assure that sensitive technologies are not diverted and reexported when we sell to non-CoCom countries—particularly the neutral and developing countries. Collectively, these countries comprise our fastest growing export market, despite financial problems in the Third World. Increasingly, Third World states are able to utilize controlled technologies. Although the current administration has made some commendable progress in obtaining bilateral reexport agreements with a few non-CoCom countries, our ability to control reexports remains extremely limited and problematic.

The U.S. government is currently spending over $40 million per year on export controls and export control enforcement. That, of course, does not include the considerable amount spent by the private sector on compliance and self-enforcement. To be sure, private sector costs are difficult even to estimate, but ultimately they must be included in the total direct cost of export restrictions. Forty million dollars would not be an unreasonable cost to the government if effective controls could be "purchased" for that amount. The fact is, however, that the control system we "buy" is largely a paper exercise—and perhaps even a "paper tiger." It remains extremely easy to circumvent, particularly through reexports from non-CoCom Free World countries, where enforcement of export restraint is minimal.

The answer to effective technology controls at a multilateral level lies, it seems to me, in the delicate process of compromise. More specifically, a formula must be found for the United States to yield to preferences for narrower controls, without relinquishing the leadership it should exert as the most technologically advanced member of CoCom. We need not, and should not, be satisfied with the least common denominator in CoCom. However, excessive demands for broader controls and draconian enforcement create counterproductive political strains, while bringing few real gains in total multilateral effectiveness. From my perspective, the increasing dominance of the Defense Department in the U.S. export control process, and the recent success of the Defense Department in gaining membership on the permanent U.S. delegation to CoCom, seem likely to complicate multilateral cooperation. Indeed, the heavier the demands emanating from Defense Department representatives for export control and enforcement, the greater the likelihood that internal U.S. disagreements concerning the scope of controls (and other technology transfer issues) will be conveyed to our CoCom partners.

If, as I have implied, tighter control of a narrower band of technologies, focused more completely on the highest end of the technology spectrum, is likely to be more effective and less costly, how do we get there from here? One approach taken in the new legislation is to reduce licensing requirements and procedures for transfers within CoCom itself. When fully implemented by Commerce Department regulations, this change should eliminate as much as 20% of the current annual licensing volume. Availability of a new type of multiple license, called the "comprehensive operating license," which will permit day-to-day transfers of technology among preapproved corporate affiliates within CoCom, should further reduce total license volumes.

Over the longer term, however, there is a real need for a more effective and politically acceptable mechanism for the "decontrol" of lower-level technologies. Foreign availability—that is, the availability of a given technology in the world marketplace outside the United States—remains the best criteria for decontrol, despite past failures to use it as an effective yardstick. The difficulty with decontrol on the basis that similar technical goods are freely available elsewhere is the danger that such an approach will, in effect, undermine U.S. leadership in technology transfer controls. Other nations, allied or neutral, could precipitate decontrol by simply persisting in making particular technologies available for transfer to controlled destinations.

The approach taken in the new legislation renewing the Export Administration Act is, first, to put a greater burden on the executive branch to disprove or eliminate foreign availability when a reasonable case is presented by U.S. industry, and, second, to allow 18 months for the executive branch to persuade the source of foreign availability to eliminate it. If foreign availability cannot be eliminated in that period of time, the technology in question would be decontrolled for U.S. suppliers. It is hoped that this approach will prove practical both in eliminating futile controls in some cases and in restoring controls by eliminating foreign availability in other instances. Ultimately, other nations must be convinced of the merits and reasonableness of particular controls. If controls are not convincing, foreign availability will continue. Rather than bind ourselves to ineffective unilateral controls, the new legislation would simply eliminate controls after a reasonable effort has been made to achieve multilateral controls.

It remains far easier to add controls than remove them, and further additions are likely. Work is actively underway in the executive branch to expand existing controls more thoroughly to cover technical data, software, biotechnology, and other forms of know-how. In a report issued with much fanfare in September 1985, the Defense Department identified some Western targets of Soviet efforts to acquire Western technology. Many of these targets consist, in fact, of unclassified government and scientific information. Whatever the benefit of expanded efforts to restrict such transfers, reduced freedom of information and scientific exchange would certainly be one of the costs. In the House of Representatives at least, I think there would be little support for the expansion of controls that would impose such costs. As difficult as it is to justify loss of trade in the face of major deficits, it is even more difficult to justify loss of domestic informational exchange on which so many of our technological innovations depend.

The two-and-a-half-year struggle to renew and revise the Export Administration Act has put considerable strain on the already overburdened export control bureaucracy. Much time and energy have been devoted to attempting to "protect turf," increase bureaucratic influence, and achieve major changes in policy in one direction or another. Disagreements over policy and the appropriate roles of various agencies and the Congress itself have, in some cases, created animosities and distrust even at a personal level among key players in the politics of technology transfer. Now we need to set aside these differences, and personal or institutional ambitions; that is, we need to "lower our voices." Full attention needs to be given to implementing the control program, complicated as it is, and to do so in a cooperative spirit. While it is not perfect, that system is at least partially effective in delaying and denying critical technologies to potential adversaries.

I wholeheartedly agree with the admonition of former Under Secretary of Commerce Lionel Olmer that we ought not be too "clinical" about export controls. Looked at clinically, there are many imperfections. On the other hand, those who—from ideological zeal or other motives—demand near perfection invite extensive additional costs that would be associated with a "clinically tight" system. Those costs would be both financial and political. The private sector would bear much of the financial cost stemming from added self-enforcement requirements, since it is extremely unlikely that even those in the Congress who support stronger controls would be willing to devote substantial new government resources to pay for them. Even so, the greatest cost of such an approach could well be the complete collapse of multilateral cooperation.

We should now work together—legislative and executive branches, as well as the various agencies with particular responsibilities within the executive branch—to make the best of the new legislation. The time for any major changes in policy and practice will come with the next renewal in 1989. In the meantime, predictable implementation of the existing system without radical changes will enhance its effectiveness by encouraging multilateral cooperation, and will minimize unnecessary costs both to the business community and to the international trade position of the United States.

15

THE CHALLENGE OF INDUSTRIAL ESPIONAGE

Phillip A. Parker

In this chapter, the term "industrial espionage" is meant to describe the efforts of hostile intelligence services to acquire Western technology—particularly technology from the United States. Before addressing this issue, however, it would be useful to review certain definitions and responsibilities adopted by the U.S. government in dealing with technology transfer issues. To begin with, the term "espionage" has a unique meaning to the Federal Bureau of Investigation (FBI), and there are certain criteria that must be met in a successful espionage prosecution. First, national defense information that is protected must have been *compromised.* This means that the information or technology in question must be classified for national security reasons and controlled accordingly. Second, the information must have been *transmitted.* This transmission must have occurred in either a written manner or, if orally, must be traceable to a document. Finally, the information must have been transmitted to a foreign agent or nation with the intention of aiding that nation or injuring the United States.

This is a very specific definition of espionage, and a much narrower one than is normally associated with "industrial espionage." Dual-use technology, for example, is not classified; according to the above criteria, therefore, the transfer of dual-use technology is not—insofar as FBI responsibilities are concerned—a classic case of espionage. Dual-use technology is controlled under the Export Administration Act, which is primarily the province of the Department of Commerce and the U.S. Customs Service, by virtue of their responsibilities for monitoring traffic through U.S. ports. Similarly, most arms are not classified. The export of arms is controlled under the Arms Export Control Act, which is administered by the Department of State and enforced by the U.S. Customs Service.

It is not my intent to imply that the FBI has no role in the prevention of the illegal export of dual-use technology, arms, or munitions. The FBI becomes involved primarily through our foreign counterintelligence investigations. There are, in addition, several criminal statutes, for which the FBI has primary responsibility, that address violations of either the Export Administration Act or the Arms Export Control Act. Specific examples would include the interstate transportation of stolen property (ITSP), fraud by wire, theft of government property, mail fraud, and others. The most famous export-related ITSP case occurred in 1983, when the FBI criminal investigative division set up a fence operation to combat the "gray" electronics market—that is, illegal dealing in stolen or counterfeit electronics parts. The case resulted in the conviction of a Japanese businessman, who walked into the fence operation having contracted for the illegal transfer of technology. Had an individual representing the USSR walked in instead, the FBI would have uncovered a violation of the Export Administration Act, in which case the FBI would have continued to use this investigative technique. Finally, in addition to its other tasks, the FBI has certain responsibilities for counterterrorism, which often also involve the illegal transfer of arms.

During foreign counterintelligence investigations, referred to as FCI investigations, the FBI frequently uncovers attempts to export dual-use technology illegally. Counterintelligence is defined very specifically in Executive Order 12333 as

information gathered and activities conducted to protect against espionage, other intelligence activities, sabotage or assassination conducted for or on behalf of foreign powers, organizations or persons, or international terrorist activities, but not including personnel, physical, document or communications security programs.

In other words, the specific definition of the counterintelligence role of the FBI is to identify and neutralize the activities of foreign intelligence officers and their agents in the United States.

The scope of this mission is extensive. There are over 200 establishments—embassies, consulates, trade offices, for example—in the United States that are of primary concern to the FBI. These establishments house approximately 4,000 officials, one-third of whom are known or suspected intelligence officers. This official presence is augmented by at least 14,000 students and more than 90,000 visitors per year. It is evident to the FBI that a significant percentage of these groups may be engaged in technology transfer. Thus, while the Export Administration Act is not an FBI statute, if the FBI has evidence that hostile intelligence services are involved in violations of the EAA, Executive Order 12333 quoted above is broad enough to include export control issues in the scope of its FCI investigations. However, our involvement is very selective, primarily because of the lack of specific responsibility under the statute.

For example, FCI investigations of known and suspected Soviet bloc intelligence officers in the United States have not uncovered a great deal of evidence that these officers are actively engaged in the illegal export of dual-use hardware. For the most part, Soviet successes in this area have not required the direct involvement of these officers. Rather, they result from complex international business transactions in several countries, orchestrated from within the USSR. The acquisitions are normally accomplished through middlemen, freight forwarders, and unscrupulous businessmen. These types of activities are often better neutralized through export control enforcement than through counterintelligence responses.

In the KGB, for example, officers of "Line X" are primarily responsible for the collection of science and technology intelligence. These officers spend much of their time collecting publicly available information. This activity includes subscribing to publications, writing for company literature, collecting handouts at conventions and symposia, and obtaining transcripts of technical presentations. Line X officers target municipal, academic, and government libraries. Initially, the United States believed that this collection was indiscriminate, but it now appears that the program is focused by and responsive to requirements designated at the KGB center.

The Soviet military intelligence apparatus, the GRU, also responds to tasking from Moscow in the collection of scientific and technological information. Those GRU officers in the United States, who are overt military attachés, actively collect militarily related scientific and technical information. These officers visit libraries and chambers of commerce during their official reconnaissance travel, in order to collect information about the locality they are visiting. As with the KGB's Line X officers, there is no significant evidence that the GRU officers acquire dual-use hardware. However, they avidly collect openly available technical data. In their clandestine work in the United States, GRU officers focus on the collection of classified military technology. The FBI's primary concern is the threat incurred via the GRU and KGB recruitment of Americans who will provide the needed technology.

The FBI also believes that all Soviet officials, not just intelligence officers, are charged with collecting scientific and technological intelligence. The State Committee for Science and Technology (GKNT) annually publishes a book of collection requirements principally for nondefense Soviet industries. All Soviet officials must fulfill their collection requirements as designated in this book each year. This is not spy work; it focuses primarily on collecting company brochures or other openly available technical data. It is interesting, however, that Soviet authorities classify the requirements book as "secret"; assignments to collect are also considered secret, even though the information being sought is unclassified.

The FBI also realizes that Soviet exchange students are very active in the collection of vital information. Many of these exchange students are co-opted by the KGB prior to their arrival in the United States. Because of the technical nature of their studies, such students often have access to publicly available information, with which they are able to assess state-of-the-art technologies. In many cases, they may even gain access to closed conferences or seminars. Trained students and scientists, moreover, are likely to be more adept than intelligence officers at eliciting information from U.S. scientists; but whatever their precise role may be, they are required to report their contacts to Soviet authorities. They may be instrumental, therefore, in arranging introductions of valuable contacts to intelligence officers, who can further evaluate and pursue the connection, if warranted.

A recent intelligence community study shows how voracious is the Soviet appetite for unclassified, seemingly innocuous technical data. FBI observations provide evidence that this is indeed the case. The problem is extremely complex for a free society. Our question remains: What type of controls should a free society place on unclassified information to keep it out of the hands of potential adversaries?

The following is a summary with a description of what the FBI is doing to halt the illegal flow of technology:

- The FBI will continue to focus its efforts on stemming the loss of classified technology. We have been fairly successful in the recent past, but the problem is still pervasive.
- The FBI will continue its development of a counterintelligence awareness program, with the intent of sensitizing defense contractors to the threat posed to their personnel, facilities, and operations by hostile intelligence services.
- The FBI will continue to pursue joint investigations and operations with the Department of Commerce and the U.S. Customs Service.
- The FBI will continue to collect intelligence on illegal activities and relay it to other pertinent agencies for their investigative use.
- Finally, the FBI will continue to participate in interagency, industrial, business, and academic groups that are working together to cope with this issue of East-West technology transfer in general, and industrial espionage in particular.

16

THE EVOLUTION OF TIGHTER U.S. EXPORT CONTROLS

Vitalij Garber

From the perspective of one who has participated in the administrative side—as opposed to the legislative side—of government, it is my view that the current concern of the United States over the transfer of technologies in the context of East-West trade traces its roots to the 1970s. After the heyday of détente, several reasons for a greater degree of concern regarding this sort of transfer became apparent. Thus it seems appropriate to begin by discussing these developments, and to move from this background to a consideration of the evolution of U.S. export control policy.

Two specific developments stand out as playing significant roles in bringing about renewed interest in the potential implications of technology flows. The first of these was—and is—the increasing importance of conventional armaments. Prior to this development, the United States perceived no real cause for concern over the balance of conventional arms, either in qualitative or quantitative terms. That we could enjoy this luxury had much to do with our adoption of a tripwire nuclear strategy.

With the changes in the nuclear balance occasioned by the 1970s, however, such a strategy could no longer provide a credible deterrent. U.S. national security policy began to place increasing emphasis on the ability to deter war in the realm of conventional arms as well. These armaments require a broad spectrum of available technologies, many of them applicable in the commercial/industrial realm as well—the "dual-use" technologies. Absent the ability to deter through the quantitative strength of our conventional arsenal, the importance of maintaining qualitative—that is, technological—superiority in these weapons simultaneously emerged as a critical national interest.

The second development was, of course, the American disillusionment with Soviet behavior during the era of détente. The incentives that were proffered as a part of the policy of détente—that is to say, the "carrots"—did not produce hoped-for results in the international arena. Attempts to increase Western leverage over Soviet actions by drawing the USSR into a fairly liberal trade regime and technology transfer program also failed in this regard. Indeed, a rather contrary result became apparent. The Soviets had been able to save considerable expenditures of money and research effort in the implementation of their military programs, the pace of which—in spite of détente—continued unabated.

With these developments in mind, let us consider the U.S. approach to these questions in the early 1970s. The most striking contrast between then and now is the far more restrictive view of West-West trade, relative to East-West trade. This is particularly notable in the area of munitions. This approach continued through both the Nixon and Ford presidencies. During the latter administration, responsibility for munitions transfers to Western nations rested with the Department of Defense (DOD), which took a cautious view of any and all requests. By contrast, exports to the East were the responsibility of the Department of Commerce, which eagerly sought all possibilities to provide the "carrots" of détente.

During the Carter administration, the Department of Defense embarked on a two-pronged effort to change the American approach to munitions technology transfer. The first aspect of this was an attempt to centralize decisionmaking on these questions under the aegis of the Defense Department. One result was the creation of the new post of Deputy Under Secretary for International Programs and Technology. This was an attempt to counter what was perceived as an excessively liberal bias on transfer issues within the bureaucracies of the Departments of State and Commerce, as well as in the DOD policy branch.

The second part of the effort attempted to bring about a reversal of the situation regarding West-West and East-West trade. The Office of the Under Secretary for Research and Engineering took the lead in tightening controls of exports to Eastern bloc nations, while relaxing restrictions on transfers to NATO allies. This period culminated with the invasion of Afghanistan, after which virtually all trade in high technology with the Soviet bloc was terminated.

As a result, the average period of review for the approval of requests to transfer technology through trade flows was shortened. It became relatively easy to maintain a two-week turnaround time for most requests. The reason for this was simple: the political situation brought forth much firmer guidelines for decisionmaking. Many more cases thus became clear-cut and easily decided. Two other factors contributed to a more efficient and expeditious evaluation of such requests. Of great importance was the computerization of the process, and the ability thus provided to handle great amounts of information in a much shorter time. Finally, the establishment of the Militarily Critical Technologies

List (MCTL), accomplished with the cooperation of industry, provided a much clearer framework upon which officials could base their decisions.

With the present administration, the change from previous form has been in the increased emphasis placed on enforcement. The pattern of case processing and the basic philosophy guiding policy in East-West technology transfer has not changed. The increased emphasis on enforcement, however, and the higher level of attention addressed to Soviet methods of clandestine technology acquisition are indeed departures from prior administrations. It should be noted, however, that in the view of some observers, this has not been so much an initiative on the part of the current administration as it has been a response to an increase in the scope of Soviet activity in this area—essentially a reflection of success in U.S. efforts to tighten its controls.

This tightening was due in part to unilateral U.S. decisions, as we have seen. Also significant, however, was the change in the American approach toward the CoCom allies. Abandoning the lenient approach of past years, which had focused on persuasion and diplomacy, the administration opted instead for a "hardball" approach, requiring firm commitments to multilateral trade control undertakings and denying certain West-West transfer requests to make the point. In consequence, the allies began to take the view that the Department of Defense had adopted a universally negative attitude on West-West trade, even though far and away the bulk of cases had been approved. The resultant climate of uncertainty spilled over into many areas of trade with our allies. Yet, ultimately, the allies became more sensitive to the growing problem of technology transfer to the East. The actions of the administration brought about as well a far greater role for the NATO defense community in trade matters.

What, then, does the future hold? In my view, the conservative trend vis-à-vis the Soviet Union will continue, through the tenure of this administration and beyond. The administration has recognized the necessity of building a stronger multilateral consensus—that is, with the CoCom nations—in designing and implementing trade control policy. The necessity of developing this consensus springs from the changing nature of defense, to which reference has been made. A very minor fraction of our future conventional arsenal will be based on traditional technologies. In contrast with past needs, a tremendous share of our future defense requirements—perhaps as much as 90%—will depend on dual-use technologies. Examples of this are guidance, sensor, battle-management, and communications technologies. In turn, the development of such capabilities will depend on the strength of the dual-use technological base of the Western countries, areas such as information technology, processing technology, and sensor technology. Thus, the areas of defense that will be crucial in the future will not be traditional ones. Rather, they will be command systems, electronic warfare systems, and the sensor and control systems on which air defenses depend.

Faced as we are with a much smaller population base upon which to build our conventional defense, we will be forced to depend on sensors deep behind enemy lines, and on the use of "smart" ammunition. Indeed, the Strategic Defense Initiative (SDI) itself—which may well have implications for conventional defense—is primarily based on dual-use technologies. The point is that much of our recent focus on defense issues, initiatives taken in both the strategic and conventional realms, rely heavily on dual-use technologies, technologies with important applications in the private sector. We must not forget the vital role played by these technologies in building the strength of our commercial economy.

As a result, it will be increasingly necessary for us to deny these technologies to our adversaries. Building standing armies large enough to match the Warsaw Pact man for man is politically infeasible, both in the United States and in NATO-Europe. We are constrained, therefore, to find an equally effective alternative, one which can credibly deter the huge tank armies and artillery batteries of the other side. High technology offers the West just this leverage; it gives us both economic strength and military security.

In order to realize the fullest advantage of this leverage, however, it is necessary that military-related technologies move throughout the alliance. NATO command and control systems, air defenses, and capabilities—for example, those required in the Follow-On Forces Attack (FOFA) concept—involve *all* the allied countries. So also will the Strategic Defense Initiative—if not in the development phase, then surely as the technologies developed begin pushing at the frontiers of strategy.

It is necessary, therefore, for the United States to assure the cooperation of its allies in protecting the security of the technologies involved. Defense strategists and political thinkers on the other side of the Atlantic have come to recognize this necessity as well. It is now a matter for open discussion among our open societies, in order to build the consensus needed to ensure that nations will voluntarily forgo the potential gains from trade in dual-use technologies in the interests of alliance security. We do not, and cannot, seek the cessation of all such trade; it is simply not a practical alternative. Instead, we must seek to undertake jointly the costs of abstaining from such trade in highly sensitive, critical areas. Given the nature of the threat we face, and that of the alliance we have, I see no alternative.

17

A BUSINESS PERSPECTIVE ON EXPORT CONTROLS

Hugh Donaghue

There are today four sets of export controls, overlapping and interplaying with one another. We have the national security controls and the foreign policy controls of the Export Administration Act (EAA). Additionally, we have the Memorandum of Understanding (MOU) between the Departments of Defense and Commerce, a document which affects some 15 countries on a number of products. But it is a shifting target, in a sense, because its contents can be changed, and we do not know (or, we are not supposed to know) just exactly what those contents are. Finally, we have the Nuclear Nonproliferation Treaty, a set of controls administered by another interagency committee of the government affecting all countries which are nonsignatories of the Nonproliferation Treaty. These four sets of controls interact; they play upon one another; and the real problem is trying to understand exactly what they imply in the case of a particular transaction.

From my company's viewpoint—and, I believe, from the viewpoint of most of the high-tech companies—high-technology trade with Eastern Europe and the Soviet Union virtually disappeared after the Soviet invasion of Afghanistan in December 1979. This is probably what led to the illegal acquisition program. It seems most likely that the effectiveness of the control mechanisms imposed after the invasion, as difficult as they are to deal with, have played at least some role in bringing about the increased Soviet emphasis on illegal acquisition.

After Afghanistan, the high-tech community offered few objections to the actions taken by our government, because they were seen as right and proper. As a matter of fact, two years after the event, we at Control Data had a decision to make on this very point. We had received an export license shortly before the invasion of Afghanistan, and the goods concerned had been shipped—legally—to Germany. At the time of the clampdown, they were in transit from Germany to Moscow. We had a debate, because there were some penalties to be incurred if we did not deliver, and the Soviets knew that we had the license. But the decision of the company was that it was only right to stop that shipment and face whatever penalties resulted, because the government had taken its action, and we therefore were obliged to follow suit.

When a government takes these sorts of decisions involving sales in the context of East-West trade, it is one thing to cut off those sales entirely. Our concerns during this particular cutoff were for the several "on-site monitors" we had in the Soviet Union in various facilities scattered around that country, and the impact it would have on them when it came to restricting the delivery of spare parts. This situation came as the result of a commitment we made to our government, so it set in motion a complex set of discussions. In these discussions, the company had essentially two objectives. First, we expressed our view that we indeed had the right to keep spare parts moving into the Soviet Union, per agreement, and, second, we wanted to withdraw those people if we were not going to be able to keep our end of the bargain.

This is the sort of complexity brought about by such decisions. We in the exporting community are more concerned about these sorts of difficulties than about specific actions, such as that taken in response to the Soviet attack on Afghanistan. It is the "spillover effect," a concern over diversion of legitimate high-tech products and technology product sales to Free World countries, that gives the community greatest concern. We have noticed that a number of questions have cropped up regarding certain countries, and we have seen delays in the licensing process where these countries are concerned. We have seen the tightening up of the distribution of license controls; I personally am one who felt such an effort was very much needed.

But Washington still exerts many unilateral controls—under either the national security, foreign policy, or nonproliferation control regimes. It seems to me that in doing so the U.S. government is creating an atmosphere which makes American companies less and less competitive in the world marketplace. There is a tremendous need for greater dialogue between companies that are doing business abroad and our government decisionmakers in this area. The issue of "reexport" controls is another major problem for U.S. exporters and another important area requiring dialogue between government and the private sector.

Another example is the case of distribution licenses. Here again we see the Department of Defense (DOD) playing nearly as large a role as the Department of Commerce, and no one should be surprised that the difference in perspective between the two departments—particularly in the case of certain countries—has not made the process less confusing or more predictable. Recently, we had to take the step of removing one of our overseas distributors from the distribution list, because some question had arisen about that company. Later, as the investigation proceeded and was completed, we found the allegations were untrue. The Department of Commerce informed us that they were going to put them back on the list, but after four months, the case was still undergoing DOD review. Somebody within DOD still had the view that the original premise, and the allegations which resulted, were true. In short, they did not get the word in a timely fashion. This kind of approach and the resulting confusion adversely affects the competitiveness of the export community.

The interplay of U.S. foreign policy and export controls (and specifically, as export controls apply to high technology) is another problem area for U.S. exporting industries. Perhaps the best case for purposes of illustration is the computer industry. For many years, computers have been used as an instrument of U.S. foreign policy. Sales of computers have been withheld from countries to show our displeasure over their conduct; conversely, sales have been encouraged to further specific foreign policy goals. In many instances, computers have been either the carrot or the stick in the U.S. government's effort to reward or punish other governments in the realm of foreign policy. Let me offer a caveat here. I am not stating a position as to whether these policy decisions are right or wrong. I am simply saying that control over trade in computers is used for these purposes. The restrictions placed on some computer sales to South Africa during September 1985 eloquently demonstrate this point.

The use of computer technology as a foreign policy tool has a 20-year history. Neither IBM nor Control Data could sell large-scale computers to France in 1966, because at that time France was not a signatory to the Test Ban Treaty. That brought into being what was known as *Plan Calcul,* which in turn resulted in the birth of the French computer industry. Of course, France did one other thing many other nations were not able to do: It put a demand on gold for Eurodollars during the summer of 1976. This led our government to focus on the problem in a way that no American company could. The result of this was the so-called Fowler-Debrais agreement reached in 1976. Note that this agreement was not between their Ministry of Industry and our Department of Commerce; rather, it was negotiated and concluded at the IMF meeting of September 1976. Thus, the pressure placed on gold by another nation led us to arrive at an agreement that had direct implications for the export of computers to that nation. In this case, trade in computers was used as an instrument in what essentially was an area of international economic policy.

In the early days of détente, it appeared that Control Data was again the "carrot" to be used for whatever policy purposes our government sought. We were encouraged by the U.S. government to do business, and we of course did it willingly. As a result, one had such examples of technology transfer as the Kama River truck plant and the sale of IBM equipment. Control Data sold a number of computers to various Soviet ministries concerned with geology. After the invasion of Afghanistan in December 1979, all ceased. The criticism here is not that the government's policy changed, but that *as* it changed it reflected badly upon those firms in the computer industry doing business in the Soviet Union. We had begun in business there when it was good policy to do so; once it was no longer good policy, however, what were we to do? After all, our reputation as businesses is at stake.

In a recent booklet distributed by the Department of Defense, reference is made to the *Ryad* computer series. This series is based upon the technology of the IBM 360 and 370 series. Somehow, the Soviets were able to acquire all of that technology. In an earlier chapter, Richard Perle mentioned the notion of "copy" in this regard. There is a subtle distinction to be made here. These computers are *not* copies; they are copies of the *architecture*. These machines have been made so that they can run on IBM software. Many of you remember that we had one company here in the United States—RCA—that went under trying to do exactly the same thing. And yet we praise the Soviets for doing the same thing a little later on. Subtleties like that sometimes emerge from the computer industry. Perhaps being part of it I am overly sensitive to them, but I sometimes wonder if the full story is being told.

Something similar occurred in the case of the People's Republic of China (PRC). In the early days of the new relationship with that country—August 1974—Control Data signed two computer sales agreements there. This, of course, was a period when U.S. policy was in tremendous flux. A number of people wanted very much to deal with the PRC, to provide the Chinese with the high technology they were requesting. Others in the government were adamantly opposed. The 1974 sale took two-and-a-half years to receive approval. These two simple sales of $6 million ultimately had to be approved by the president of the United States, which took place in October 1976. Even today, though our attitude seems to have really changed in some parts of the government, we find that in the case of high technology transfer to the PRC, our government's attitude remains one of ambivalence. We have removed the PRC from its unique category, and put it into the category of the Free World. But it is the only Free World country that has its cases channeled through the Coordinating Committee (CoCom). We continue to meet resistance in trying to achieve any "bump" licensing for the PRC, as had been promised to the private sector by the Department of Commerce in the early 1980s. In order to sell certain computers to the People's Republic, we still have to accept onerous conditions; indeed, it is difficult to imagine why the Chinese agree to them at all. An example is the requirement that a computer console be located in an isolated room on PRC territory, allowing them no access to it. Can you imagine something like that happening here or in other parts of the world? In my view, then, although in some parts of the government the attitude toward technology transfer with the People's Republic of China may have changed, in other parts it is as yet unacceptable.

By way of conclusion, let me offer one final case history which demonstrates what can happen to a company trying to support its government's activities when policy changes. I do this in the hope that some lessons for the private sector may be found therein. I readily admit that I have not been able to discern these lessons, but I am nonetheless sure that they exist.

On July 6, 1968, the United States and Romania signed an agreement on scientific-technical commercial cooperation. Concurrently, several senior members of Control Data's management met with some of the Romanian delegation. They were asked what Control Data's plans were for doing business in Eastern Europe, and whether there were any specific plans with regard to Romania. We responded affirmatively, even though we had nothing in mind at that time. Later, we learned that Romania had entered into negotiations with both CII of France and ICL of Great Britain, involving the transfer of mainframe computer systems technology. The Romanians then asked us to propose a comparable transfer involving one of our low-end mainframes; we indicated our willingness to do so.

In discussions with the U.S. government, we were told to "cool it," that it was not in the cards at that time. In my view, this was an acceptable response. In September 1968, after the Soviet invasion of Czechoslovakia, it appeared for a time that Romania might be invaded also. The U.S. government then issued some strong warnings, and seemed to move closer politically to Romania, perhaps trying to wean it away from the Soviet bloc. President Ceausescu visited the United States in 1970 and, at that time, discussed Romania's desire to enter into some high technology agreements with U.S. firms. He was encouraged to do so by our government. Soon thereafter, we began discussing with Romania the possibility of their manufacturing some of our peripheral equipment, specifically card readers and printers.

Romania was then in the process of drafting a new law to allow joint ventures with Western firms, as well as the repatriation of profits. This law was the first of its kind among the nations of the Soviet bloc. As a result of this development, and as a result of a number of discussions with our own government, we decided that it was in the best interests of Control Data and the U.S. government to allow the transfer of printer and card technology to a new plant to be set up as a joint venture (ROM/CD)—55% owned by a Romanian agency and 45% owned by Control Data. The decree was actually passed in November 1972, and we signed the agreement. At that time, Assistant Secretary of State Ken Rush said he was seeking to encourage U.S. businessmen to sell, invest, and buy in these countries as opportunity and confidence permitted; doing business in Eastern Europe was seen to be fully consonant with U.S. national interests. Moreover, Rush cited what we were doing in Romania as the model.

As we look at it now over ten years later, ROM/CD is the only U.S. joint venture operating in Romania. I do not know of any other high technology joint ventures there or in any other part of Eastern Europe. Until recently, ROM/CD was considered a model of U.S. innovation and cooperation. Until this administration, every secretary of commerce (as well as many other high-level government officials and dignitaries) had visited our plant. On October 15, 1984, ROM/CD celebrated its tenth anniversary. To remain competitive, it must receive a continuous flow of technology; without some guarantee of this flow, the continued well-being of the joint venture will be threatened. But, again—as in the case with the Soviet Union—attitudes within the U.S. government have changed, for whatever reason. The flow of technology to ROM/CD has been cut off, and its continued existence is threatened. We have, then, yet another example of the carrot being offered, a company being encouraged to enter into a long-term relationship, a policy change, and a U.S. company out on the limb—after having originally acted in what it was given to understand was the national interest. Similar examples exist regarding countries such as India and other Free World countries.

The lesson I gain from this case is that of a great need for more dialogue between those people in the private sector out there on the frontiers of trade and those in the government developing the "export guidelines." The policy comes from above (as it certainly should) and the regulations come from below. But between policy and regulation, some dialogue with industry is necessary. Full discussion of the implications of these regulations *before* they are put into concrete would go a long way toward ending the resentment U.S. exporters feel toward the government's trade policy. If these steps are not taken, U.S. exporters will be seriously disadvantaged, and their competitiveness in the world market will diminish.

PART 6

TECHNOLOGY TRANSFER AND U.S.-ALLIANCE RELATIONS

18

COCOM AFTER 35 YEARS: REAFFIRMATION OR REORGANIZATION?

Robert Price

Our Coordinating Committee (CoCom) allies share the U.S. view that the fundamental premise for national security controls is to prevent significant technologies with military application from going to the Soviet Union or its satellites. That premise has been held even more strongly by our allies over the past five years, as we have learned more about the Soviet campaign to acquire Western technology legally and illegally for its weapons and military equipment projects.

BACKGROUND, OBJECTIVES, AND MEMBERSHIP

CoCom is an informal consultative organization, established in 1949 to coordinate trade controls on the export of strategic items to communist countries. It is based on the concept of multilateral cooperation and coordination among allies, recognizing that no country has a monopoly on high technology. Its fundamental objective is to restrict the export of those goods and technologies which would make a significant contribution to the military potential of the targeted countries—the USSR, other Warsaw Pact countries, Albania, and communist countries in Asia (North Korea, Vietnam, and the People's Republic of China). Member countries are those in NATO (except for Iceland) plus Japan. CoCom has no formal relationship with either NATO or the OECD. The organization is not based on any treaty or executive agreement. Decisions are taken by unanimous vote, and its deliberations by mutual agreement are confidential. Indeed, until recent years, its very existence was classified.

Located in Paris and housed in a U.S. Embassy annex, CoCom has a small secretariat staff of approximately 25 and a modest budget of about one million dollars. The U.S. delegate to CoCom and his deputy are State Department foreign service officers, who are joined by teams of U.S.-based technical experts and interagency policy-level officials during specific negotiations. The key U.S. departments involved in "backstopping" CoCom are State, Commerce, Defense, Energy, and others as appropriate.

Other countries are generally represented by officials either from their OECD delegation or attached to their Paris embassies (economic ministries). Over the years, CoCom has adopted and revised various basic regulations and procedures; these are not codified in a comprehensive set of by-laws, but rather are found in records of discussion and certain key decisions and recommendations. Among the more important of these documents is the list of items controlled, the most recent and comprehensive revisions of which were completed in 1984.

MAJOR FUNCTIONS

Establishment and Review of the Three Embargo Lists

The three international embargo lists are the munitions, atomic energy, and international lists. The third list includes dual-use products and technology that have both civilian and military applications. All three are revised during periodic list reviews as well as on the basis of ad hoc proposals submitted by member governments. Since the establishment of CoCom, the latest and perhaps most comprehensive list review was completed in July 1984. For the first time, certain computer software and telecommunications switching equipment were explicitly controlled. In addition, stricter controls have been implemented for small, militarily relevant computers, while controls have been removed on a range of lower-performance computers.

Among other items CoCom has brought under control are spacecraft and launch vehicles, large floating docks, gas turbine engines and their technologies, robots, and advanced composite materials and their production equipment. CoCom agreed to shift to a continuous or segmented list review in the fall of 1985, as opposed to the previous practice of a formal list review every several years. Under the new procedure, the list will be divided into four major divisions, each of which will receive annual (though not necessarily simultaneous) review.

Review of Exceptions

CoCom procedures permit member governments to export embargoed items to proscribed countries where the risk of diversion to military purposes is sufficiently small. In some cases, exceptions to normal export controls are allowed at national discretion, and in other cases following unanimous agreement by the committee.

Apart from the list reviews, consideration of such cases is the major function of CoCom. Some 4,000 requests for exceptions are submitted annually by member governments for committee review. The United States submits more than half of these cases, and the overwhelming share is for proposed exports to the PRC.

Since the Soviet invasion of Afghanistan, CoCom has adhered to the de facto practice of denying exception cases to the USSR, except in a few limited areas. Cases appear on CoCom's agenda in accordance with specified time limits; within these limits, if member governments cannot present their positions when the cases appear on the agenda, they are granted additional time for study. Although procedures provide a final time limit for the presentation of positions, additional time is given for receipt of answers to questions asked. Processing time for most cases is under 90 days.

Coordination of Export Control Enforcement Activities

This is the third major function of CoCom, which is carried out through the CoCom Subcommittee on Export Controls. Since 1982, the subcommittee has met twice yearly. Its mandate encompasses programs for increased cooperation among enforcement and investigatory agencies and greater harmonization of export licensing procedures. Among the most important issues addressed have been approaches to non-CoCom countries to urge cooperation in measures for better protection from diversion of in-transit goods and those in storage in bonded warehouses.

RECENT COCOM ACTIVITIES

Conclusions of the February 1985 High-Level Meeting

CoCom's third high-level meeting since 1982 reflected continued policy-level interest in strengthening the organization, administration, and enforcement of the CoCom embargo. The meeting confirmed a general appreciation among the CoCom partners of the need to protect adequately sensitive Western high technology. It assessed progress on a number of initiatives over the past two years, including the recently concluded 1982-1984 list review, and endorsed a framework for easing the burden of China cases in CoCom. It also reconfirmed a general commitment to intensify efforts to achieve greater third-country cooperation with CoCom controls.

Segmented List Review

The segmented list review, endorsed at the high-level meeting, entered into force in the fall of 1985. Technologies as well as products will be assessed for possible inclusion in the control lists for a four-year period. A major benefit of the new procedure will be the more timely publication each year of modifications in the list, rather than a single massive revision every several years as in the past. The procedure will also rationalize the work program for the staff of the CoCom Secretariat, as well as for participating governments. Segmented review of one of the four major product/technology divisions that now comprise the list began in November 1985.

Deliberations Over China Case Processing

CoCom countries agreed at the last high-level meeting that China's present policies, as well as the rapidly growing number of China cases in CoCom, warrant the accordance of more flexible treatment to exports of high technology to China. (83% of the 3,199 CoCom exceptions cases in 1984 were for China.) In 1985, a CoCom ad hoc group developed a number of proposals to expedite handling of certain PRC cases. If these procedures are effectively implemented, it is anticipated that the China caseload in CoCom will be reduced significantly, thus enabling CoCom to devote greater attention to higher-priority Warsaw Pact country cases.

Coordination of Export Control Initiatives in Non-CoCom Countries

As CoCom has progressively strengthened enforcement efforts within CoCom parameters, it has become increasingly evident that the Soviet Union and its allies are seeking CoCom-controlled technology via non-CoCom countries. The United States and certain other CoCom countries have individually dealt with this issue through bilateral contacts with certain key exporting countries not participating in the CoCom system. In a 1984 decision, CoCom agreed to accord higher priority to these initiatives, and to coordinate member contacts with third countries. Since then, the United States and its CoCom partners have had discussions with a number of countries that import significant quantities of CoCom-controlled technologies from CoCom sources and/or indigenously manufacture CoCom-controlled products. The U.S. objective is to obtain the active cooperation of those producer countries in tighter export control—specifically, the denial of CoCom-controlled products and technology to potential U.S. adversaries. In this connection, it is worth recalling that the new Export Administration Act of 1985 contains a provision whereby U.S. authorities may grant CoCom-like trading privileges to third countries that cooperate fully on export control issues.

CoCom Modernization

In response to CoCom's expanding role in monitoring technology transfer to communist countries, CoCom members have agreed on the priority need to upgrade and modernize the CoCom organization and its secretariat. By 1985, the United States had committed $2 million to this process, which will help provide for the badly needed construction of expanded facilities, for additional word processing equipment, and for other improvements to the secretariat organization.

CoCom recently agreed to the creation of several new positions on the secretariat staff, which should significantly augment technical expertise and expedite the processing of export control exception cases. The United States is highly pleased with the strong commitment shown by the CoCom partners to the modernization of the organization; budgeting contributions are now increasing some 20% from year to year.

While CoCom is not a perfect organization, it has served the alliance remarkably well in limiting damage to Western security interests due to uncontrolled trade with our potential adversaries. The United States and its alliance partners intend to continue to devote major efforts and resources to this important undertaking.

19

TECHNOLOGY TRANSFER AND ALLIANCE RELATIONS: A WEST GERMAN PERSPECTIVE

Manfred Von Nordheim

In considering the question of East-West technology transfer, it is clearly important to identify the major sources of technological leaks to the Soviet bloc, and to alert the business and policy communities on both sides of the Atlantic to the scale of the problem. The question is: What can and ought to be done about it? It is at this point—when the pros and cons of alternative export controls are being weighed—that consensus among the Western allies begins to fall apart.

Several contributions to this collection address the substantial costs inflicted upon the West by the illegal export of high technology items to the East. Not only do the Warsaw Pact countries save enormous resources by obtaining technology from the West by legal and illegal means, but the West then has to invest heavily to protect itself against Soviet bloc military capabilities, which have been increased with the help of those same Western technologies. However, what has not been adequately discussed is the cost that *we* in the West could incur if we were to engage in an all-out effort to shut down these technology leaks.

For example, concern has been expressed about the large number of foreign students in the United States. Surely, a potentially significant source of the loss of technology could be eliminated by drastically reducing the number of foreign students attending American universities. But consider the costs of such a drastic measure, both on overall allied relations and on future scientific-technological exchanges in particular.

In this same vein, there is the question of the degree to which scientific meetings, exchanges, and literature will remain open. One great advantage that the West has is the open exchange of information and the open discussion of opposing views. To clamp down on this openness in order to deprive the Soviet Union of high-technology insights may well inflict greater damage on us than the gain the other side might otherwise achieve. Indeed, one of the reasons why the West has a commanding lead over the East in the sciences is precisely the Western tradition of free and open inquiry.

Unfortunately, I fear that the clampdown on exchanges between scientists even within the West has already progressed more than most of us realize. All one has to do is study the announcements in the *Commerce Business Daily* to notice how many briefings and meetings explicitly exclude the participation of foreigners—not just Soviet bloc country representatives, but *all* foreigners. If this trend continues, one cannot exclude the possibility that sometime in the future we will see similar meetings in Europe closed to U.S. citizens. If this approach continues to develop unchecked, are we not hurting ourselves most of all? U.S. Under Secretary of State William Schneider has stated that we must engage in more cooperative ventures in the NATO armament field, and he notes that a number of positive developments have occurred recently, or are about to take place. How many transatlantic ventures will *not* take place because companies or individuals on both sides of the Atlantic may come to the conclusion that the advantages of such cooperation may not outweigh the extra work and the potential trouble involved in adopting mutually acceptable security precautions against "technological theft"?

As a result of tightened export controls, which often seem excessive and erratic from the European perspective, one perceives a trend in Western Europe to become less dependent on certain critical items imported from the United States. As a consequence, the West is hurting itself most, because we end up not doing what we can do best—namely, producing in great numbers and reducing costs. It would be a mistake to assume that West Europeans are not concerned with the loss of technology to Soviet bloc countries. They are indeed concerned, because they know very well that Soviet technicians are very quick to adapt certain technologies from the West to military use. The White Paper on Defense published in the spring of 1985 by the Ministry of Defense of the Federal Republic explicitly draws attention to the qualitative improvements so achieved in Warsaw Pact armaments.

In many respects, the fundamental disagreement between Western Europe and the United States has to do instead with the broader question of the extent to which trade between sovereign nations can and should be used as a political weapon. There is no easy answer to this question, but the way we answer it will be determined to a large extent by the role played by trade in our respective societies. About 30% of West Germany's GNP is directly affected by foreign trade, and in other West European countries these figures are quite similar. By contrast, in the United States, foreign trade accounts for only about 7% of GNP. Hence, it is only natural that the outlook on foreign trade should be dissimilar.

One also has to consider that West Germany no longer enjoys a trade advantage due to low wages. Challenged by some trade competitors who can pay their workers less, and by others who have achieved high quality standards (e.g., Japan), it has become all the more important today for West Germany to maintain its reputation as a solid and reliable trade partner. Trade sanctions, especially when coupled with a switch-on, switch-off foreign policy, are poison to this kind of reputation. As a consequence, Europeans will be found extremely reluctant to follow the United States when it wishes to impose sanctions or embargoes. West Germans in particular well remember that in the past the West twice engaged in a pipeline boycott against the USSR—and that in response the Soviet Union engaged in a major push to develop its own pipeline-related industry. So, too, in addition to lost business opportunities, the Europeans have to ponder whether or not they should "reinvent the wheel"—that is, whether or not to commit substantial development funds to become independent of crucial U.S. technologies (such as gas turbines for pumping stations) that may be embargoed insofar as East-West trade is concerned.

This is not at all to suggest that, in the view of West Europeans, trade with Soviet bloc countries should flow completely unhindered, or that there should be no restraints on technology transfer from West to East. Europe is just as much in favor of restricting the flow of crucial technologies as are U.S. policy officials, especially when military applications may be involved. The dispute centers around the question of where to draw the line between critical and noncritical technology.

In view of the close and mutually beneficial trade relationship among Western nations, it should be clear that the issue of trade with, and technology transfer toward, the East cannot be solved by fiat, by attempting to impose policies unilaterally on an alliance comprised of free and sovereign nations. Just as the Europeans ought to take U.S. concerns about the flow of military-related technology to the East more seriously, the United States ought to realize that on a case-by-case basis, valid disagreements may exist between what is critical and what is not, and that there may be differences on whether proposed general restrictions serve any useful purpose. U.S. Assistant Secretary of Defense Richard Perle has warned that the domestic consensus in the United States tends to break down when American businessmen, who adhere to U.S. restraints on trade and technology, see their business going to European and Japanese firms adhering to a different policy. While this point is well taken, one should also realize that domestic consensus in Europe and Japan on restrictions toward trade with the East also is endangered, if there is widespread feeling that U.S. demands and policies are unreasonable. Certainly it should be clear that a policy agreed to by all allies—even if considered still too lax by the United States—is preferable to, and likely to be more effective than, a go-it-alone U.S. policy. Hence, it is imperative that on the issue of East-West trade and technology transfer, the nations of the West develop a reasonable and enforceable common policy.

20

THE WEST-WEST DIMENSIONS OF EAST-WEST ECONOMIC RELATIONS

Henry R. Nau

The sources of controversy in the alliance over the role of technology in East-West relations are numerous. The most important is the *strategic* dimension—the different views within the alliance of the relationship between East-West economic activities and East-West strategic conflict. This dimension explains much of the high-level political dispute within the alliance over the past decade on East-West economic issues (e.g., the pipeline controversy of 1981-1982). When views diverge significantly at this level, other sources or dimensions of controversy are compounded:

- the *international* dimension, involving relations with CoCom (the Coordinating Committee for export controls among allied countries) and with non-CoCom, Western countries
- the *national* dimension, involving relations among different agencies within a single country charged with responsibilities for various security or economic aspects of trade and technology flows, and
- the *industrial* dimension, involving relations between business and government seeking a balance between commercial interests in product and technology exports and security interests.

In recent years, significant progress has been achieved in narrowing differences at the strategic level. This progress, in turn, has facilitated some improvements in the international and national dimensions of East-West economic relations, including important CoCom decisions in the summer of 1984, and passage by

Congress in the summer of 1985 of the long-delayed Export Administration Amendments Act of 1985. The spotlight now turns to the industry level, where improvements are still pending—improvements which hinge to a great extent on the smooth integration of the Defense Department's new role in reviewing individual validated and multiple licenses of controlled goods and technology exports among Western countries.

These developments offer a new opportunity to place the issue of East-West trade and technology relations on firmer ground within the alliance. The prospects are neither as gloomy as some analysts assume, who focus on the conflicts of recent years, nor as assured as other advocates may believe, who see recent progress largely as a result of unilateral U.S. options and pressure.

THE STRATEGIC DIMENSION

Three basic views may be identified in the alliance concerning the relationship between economic ties and strategic conflict.[1] The first view, more popular in Europe than in the United States, holds that economic relations between East and West can help, over time, to *resolve* basic strategic and political conflicts between the United States and the Soviet Union. Accordingly, this view encourages economic cooperation and seeks to limit restrictions on strategic technologies to a bare minimum. Economic activities offer mutual benefits and establish a common stake in peaceful international relations. They are said to contribute to decentralization and greater pluralism in the East and to an awareness of the limitations of markets in the West. By so doing, they supposedly encourage a convergence of structures and expectations that ultimately removes or at least significantly ameliorates the central conflict between the two types of societies. As this conflict diminishes, resources formerly devoted to military defense can be safely diverted to more peaceful social and economic purposes. Restrictions on strategic trade and technology flows can be further relaxed. Various perspectives on détente are incorporated into this view, differing largely in terms of the extent to which they foresaw the narrowing of fundamental differences and the degree to which they favored reducing defense expenditures to finance social objectives.

A second view, which may be considered mainstream in the United States, holds that fundamental political conflicts between East and West are deep-seated and unlikely to be affected by economic relations, which in any case are themselves limited by differences in basic economic and social structures. According to this view, economic relations between East and West are primarily useful in *managing* conflict, not significantly resolving it. Thus, economic relations are subordinated to the requirements of maintaining strategic and political equilibrium—in short, to the operation of deterrence. Strategic technologies are defined more broadly and protected more carefully through tougher export control licensing and enforcement systems. Nonstrategic trade may also be useful from time to time as a foreign policy tool to communicate intentions between the superpowers and signal their approval or disapproval of one another's actions. Together with defense and political measures, trade cooperation and sanctions condition the atmosphere of superpower relations, which is the essence of deterrence. In this sense, economic relations do not substitute for, but supplement, defense measures. The unique quality of economic initiatives seen from this perspective is that they may be used more readily to signal approval or disapproval, as they are less risky than military moves. To be effective, however, economic steps must ultimately be backed up by the threat or promise to do something further. In this second view, therefore, economic relations are inextricably embedded in the array or "ladder" of policy instruments for escalating threat and managing deterrence.

A third view, which has been strongly held in the United States at various times, sees economic relations between East and West as a means not of resolving or managing conflict with the Soviet Union, but of *waging* and ultimately winning this conflict through economic warfare. This view, like the first view, sees the conflict eventually ending. However, conflict termination is achieved not by compromise but by weakening the Soviet state, forcing it to face the inefficiencies of its own economic system and the costs of its unrelenting military buildup. By compelling tradeoffs among economic and defense objectives within the Soviet Union, economic restrictions affect not only the psychology of deterrence between East and West (as in the second view), but, in the end, the physical, military balance itself. The conflict diminishes as the Soviet Union retreats or changes its basic character in the presence of superior U.S. power. ·

There are numerous variants to these perspectives; the three views actually define a spectrum of thought rather than discrete positions. Two variants deserve special mention because they play a more visible role in the contemporary alliance discussion. A variant of the first view holds that economic relations in Central Europe, and specifically between East and West Germany, may someday resolve a major subconflict in East-West relations—namely, the division of Germany. According to this view, held by many in the FRG, expanding intra-German economic relations create a necessary, though probably not sufficient, condition for eventual German reunification. If reunification involved some element of neutralization (which it probably would), Germany would be able, in effect, to withdraw from central aspects of the East-West conflict. Thus, from its perspective, expanding East-West trade may help someday to resolve an important conflict. A variant of the third view argues that intensive economic development within the United States and the West may eventually provide the basis for reestablishing

Western superiority over the Soviet Union. In this event, the East-West conflict becomes less troublesome and in that sense ends by not weakening the Soviet state, but by dramatically enhancing U.S. strength. The desire for a technological breakout, which at least some supporters of the Strategic Defense Initiative appear to hold, is a reflection of this point of view.

A DECADE OF DISPUTE

In the early and mid-1970s, the center of gravity among the views outlined above shifted significantly toward the first perspective. While Richard Nixon and Henry Kissinger may have intended their use of economic cooperation with the Soviet Union to be merely a "carrot" in the process of managing deterrence, they did talk about establishing a Soviet stake in the international economy.[2] Détente enthusiasts in Europe and the United States went further and spoke glowingly about the prospects of convergence. A series of international agreements—Berlin, SALT I, the ABM Treaty, the Vietnam peace accord—coincided with the expansion of economic relations and seemed to suggest that the underlying conflicts (or at least some important elements of them) were on the way to being resolved. The point at which détente clearly went beyond the intentions of Nixon and Kissinger came when the United States began to cut back significantly on military expenditures, using the so-called Vietnam "peace dividend" to expand welfare and other domestic social programs.

In retrospect, the mistaken expectation of the détente era was not that economic relations might be useful as carrots to manage deterrence more effectively, but that these relations could resolve significant political conflicts, thereby lowering the requirement for deterrence and permitting the reduction of military expenditures. Ironically, the United States fell for this seductive tradeoff notion that military resources could be safely diverted to economic purposes to a far larger extent than the Europeans. This was particularly true with the Germans, who maintained the growth of their military outlays in the 1970s. On the other hand, Europeans tended to overstate the significance of the conflicts that were being ameliorated in this period, largely because these conflicts, such as Berlin, were centered in Europe.

Thus, economic relations with the East expanded in the 1970s on the basis of what was perceived at the beginning of that decade as a stable strategic balance between the United States and the Soviet Union. In the course of the decade, however, this balance progressively deteriorated as the United States unilaterally disarmed. Economic relations that initially supported the improved management of deterrence gradually became potential new threats, taking shape as economic avenues through which the Soviet Union might apply subtle political pressure and exacerbate the loss of confidence in Western defense capabilities.

This atmosphere constituted the background against which U.S. policy shifted once again in the late 1970s back toward emphasizing the requirements for managing deterrence and, in the eyes of some, toward restoring American superiority, or a "margin of safety" as it was called. This shift toward the second and third views outlined above predictably sparked turbulence in alliance relations. Europe clung to the first view even as its ability to maintain military outlays weakened under the increasing economic pressures of the late 1970s. Many groups in Europe, especially the various political parties in Germany, grew more united in their expectation that economic relations, at least between the two Germanies, could someday resolve the troublesome German question. The United States, on the other hand, swung rather widely (some say wildly) toward the second and third views, using economic relations exclusively as sticks (e.g., the Afghanistan and Polish sanctions) for managing deterrence, while talking about broader embargoes to weaken Soviet society. (This sort of talk was always stronger than the subsequent action, however, as reflected in the lifting of the grain embargo.) Some emphasis was also placed on the development of technological breakthroughs to enhance U.S. strength, which might eventually win the conflict with the communist system.

FROM CONFLICT TO NEW CONSENSUS

What has emerged from this titanic struggle of basic views on the relationship of economic relations to strategic conflict is a reconsolidation of alliance perspectives around the second view. Helped by the coming to power of conservative governments in Britain and Germany and a strong defense-minded socialist government in France, the United States has pulled the consensus back toward the deterrence perspective. The greater military self-confidence of the United States and the West has also made less likely new political crises that might once again precipitate controversial foreign policy controls, such as the gas pipeline embargo.

Much depends now on how these gains of the past few years, paid for in debilitating alliance conflicts, will be exploited in the somewhat calmer atmosphere that currently prevails. If the United States fails to maintain its defense watch or its high priority for East-West trade issues in CoCom, NATO, OECD, and IEA (as it has been known to do), a unique opportunity will be lost, and the alliance will set itself up for another serious controversy when the next crisis erupts.

The first step is to recognize that East-West economic relations are not significant enough by themselves to resolve any of the major conflicts dividing the United States and the Soviet Union. East-West trade flows, even if they begin to increase again after the recession- and debt-imposed lull of the past few years, are marginal in any aggregate sense to the economic well-being of Western countries. (The one potential, though not current, exception to this conclusion may be the Federal Republic of Germany, where East-West trade flows today represent less than 10% of West German trade, but loom larger in the expectation of eventual reunification.) These flows are more important to the Soviet Union and its allies, as recent reports on Soviet strategic gains from Western technology inflows make clear.[3] But, as two astute observers of East-West trade issues observe, "there is no evidence that the Soviet Union will make significant political concessions—or refrain from pursuing major foreign policy interests—if the West denies it goods that contribute only a limited amount to its economic development." "Quite simply," these observers conclude, "the means and ends are totally disproportionate."[4]

Hence the only sensible perspective for managing East-West economic relations is the deterrence perspective. The United States should be particularly careful not to depart from this perspective, given the fact that its allies are more prone to embrace it—as opposed to a more confrontationally-oriented perspective—especially once the United States hints that it may be leaning this way itself. Soberness about U.S.-Soviet differences, therefore, is more appropriate than sentimentality.[5]

Moreover, in using economic ties to manage deterrence, the United States must recognize that economic "carrots" or "sticks" are only effective if they are used as integral parts of broader policies and not as substitutes for, or in isolation from, these other policies. Carrots, for example, work only if they are supported by broader policies to improve relations (as was the intent, at least, in the Nixon-Kissinger initiative). Lifting the grain embargo in 1981 was much less effective as a carrot because it ran against the "grain" of other, more militant policies of the administration at the time.[6] Similarly, sticks work only if they are supported by other actions, and ultimately by the threat to escalate to more severe actions—political or military—if the crisis persists. Unless the United States is prepared to support sanctions with broader measures, it should probably refrain from such actions or impose them only on a temporary basis. This would ensure that "lightswitch diplomacy," as it has been called, is implemented only when the stakes are very high or when economic losses, which may be severe over the long-term when U.S. exporters lose markets to more reliable suppliers, can be limited.[7]

Improvements and stability along the strategic dimensions of West-West disputes with respect to East-West economic relations create opportunities for improvements in other dimensions. Assuming that strategic consensus persists, the critical developments in West-West relations over the next few years will occur in CoCom, national export control programs, and industry-government relations.

THE COCOM DIMENSION

For more than 25 years after its establishment, CoCom operated without high-level political guidance. As a result, it continued to function relatively smoothly into the 1970s even as high-level political disagreements over East-West trade escalated. The price was the decreasing ability of CoCom to make difficult decisions—on computers, for example. As the pace of technology quickened, CoCom became less and less relevant to the task of protecting Western strategic technology.

Under the consensus forged by the Reagan administration, CoCom has been revitalized. Three high-level CoCom meetings, the last in February 1985, have led to substantial improvements, including

- a new agreement on computer controls
- new controls on high technology items such as robotics (both hardware and software), spacecraft, advanced printed circuit boards, manufacturing equipment for printed circuit boards, and advanced aeroengine technologies
- tighter controls on communications switching equipment, software, numerically controlled machine tools, electronic-grade silicon, semiconductor manufacturing equipment and turnkey plants, and
- continuous list review to keep pace with steadily changing technology, rather than periodic review as in the past.[8]

CoCom is undergoing a major renovation of facilities to enlarge its quarters, upgrade automation, and increase its staff. Consideration is being given to the creation of a Defense Experts Group, which, although not a formal part of CoCom, would advise CoCom on the military uses of technology and on the prospects for Soviet reengineering of advanced equipment.

All of these improvements are long overdue. They help the allies and the United States alike, because the stronger CoCom is politically and administratively, the more likely it will serve to reconcile continuing differences between the United States and its allies. The controversies of 1981-1982 occurred at the highest political levels (i.e., among heads of state and government) in part because there were no existing vehicles to handle such disputes effectively. A CoCom more capable of making difficult decisions which are accepted as fair (as were the decisions enumerated above) spares the alliance unilateral actions by one member or another and consequently more troubling controversies.

As CoCom controls are strengthened, the leakage of strategic technologies from non-CoCom countries becomes a larger problem. The administration has addressed this problem through an intensive campaign to negotiate bilateral arrangements with non-CoCom countries, establishing CoCom-equivalent or at least improved national controls for technology transfers. Austria, Sweden, and India have concluded recent agreements with the United States, while extensive talks are underway with the more advanced developing countries, particularly in Asia.

THE NATIONAL DIMENSION

International negotiations within CoCom and with non-CoCom countries have contributed to a strengthening of national controls. France, the United Kingdom, and Canada have reorganized their decisionmaking procedures in recent years, enlarging the role played by considerations of defense. Austria has passed new legislation, strengthening the legal basis for enforcement of export controls. With the increase of international cooperation, national intelligence capabilities have been improved.

The decisionmaking process in the United States, especially the role of the Department of Defense, was the leading source of controversy in the recent overhaul of U.S. export control legislation. Having been given the right in the 1979 legislation (Section 10g) to review individual export licenses to controlled countries, the Department of Defense sought this same right in the new legislation with respect to CoCom and noncontrolled, non-CoCom countries. The Department of Commerce and American business strongly opposed this extension of authority, fearing the cutoff of legitimate technological transfer among Western countries. The issue was decided administratively by the president in a January 1984 Executive Order. This order enabled the United States to take a unified position in CoCom decisions in 1984 on computers and other list review items. Nevertheless, ambiguities remained, and the president issued further orders in January 1985, which specified some 15 noncontrolled countries to which exports of seven product categories would be subject to case-by-case review in the Pentagon.

Congress ultimately refused to reinforce this arrangement in the new legislation. This is regrettable, since failure to resolve the issue legislatively leaves the various bureaucracies free to carry on the debilitating internecine warfare of the past few years, enlisting their respective congressional allies in the process. The end result may be continued delay and frustration in the license review process, with new charges that the Department of Defense review role is crippling America's exports.

The Department of Defense has a legitimate role to play in West-West license review. It is the agency charged with the responsibility for America's strategic technology investment and therefore also with its protection. To be sure, it has to play its role expeditiously and fairly. The Department of Defense began formal review of individual West-West validated license applications in February 1985. In the first two weeks, it screened 1,123 cases and requested hard-copy files of 178 of these cases. Of the latter, all were processed on the first day the documents arrived at the Department of Defense. According to the law, the Defense Department has seven days to review the applications and 15 days to request and review the hard file on a particular case. Clearly, the Department of Defense has a stake in streamlining its participation in the review process. But success requires the cooperation of all agencies. Anyone who has worked in the U.S. bureaucracy knows that there are not only invisible, but often legitimate, ways to stall decisions. A clearer legislative resolution of this issue would have minimized such opportunities.

THE INDUSTRIAL DIMENSION

At the moment, the role of the Department of Defense in West-West review extends only to individual validated licenses. It does not involve the multiple licenses—distribution and comprehensive operations licenses.

The new legislation eliminates the qualified general license which previously authorized multiple exports. In its place, it identifies four specific validated licenses authorizing multiple exports to noncontrolled countries:[9]

- *Distribution licenses* authorize exports of goods to approved distributors of users of the goods.
- *Comprehensive operations licenses* authorize exports and reexports of technology and related goods, including items from the list of militarily critical technologies, from a domestic concern to and among its foreign subsidiaries, affiliates, joint ventures, and licensees that have long-term, contractually defined relations with the exporter.
- *Project licenses* authorize exports of goods and technology for a specified activity.
- *Service supply licenses* authorize exports of spare or replacement parts for goods previously exported.

These licenses, particularly the distribution (DL) and comprehensive operations (COL) licenses are the key to the smooth flow of West-West trade and technology transfer. Unlike individual validated licenses, they do not require review of each transfer. The DL authorizes a particular recipient in noncontrolled countries, rather than a particular transaction, and permits the shipment of goods to that foreign consignee as long as the latter is judged reliable with respect to the prevention of diversion of goods to controlled countries. The COL authorizes a particular multinational company or network of related companies within noncontrolled countries, and permits the transfer of technology within that company or network as long as the latter's system of internal control is approved. Together, the DL and COL allow for repeated transfers of both goods and technology within the West without review of each transaction.

The problem at this point is the lack of confidence in the distribution license and the lack of experience with the comprehensive operations license. As William T. Archey, then-acting Assistant Secretary of Commerce for Trade Administration testified in 1984, "the entire period of the 1970s. . .saw a major erosion of the regulations governing the distribution license program."[10] From 1977 to 1984, no audits of foreign consignees receiving distribution licenses were conducted, even though one of the last audits in 1977 turned up over 111 violations. In 1984, the Department of Commerce hired 25 new people and began to conduct audits once again. It will take time, however, to reestablish the credibility of the DL. The president's directive authorizing Department of Defense review of West-West transfers apparently extends to DLs, as well as to individual validated licenses. But as of the summer of 1985, the Department of Defense was not involved in the DL audits, and there is clear dissatisfaction in the Department of Defense with many distribution centers currently licensed, especially in the Asian-Pacific area.

A new mechanism, the COL deals with technology rather than products. Accordingly, it is part of the difficult and controversial process of extending export controls to technology and technical data. (It is the industrial counterpart to the attempts to control, in one way or another, flows of scientific and technical information among universities and professional societies.) In effect, it asks industry to impose self-controls or to design an internal control system that meets the standards of the government licensing community. Presumably, once established, the internal control system of a multinational company or a network of related firms would be audited periodically—every one or two years—to ensure compliance with standards. This procedure would be far less intrusive than review of each individual technology transaction, which was never practical to begin with.

CONCLUSIONS

It will take perhaps years to build confidence in the licensing arrangements for West-West trade and technology transfer. In the meantime, strategic circumstances may change or crises may emerge which will once again disrupt alliance cohesion and CoCom export control cooperation. There is little one can do about these possibilities.

Nevertheless, the current calm in both CoCom and U.S. export control procedures should be exploited to press forward the progress achieved in recent years and to establish experience—and confidence—in the West-West licensing process. The U.S. government must maintain and continue to press its priorities in CoCom and in bilateral arrangements with non-CoCom countries. Official controls are the first line of defense in protecting the West's strategic technology investment. The stronger and more effective these controls are, the less concerned the Department of Defense and others will be about strategic and technology flows within the West. In this sense, there is a tradeoff between East-West and West-West controls. Part of the U.S. bargaining leverage with its allies and friends is the willingness to ease West-West transfers if foreign partners strengthen their East-West controls.

Finally, easing West-West transfers depends critically on the smooth operation of the new Department of Defense authority to review selected individual validated licenses for transfers within the West and the early extension of this review role to DLs and COLs as well. Only with the Department of Defense fully integrated into the export review process can one expect some abatement of the bureaucratic warfare of recent years. While tensions will necessarily remain between the Departments of Commerce and Defense, and between the U.S. government and industry, the extreme charges of bad faith and hidden motivations in these relations must be silenced over the next few years, just as the emotional charges that fueled the pipeline controversy several years ago have been silenced in recent alliance relations.

NOTES

1. My thinking in this section has been stimulated by an insightful paper by Richard E. Bissell, "Strategic Parity and Economic Deterrence," presented at the Annual Convention of the American Political Science Association, New Orleans, Louisiana, August 30, 1985. See also my essay, "International Technology Transfer," *The Washington Quarterly,* Winter 1985, pp. 57-64.
2. See, selectively, their respective memoirs, Richard Nixon, *RN: The Memoirs of Richard Nixon* (New York: Grosset and Dunlap, 1978) and Henry Kissinger, *White House Years* (Boston: Little, Brown, and Company, 1979).

3. See *Assessing the Effect of Technology Transfer on U.S./Western Security: A Defense Perspective,* Office of the Under Secretary of Defense for Policy, Department of Defense, February 1985; and new reports released by the Defense Department and reported in the *New York Times* and the *Washington Post* on September 19, 1985.
4. See Ellen L. Frost and Angela E. Stent, "NATO's Troubles with East-West Trade," *International Security,* 8:1 (Summer 1983), pp. 179-201.
5. In this respect, the Reagan administration's approach to the Gorbachev-Reagan summit meeting in November 1985 was right on course.
6. On this point, see Bissell, op. cit.
7. In the case of Afghanistan and Poland, for example, the United States imposed economic sanctions even though it was clear that it was not prepared to use stronger measures, such as military force, if the sanctions failed. Yet in both cases, it was clearly necessary to do something to signal disapproval of Soviet actions. The best solution may have been to support the sanctions with strengthened military or political measures within the alliance (e.g., unscheduled maneuvers), designed not to threaten intervention in the existing disputes, but to raise uncertainty in Soviet calculations should it contemplate another "adventure" in some other vital area. Or, failing the willingness to do that, the sanctions should have been announced as temporary at the outset, because they will be lifted eventually in any case—if no more severe action is planned—and usually as a result of domestic pressures betraying weakness rather than resolve.
8. See Department of Defense, *The Technology Security Program,* A Report to the 99th Congress, First Session, February 1985.
9. See Ronald Pramberger, "Section-by-Section Comparison of the Export Administration Act of 1979 (as amended) and the Export Administration Act of 1985," for Conference sponsored by the Chamber of Commerce of the United States of America, July 18, 1985.
10. See *Enforcement of the Export Control Enforcement Act,* Hearing before the Committee on Banking, Housing, and Urban Affairs, U.S. Senate, 98th Congress, 2nd Session, April 2, 1984, p. 55.

PART 7

CONCLUSIONS

21

WEST-EAST TECHNOLOGY TRANSFER: IMPLICATIONS FOR U.S. POLICY

Charles M. Perry and Robert L. Pfaltzgraff, Jr.

In recent years attention has been focused on a series of espionage cases that involve the theft of U.S. defense secrets sold to the Soviet Union, as well as the defection to the East of highly placed persons in the West German government. Such examples represent only the most publicized elements of a vast Soviet effort to acquire sensitive information from the open societies of the West in support of the military machine of the Soviet Union. According to a Department of Defense study released in 1985:

Virtually every Soviet military research project—well over 4,000 each year in the late 1970s and over 5,000 in the early 1980s—benefits from these technical documents and hardware. The assimilation of Western technology is so broad that the United States and other Western nations are thus subsidizing the Soviet military buildup.[1]

It is estimated that the Soviet Union has saved the equivalent of several billion dollars by the acquisition of military technologies from the West.

The Soviet collection network is orchestrated at the highest level by the Military Industrial Commission (VPK) of the Presidium of the Council of Ministers. The commission issues orders for the acquisition, by legal or illicit means, of military and dual-use technologies—including blueprints, product samples, and test equipment—to improve the quality of Soviet weapons and related military equipment. The Ministry of Foreign Trade, together with the Soviet intelligence services—the KGB and GRU and their surrogates in East European communist states—administer a parallel effort designed to obtain advanced technologies—such as those relating to microelectronics, computer machinery, robotics, communications, and diagnostic and other equipment—in order to increase the quality and quantity of the output of the weapons industry in the Soviet Union. Assignments for specific technology acquisition are given by the Soviet intelligence apparatus to its East European counterparts, whose worldwide activities are coordinated by the Soviet Union. The intelligence services of East Germany, Hungary, and Poland are said to have been among the most successful in obtaining classified information and export-controlled defense-related products for the Soviet military establishment from the West.

In this collection effort, the Soviet Union has targeted a variety of potential sources for sensitive information. These include defense contractors, especially those of the aerospace, chemical, and petrochemical industries. Among the other objects of the Soviet collection effort are foreign trading firms, academic institutions, electronic data bases, and scientific conferences attended by representatives of the Soviet scientific community under the auspices of the Academy of Science of the USSR. Other Soviet agencies, such as the State Committee for Science and Technology and the State Committee for Foreign Economics, send to scientific meetings delegations whose members are involved in the overt collection of information, much of it having no immediate and obvious military application, but who are co-opted from time to time to gather weapons-related technological data.

The Soviet Union is using a large number of front organizations as a means of circumventing Western restrictions on the Soviet purchase of sensitive technologies. For this purpose, the Soviet Union makes use of diverters who work either for set or negotiated fees, or for a commission in the form of a percentage of the purchase price. More than 300 firms operating in more than 30 countries have been identified by the U.S. government to be engaged in the diversion of technology to the Soviet Union.

The use of such mechanisms incurs for the Soviet Union minimal risk or legal liability. There is little or no direct contact with the diverter, who usually enjoys autonomy in operational decisions such as contacting the front organization, making the purchase, and arranging for storage and delivery of the required technology. The use of trade diverters supplements the activities of the Soviet intelligence services, while minimizing the likelihood that KGB and GRU operations will be exposed or compromised.

In the last decade, this multipronged Soviet technology acquisition apparatus has yielded handsome dividends in aerospace projectiles and explosives, armor, electro-optics, missiles, communications, radar and computers, nuclear and high-energy lasers, electronics and microelectronics, chemicals, electrical equipment, and petrochemicals. As a result of technologies incorporated into Soviet weapons systems, copied from Western systems by reverse engineering, the Soviet Union has virtually eliminated the lead once enjoyed by the United States and its allies in such military systems as tanks, artillery, and antitank and surface-to-air missiles.

It is said that an average of over 5,000 Soviet military equipment and weapons research projects for each year in the present decade have benefited from hardware and technical documents obtained by the Soviet Union from the West. Western technology has helped the Soviet Union to reduce its weapons acquisition cycle by as much as two years in projects advanced in status, such as self-aiming aviation cluster munitions, or by as long as five years in the case of projects at an earlier stage of research. Moreover, the Soviet Union has used data on the F-18 fire control radar as the technical basis for a new lookdown/shootdown radar system for the latest generation of Soviet fighter aircraft.

The Reagan administration has taken steps to limit the transfer of technology to the Soviet Union, including the development of up-to-date export licensing procedures and the modernization of CoCom, the organization consisting of Western advanced industrial states formed nearly two generations ago to control East-West technology transfer. The need for more effective means to limit such transfers is apparent. Faced with the quantitative advantage possessed by the Soviet Union in most indicators of military power, the United States has relied upon the qualitative edge conferred by our technology. This cannot be allowed to be dissipated through the transfer of such technology—legally or illegally—to the Soviet Union.

KEY TECHNOLOGY CATEGORIES

Without access to classified data, it is difficult at best to identify with any precision the kinds of Western technologies that the Soviet Union will seek to acquire in the years ahead. Published lists of current technology transfers from West to East are useful only as crude indicators of future trade. They generally provide no more than gross dollar values for broadly defined commodity groups (electronics, transistors, chemical materials, etc.). Such lists, moreover, tend to focus almost exclusively on hardware exchanges, paying scant attention to the fact that the provision of training, design criteria, and technical documentation—the so-called "know-how" dimension of technology transfers —has become an important (and growing) aspect of trade with the Soviet Union.

Nevertheless, by combining publicly available data on current technology transfers, together with what we now know about major bottlenecks in the Soviet economy, it is possible to identify general categories of Western technologies—and to a lesser extent, specific technical commodities—which the Soviet Union is likely to seek to acquire in the late 1980s and beyond. What follows is a brief survey of several categories, access to which Moscow can be expected to assign a high priority over the next decade. For the most part, such technologies consist of "dual-use" systems, the transfer of which could form a source of contention between the United States and its NATO-European allies, and the augmentation of which could carry significant benefits for the overall military-strategic posture of the Soviet Union, as well as for the Soviet economy.

Oil and Gas Technologies

In order to maintain hard currency earnings from energy exports, Moscow in the early 1980s placed high priority on improving the production and transportation network for Soviet oil and gas, giving special attention to the tapping of Siberian/Arctic and off-shore resources (e.g., in the Barents and Baltic Seas). Indeed, the eleventh Five-Year Plan (1981-1985) alone called for the construction of some 48,000 kilometers of gas trunk lines, including six major lines from Western Siberia to European Russia, one of which is the Urengoy pipeline for exports to Western Europe. The present Soviet Five-Year Plan (1986-1990) sets forth production goals that include substantial imports of advanced technologies such as oil and natural gas equipment. What distinguishes the second half of the 1980s from the earlier years of the decade, however, is the sharp decline in world oil prices, the effect of which has been to produce a hard currency shortfall for the Soviet Union. Nevertheless, Soviet technology procurement needs in the West and Japan are likely to have as their focus:

- Fluid and gas-lifting equipment, especially high-capacity submersible pumps
- Deep drilling equipment for oil/gas deposits in the Caspian Sea and Arctic zones
- High-quality drilling bits, rigging steel, and drill pipes
- Advanced geophysical/seismic equipment for oil/gas exploration
- Large-diameter transport pipe, pipelaying equipment, and associated oil/gas transmission systems (compressor stations, turbines, etc.)
- Enhanced oil recovery technology
- "Sour gas" gathering and treatment facilities.

Apart from American companies, much, if not all, of this equipment can be bought from European firms, including those involved in the gas pipeline deal of the early 1980s. Moreover, in addition to strengthening the Soviet industrial base and sustaining Moscow's leading position in the world energy market, these technologies, it must be noted, also can have a more direct military impact. Sophisticated acoustic/seismic equipment, for example, could have useful antisubmarine warfare (ASW) applications; and integrated pipeline systems, linked to Eastern and Western Europe, will improve Warsaw Pact fuel mobilization-distribution capabilities.

Coal and Nuclear Power Technologies

Only slightly lower among Soviet energy priorities than oil and gas development is the expansion of coal and nuclear power capacities. Among the effects of the Chernobyl disaster in April 1986 is likely to be a Soviet interest in the acquisition of more sophisticated technologies from the West for nuclear power plants. In addition to their role in helping to diversify the Soviet energy economy, new coal and nuclear power technologies (as well as energy conservation technologies) represent essential components of Moscow's future energy diplomacy and export strategies. Among the items found in the West that would contribute most directly to Soviet development plans are:

- Advanced coal extraction technologies and mine mechanization equipment
- More efficient methods for conventional coal-burning, especially the fluidized-bed technique
- Coal conversion technologies for exploiting Siberian deposits, most notably gasification facilities
- Coal-slurry pipeline equipment
- High-temperature, gas-cooled nuclear power reactor (HTGCR) programs, which could produce processed heat for coal conversion plants
- Nuclear fuel-handling and waste disposal techniques
- High-voltage (HV) electric power lines and terminals, as well as new cable technology, for long-distance electricity transmission.

As for West European sources for these and related technologies, the Federal Republic of Germany stands out as the most likely supplier of coal production and conversion equipment. It is conceivable that some of the nuclear technologies noted above could have weapons program applications: For the most part, however, coal and nuclear energy developments will have an indirect impact on Soviet military power, bolstering the defense industrial base and adding flexibility to the energy security structure.

Strategic Mineral Production and Processing

In the resource management field, another pressing requirement for the Soviet Union is the need to modernize production and processing capabilities for nonfuel minerals, especially with respect to strategic commodities, such as chrome, cobalt, platinum group metals, and manganese. Soviet needs in this arena include:

- Advanced exploration and ore extraction techniques suitable, in particular, for use in arctic conditions
- Heavy-duty, all-weather, earth-moving equipment
- Mechanization of mine and minehead operations
- More efficient smelting/refining and beneficiation techniques, especially for low-grade ores
- Computerized plant management systems.

To a large extent, research and development related directly to the exploitation of strategic minerals is concentrated in the United States, Canada, Australia, and South Africa. There are, however, a few key European firms that could provide the Soviet Union with essential production technologies and management assistance, most notably from France and the Federal Republic of Germany. Japanese companies, such as Sumitomo Metal Mining, might also emerge as important suppliers for certain exploration and extraction operations. It is worth noting as well that, quite apart from upholding the Soviet Union's position as a key world producer and exporter, the refurbishment of strategic mineral mining and processing facilities contributes directly to the Soviet defense potential, inasmuch as strategic minerals and metals remain vital to the production of modern weapon systems and associated technologies.

Metallurgy and Material Science Innovations

Closely related to the strategic mineral issues discussed above is the Soviet Union's ongoing interest in gaining access to Western innovations in the fields of metallurgy and material science. Here, Moscow's shopping list is likely to call for the acquisition, by direct and indirect means, of:

- New techniques for powder- and hydro-metallurgy
- More efficient blast furnace operations

- Superalloys and specialty steel technologies, including those for high-strength, low-alloy (HSLA) products
- Advanced casting procedures for large and for complex forms, such as the "near-net shape" forging technique
- Technologies for the production, joining, and machining of composite materials, superplastic metals, and metal glasses
- Ferrite materials expertise
- Improvements in secondary recovery and scrap metal recycling.

In the years just ahead, these and similar items are likely to become increasingly widespread among the major steel producers of Western Europe and Japan, as well as among key metal consumer industries (e.g., aerospace companies and construction firms). More important still, access to a number of these technologies—especially those related to superalloys and composites—could significantly improve Soviet weapons production, most notably with respect to high-performance jet aircraft. It is worth noting, moreover, that ferrite materials are vital to the development of the "stealth" technology that will be indispensable in the designing of new generation military aircraft.

Computer Systems and Associated Electronics

Apart from the energy sector, Soviet needs are perhaps most pressing in the area of "state-of-the-art" computer products. Of particular interest to the Soviet leadership would be:

- Advanced microelectronics, including circuit design and miniaturization information
- Very high-speed (VHS) integrated circuitry
- Semiconductor electronics, especially for very large-scale integration (VLSI) and high-capacity products
- Mini-computer technology
- Computer architecture and software advances (including procedure-oriented and symbol-manipulation languages), to allow multiple simultaneous use and the integration of computer networks.

Of course, much of the best work in the computer field is being done in the United States, but major European firms are likely sources for a substantial portion of this equipment. The highly competitive microelectronics industry of

Japan looms as yet another important supply base for the Soviet Union. More to the point, however, advanced computer systems, whatever their exact sources, have contributed, and could continue to contribute, to a wide array of Soviet defense capabilities unless export controls are tightened. This is true, particularly in regard to missile guidance and weapons navigation, early warning systems (including AWACS technology), precision guided munitions (PGMs), advanced avionics and target acquisition, ballistic missile defense (BMD) operations, and military command, control and communications (C^3) networks.

Automated Machinery and New Manufacturing Techniques

Another high priority for the Soviet Union in the future will be plant modernization in the manufacturing sector as a whole, with emphasis on greater (and more efficient) mechanization to improve productivity. Among the items available in NATO countries and Japan that would be particularly helpful in this regard are:

- Precision-grinding and metal-cutting machines
- High-technology industrial robots
- Computerized inventory and industrial control systems
- "State-of-the-art" numerically-controlled (NC) machine tools
- Advanced continuous forging techniques.

In recent years, machinery sales and related equipment have become a major—perhaps *the* major—item in technology transfer from West to East, and it is likely that more than half of the machinery supplies bought in the West have been put to use in some aspect of defense production. Apart from improving Soviet industrial efficiency, Western machinery may very well bolster weapons production rates and strengthen mobilization/"surge production" potential. Such technologies, moreover, are readily available in virtually all of the major industrial democracies, although Japan has emerged as the world leader in robotics.

Telecommunications Equipment

Western telecommunications equipment is yet another prime candidate for a concerted Soviet procurement program, especially in view of the impact such technologies may have on global military communications networks, national command and control facilities, and intelligence gathering operations. Items of particular interest probably include:

- Sophisticated fiber optics
- Advanced magnetic recording/sonar devices
- Radar imaging and high-capacity photographic techniques, especially for use in space
- Remote sensor technology
- Microwave component technology
- Advancements in direct broadcast and satellite communications
- Radio/TV/video miniaturization processes.

Once again, the electronics industry of Japan provides perhaps the most attractive market for Soviet buyers, but the major electronics firms in Western Europe—the Netherlands, the Federal Republic of Germany, and Sweden—could provide much, if not all, of what is available in Japan.

Transport and Logistic Support Equipment

The transport sector remains one of the enduring deficiencies of the Soviet economy, and undoubtedly will be targeted for major efforts at improvement during future five-year plans. Western technology and management systems which might be acquired for this purpose could include:

- High-capacity, automated plants for vehicle production (e.g., the Kama River truck factory)
- Wide-bodied cargo aircraft, plus short-take-off-and-landing (STOL) technology
- Roll-on, roll-off (Ro/Ro) equipment, together with maritime logistical supply and servicing technologies
- Innovations in jet engine construction and new propulsion systems (e.g., superconductor power technology)
- Large-scale construction equipment, including oversized bulldozers, front-end loaders, and cranes.

With the exception of Ro/Ro and superconductor technologies, items such as these may not appear unique, nor do they necessarily stand beyond the indigenous design capacity of the Soviet Union. They can provide, however, significant, if somewhat indirect, input to the overall Soviet military machine, especially in the area of strategic mobility/power projection, as evidenced by the Red Army's use of trucks produced at the Western-built Kama River plant during the Soviet invasion of Afghanistan and in the protracted warfare that has been conducted by Moscow there since 1979. Based on past trade negotiations, technology transfer/plant construction deals—at least insofar as ground transport is concerned—might be arranged by Moscow with West European as well as with a variety of U.S. companies.

In helping to build up and modernize air, sea, and ground transport production facilities within the Soviet Union, Western companies actually may be providing Moscow with the capacity to compete more effectively with the West for sales and/or trade agreements in key Third World areas, and in some of the industrialized states of Latin America and Asia. For this reason alone, the potentially negative effects of such competition on the industrial bases of the West—especially with respect to the loss of important export markets—should at least be considered when assessing the costs and benefits of technology transfers.

Food Production and Processing Technology

Problems related to agriculture and food development will demand serious attention in the Soviet Union. This is especially true with respect to ongoing technical deficiencies in Soviet farm machinery. Therefore, the Soviet leadership appears to be particularly interested in gaining and/or maintaining access to:

- Combines, tractors and other equipment built in the West, to be used for seeding, planting and harvesting
- Minitractors and small-scale mowing machines to boost productivity on private plots
- Industrialized livestock management systems
- Aquaculture and fish farming technologies
- Modern food processing and packaging techniques.

To be sure, food-related technologies have only an indirect bearing on the index of Soviet military power, and, in the wake of America's "on-again, off-again" grain embargo diplomacy, there seems to be little interest, at the moment, either in Washington or the West European capitals, in closing off the West-to-East flow of information or technology for food production and management. Nevertheless, to the extent that such assistance strengthens the Soviet economy and improves efficiencies, without requiring fundamental reforms, its strategic implications may *not* be entirely benign. For the purpose of this survey, it is worth remembering as well that, while the Soviets may prefer to deal with American agricultural and food product firms, they are now beginning to buy more often from European companies located primarily in the Netherlands and Denmark, and, to a lesser extent, in France and the United Kingdom. In time, moreover, improvements in Soviet production and processing capabilities, together with Moscow's greater reliance on European technology suppliers, could erode one of the more important U.S. economic levers over the Soviet Union—namely, the provision of grain and farm machinery.

Laser Technologies

Last, but far from least, is the issue of laser technologies and related technical data, which could contribute in time to the development of "beam weaponry" and other "breakthrough technologies" in the military sphere, especially with respect to space-based ballistic missile defense (BMD), antisatellite (ASAT) capabilities, and antisubmarine warfare (ASW)/ocean surveillance systems. No doubt, much of the equipment most relevant to these capabilities already is strictly controlled in the West. Nevertheless, given the consequences of potential diversion of ostensibly civilian technologies to military purposes, extreme caution should prevail in the case of any laser-related transfers or information exchanges with the Soviet Union. This is true, especially with respect to:

- Research findings in high-energy physics, particularly in regard to directed-energy devices
- Research and development for high-voltage, high-current accelerators
- Laser applications in the "blue-green" spectrum
- Equipment useful to the construction of gas, gas dynamic, electric charge, and chemical-based (hydrogen-fluoride) lasers.

Since most of the very sensitive research into the military uses of lasers is classified, Soviet access, in other than a surreptitious manner, is unlikely. Laser research in the open commercial sector is proliferating, however, and the incorporation of emerging civilian laser technologies into future military systems—laser data control systems, for example, in defense communications networks—cannot be discounted. Soviet interest in encouraging research and technology transfers in the laser field is bound to increase, and the Western allies ought not to be caught unaware of the potential strategic implication of such trade, as they were in the case of East-West trade in first-generation computers.

On balance, then, it seems fair to conclude that each of the 10 key technology categories outlined in this chapter contains items that ought to be more carefully controlled in terms of East-West trade. Some of the equipment and technical components listed above—superalloy technology, for example—could have immediate military applications. Others, such as computer directed manufacturing technologies, may enhance Soviet military power in a more indirect fashion, primarily by strengthening overall production capabilities and by reducing inefficiencies in the industrial sector. Still other commodities—most notably energy and mineral development technologies—could challenge, in time, the economic (as opposed to strictly military) security of the industrial democracies, by helping the Soviet Union to sustain hard currency, resource exports to the West and Japan at levels that could not readily be covered, in the event of a supply disruption, by imports from other countries or by domestic supplies. In sum, technology transfers to the East—profitable as they may be—can complicate Western efforts to retain a qualitative edge over the Soviet Union while at the same time deepening alliance dependencies on foreign trade flows, such as energy supplies, that could be interrupted.

CONCLUSIONS AND POLICY RECOMMENDATIONS

A number of policy implications emerged from chapters in this volume, reflecting the broad scope of issues and perspectives involved. No effort was made to construct an overall consensus or reach a general final agreement among contributors. The following observations and recommendations are summarized:

1. A restrained U.S. export policy toward the Soviet Union and its East European allies should be pursued, in order to limit the hemorrhage of sensitive technologies and valuable technical information to Soviet bloc countries. Greater efforts, in particular, are required to:

- Retard the loss of classified information (including critical software and associated documentation), as well as "end-product" hardware and component technologies
- Identify, monitor, and expose the scope and structure of the massive Soviet technology acquisition effort, especially the clandestine activities of the Soviet intelligence services and foreign trade representatives

- Enhance communication among the Departments of State, Commerce, Defense, and Treasury, so as to improve licensing and enforcement procedures
- Deepen and extend the consensus on tighter export controls that now prevails among CoCom members, and encourage adoption of comparable control mechanisms by non-CoCom states
- Encourage higher public awareness—especially among industry —concerning technology transfer risks and concerns.

2. Broader allied agreement and cooperation in the East-West trade arena may require additional steps to streamline and simplify technology transfer (under secure conditions) within the Free World. For example, wider use of multiple licenses—especially distribution (DL) and comprehensive operations licenses (COL)—might be considered in the context of West-West trade, so that repeated transfers of goods and technologies to countries with reliable export control systems could be achieved without requiring a separate review for each transaction. Together with CoCom reforms already set in motion (e.g., continuous commodity control list review, and selective "decontrol" of certain low-performance computers), multiple licensing procedures could form the basis for a smoother and more predictable U.S. trade regime with its West European allies, Japan, and other friendly states.

3. Harmonization of licensing procedures among the Atlantic Alliance countries and Japan certainly should ease concerns in the U.S. executive branch (especially in the Department of Defense) over past inadequacies of allied export controls. Nevertheless, the West-West consensus that now prevails insofar as East-West trade is concerned may not be sustained (much less, widened) unless further steps are taken to integrate the Department of Defense more fully into the export review process. President Reagan's authorization of a Department of Defense right to review selected individual validated licenses for technology transfers within the West is a step in the right direction, and should be extended as soon as possible to apply to multiple licenses as well. As the agency responsible for strategic technology cooperation, DOD has a legitimate role to play in West-West license reviews. More importantly, the evidence to date suggests that DOD reviews will *not* unduly lengthen the review process or lead to extensive export denials.

4. Additional mechanisms are also needed to bring DOD perspectives and concerns (and those of allied defense ministries) more directly into CoCom deliberations. In this regard, plans for the creation of a Defense Expert Group within CoCom should be realized to provide "in-house" expertise on the military uses and re-engineering of advanced equipment and technology. So, too, member-state commitments to modernize CoCom facilities and data automation capabilities should be carried out without delay. Progress in

renovating and strengthening CoCom should substantially reduce the potential for "policy battles" between various branches of the U.S. government concerned with technology transfers, as well as between the United States and its allies.

5. Because neutral third countries have been a significant source of technology flow to the East, the United States should establish bilateral and multilateral agreements with newly industrialized countries and West European neutrals, in order to stem re-export of defense-relevant technologies and products to the Soviet bloc. In an effort to facilitate such agreements, the new U.S. Export Administration Act allows for the provision of CoCom-like treatment to third countries that cooperate fully on export control issues. It was suggested that allied countries should undertake similar initiatives to address the re-transfer problem.

6. Science and technology exchanges, it was agreed, form a very important (and often ignored) dimension of East-West trade relations. However, for the United States to benefit from science and technology exchange with the USSR, and to minimize inappropriate technology transfers, the following requirements should be met:

- The United States should avoid the transfer of technology in areas of Soviet technological weakness. It should act to prevent wideranging Soviet access to research facilities and U.S. industry. The United States should require equal and reciprocal exchange of data and working drafts between U.S. and Soviet scientists, as well as reciprocal rights of travel and attendance at workshops and professional meetings.
- Bilateral exchanges should be properly administered and implemented by persons qualified in administration and negotiation, and possessing in-field experience and language competence.
- Exchanges should be properly monitored and reported, and adequate resources should be allotted, to enable U.S. personnel to follow the movements and activities of participating Soviet scientists in the United States.
- Qualified analysts should properly assess and evaluate the results of joint scientific projects. Gain and loss summaries should be made available to U.S. administrators and policy offices.

7. Both the United States and its allies should design a clearer and more cautious philosophy regarding East-West technology transfer, reflecting a more realistic appraisal of Western abilities to influence long-term Soviet policy through trade relations, as well as greater appreciation of Soviet ability to convert Western products and technologies to potential military use. While the Western countries and Japan should take advantage of the limited

opportunities that exist for influencing the Soviet system, they should also be aware of the following crucial points:

- Economic development stimulated in part by Western technology may simply harden, and render more efficient, the very political system that the West hopes to change.
- Through economic and technological support of the Soviet military research and development community (which is given priority access to Western technologies), the West may encourage Soviet leaders to perpetuate current defense priorities.
- While select transfers of technology may help to encourage economic decentralization trends in certain East European countries (particularly those that enjoyed more democratic political traditions in the past), Soviet authorities are not likely to allow significant political change. Perhaps more to the point, any technology transfers to Eastern Europe will almost certainly end up in the Soviet Union in time.
- Above all, the Soviet system of resource allocation *cannot* be viewed as simply another economic system, a variety of our own. It is, in fact, a key mechanism by which the Communist Party of the Soviet Union retains central political control.

8. To some extent, of course, trade and economic ties can provide useful diplomatic levers in East-West relations. A policy of economic "carrots-and-sticks," for example, has been central to West Germany's *Ostpolitik* toward East Germany, at times bringing tangible results of great importance to Bonn (e.g., freer immigration from East to West Germany and the reunification of families). So, too, the imposition of economic sanctions and the suspension of trade relations can have a costly—if not debilitating—effect on Soviet bloc economies, at least over the short term. It must be remembered, however, that sanctions against technology transfer are likely to work most fully only if they are an integral part of a broader array of policies. Sanctions must be fitted within a credible sequence of increasingly punitive moves, and should be imposed only when the stakes are truly high enough, thereby avoiding "light-switch diplomacy," or the on-again, off-again use of trade policy as an instrument of foreign policy, which has led in the past to severe, and at times avoidable, strains in U.S. alliance relations.

9. As for Sino-American trade relations, current efforts in CoCom to facilitate Chinese access to certain categories of high technology and to expedite the handling of China-related export requests are to be commended. It would be dangerous, however, to assume that the present compatibility of complementarity of U.S. and Chinese interests will necessarily prevail over the longer term. While the current "pro-China" cast of U.S. foreign policy works in

favor of broader technology transfers, there is, nevertheless, considerable potential risk in moving ahead with expanded technology sales to the PRC without greater clarity of purpose among U.S. policymakers, together with a more realistic set of expectations as to what we can (and hope to) achieve through wider commercial ties. This is not to argue against the facilitation of U.S.-China trade, for the provision of advanced technology is likely to remain America's strongest card in dealing with the People's Republic, especially in view of Beijing's apparent dissatisfaction over the level of trade with Japan and the quality of technology available from Western Europe. It does, however, suggest that clearer policy guidance is needed if both partners—China and the United States—are not to be disappointed.

10. The United States must establish procedures, through legislation and administrative action, for greater communication between the private sector and those government bodies originating and implementing export policy. Such a dialogue between industry and government is an essential part of the task of providing the private sector with an adequate understanding of the implications of policy regulations and export guidelines. It is also a crucial prerequisite for long-term decisionmaking in the private sector. Should disagreements of the recent past between government and the private sector persist, U.S. exporters could face a serious decline in their competitive position which, in turn, can only serve to erode the very technological edge of American and Western products that all parties—private and public—hope to sustain.

For its part, the executive branch should endeavor to carry out the mandates and meet the time constraints of the 1985 Export Administration Act (EAA), as Congress intended, in order to reduce the need for excessively rigorous oversight efforts on the part of House and Senate members. This would include consolidation of the Defense Department's role in license reviews, refinement of commodity control lists, and foreign availability determinations. Predictable implementation of the existing system without radical changes will enhance its effectiveness, encourage multilateral cooperation, and eliminate unnecessary costs to U.S. businesses, thus aiding the international trade community. At the same time, those in industry could well turn their attention to the design and promotion of more effective corporate security and intelligence programs, thereby easing DOD concerns over current vulnerabilities in the private sector.

NOTES

1. *Soviet Acquisition of Militarily Significant Western Technology: An Update* (Washington, D.C.: U.S. Government Printing Office, 1985), p.i.

GLOSSARY

ABM	Antiballistic missile
AEA	American Electronics Association
AEN	Administrative Exception Note
ASAT	Antisatellite
ASEAN	Association of Southeast Asian Nations
ASW	Antisubmarine Warfare
AWACS	Airborne Warning and Control System
BAM	Baikal-Amur Railroad
BRT	Business Round Table
CBEMA	Computer and Business Equipment Manufacturing Association
CC CPSU	Central Committee of the Communist Party of the Soviet Union
CCL	Commodity Control List
CIA	Central Intelligence Agency
CMEA	Council for Mutual Economic Assistance (Bulgaria, Cuba, Czechoslovakia, German Democratic Republic, Hungary, Mongolia, Poland, Romania, USSR, Vietnam)
CMEA —Six	Bulgaria, Czechoslovakia, German Democratic Republic, Hungary, Poland, USSR
CoCom	Coordinating Committee for Multilateral Export Controls (NATO countries, except Iceland, and Japan)
COL	Comprehensive License
COMECON	(See CMEA)
DIA	Defense Intelligence Agency
DL	Distribution License
DOD	Department of Defense
EAA	Export Administration Act
EIA	Electronics Industry Association
FBI	Federal Bureau of Investigation
FCI	Foreign Counterintelligence Investigations
FOFA	Follow-On Forces Attack
GKNT	State Committee for Science and Technology (USSR)
Gosplan	State Planning Commission (USSR)
GRU	Chief Intelligence Directorate of the Soviet General Staff
HSLA	High-Strength, Low-Alloy
IEEPA	International Emergency Economic Powers Act
IMF	International Monetary Fund
ITSP	Interstate Transportation of Stolen Property
KAMAZ	Kama River Truck Plant
KGB	Committee for State Security (USSR)

MCTL	Militarily Critical Technologies List
MIT	Massachusetts Institute of Technology
MOS	Metal Oxide Semiconductor
MOU	Memorandum of Understanding
NASA	National Aeronautics and Space Administration
NATO	North Atlantic Treaty Organization (Belgium, Canada, Denmark, France, Greece, Iceland, Italy, Luxembourg, the Netherlands, Norway, Portugal, Spain, Turkey, United Kingdom, United States, West Germany)
NDSTIC	National Defense Science, Technology, and Industry Commission (PRC)
NEP	New Economic Plan
NPO	Scientific Production Complex (USSR)
OECD	Organization for Economic Cooperation and Development
PGM	Precision-Guided Munitions
PLO	Palestine Liberation Organization
PRC	People's Republic of China
R&D	Research and Development
Ro/Ro	Roll-on, Roll-off
S&T	Science and Technology
SALT	Strategic Arms Limitation Talks
SDI	Strategic Defense Initiative
SED	Shipper's Export Declaration
STOL	Short-Takeoff-and-Landing
STR	Scientific-Technological Revolution
TOW	Tube-Launched Optically-Tracked Wire-Guided (missile)
VAZ	Volga Automotive Plant (Togliattigrad)
VHSIC	Very High-Speed Integrated Circuit
VLSI	Very Large-Scale Integration
VPK	Military-Industrial Commission (USSR)

INDEX

Academy of Sciences, USSR, 4, 16, 18, 35, 76, 96, 108n, 113, 114, 116; role in science and technology, 121–123

Acquisition of Western technology: by hostile intelligence services, 178; by PRC, 141; by USSR, 3–5, 9, 12, 14, 15–21, 47, 49, 67, 70–74, 86, 91, 124, 158, 159, 176, 180, 184, 186, 189, 195, 219–224, 227, 230

"Active" technology transfer, 60, 64

Afghanistan, 162–163, 197, 228; role in Sino–American relations, 141, 145; role in U.S. economic sanctions, 208, 215n; role in U.S.–Soviet high technology trade, 183, 186–188; Soviet occupation of, 18, 127n

Agents (Soviet), 8, 18, 70–73, 167, 179

American Communist Party. See Communist Party of the United States of America (CPUSA)

American Electronics Association (AEA), 166

Ammunitions technology, 84, 85

Andropov, Yuri, 32, 33, 37–38, 41, 48, 50, 73; and Gorbachev, 51

Antisatellite (ASAT) capabilities, 229

Antisubmarine warfare (ASW) technology, 21, 223, 229

Arab–Israeli war (1973), 12

Arms Export Control Act, 86, 178, 179

Asia, 195, 211, 228; Central, 40 (See also Sibaral project); East and Southeast, 134, 135, 142, 144, 147

Association of South East Asian Nations (ASEAN). See Third World

Atlantic Alliance. See North Atlantic Treaty Organization (NATO)

Austria, 15, 72, 211

Automated machinery technologies, 226

Baikal–Amur Railroad (BAM), 40, 43, 57n

Ballistic missile defense (BMD), 226, 229

Barr, Joel. See Berg, Iosef

Berg, Iosef (a.k.a. Joel Barr), 60, 63, 68

Brezhnev, Leonid, 16, 37, 48, 49, 52, 73, 75, 76, 91, 98, 108; *apparatchiki,* 31, 33; and Gorbachev, 31–33, 37, 79

Bruchhausen, Werner, 15. *See also* Front organizations

Business community. *See* U.S. business community

Business Round Table (BRT), 166

Cadre, 45, 66, 125; Czechoslovakian, 70; Gorbachevian compared to those of Brezhnev, 28, 31–34, 55. *See also* Brezhnev, Leonid I.; "Efficient technocrat"; Gorbachev, Mikhail S.

Cambodia. *See* Kampuchea

Central Asia. *See* Asia, Central

Central Intelligence Agency (CIA), 7, 41, 75, 104n, 158–159

Chemical industry: economic growth of in USSR, 89; importation of technologies by PRC, 146; importation of technologies by USSR, 76, 220–221; in Czechoslovakia, 71, 74; Soviet, 115

Chen Bin, 139, 145. *See also* People's Republic of China, National Defense Science, Technology, and Industry Commission (NDSTIC)

Chernobyl nuclear plant (Ukraine), 103, 223

China, People's Republic of (PRC), 189, 198; acquisition of Western technology, 141; break from orthodox communism, 95; Central Committee of the Communist Party, 132; "China card" (United States), 140; "China strategy" (Japan), 136; development of nuclear weapons, 151; domestic policy of, 144, 148–150; economic reform in, 46, 95, 103, 131–151, 195; foreign policy of, 131, 137–139; "Gang of Four," 150n; and Middle East, 147; military cooperation with U.S., 131; National Defense Science, Technology, and Industry Commission (NDSTIC), 139, 145; "open-door" policy of, 132, 138–140, 144, 146–147; "pro-China" policy of U.S., 132, 233; reforms, 132, 134, 139, 140, 147; seventh Five-Year Plan, 133;

ABOUT THE EDITORS AND CONTRIBUTORS

THE EDITORS

Charles M. Perry is a Senior Staff Member of the Institute for Foreign Policy Analysis, Inc.

Robert L. Pfaltzgraff, Jr., is President of the Institute for Foreign Policy Analysis, Inc., and Shelby Cullom Davis Professor of International Security Studies at the Fletcher School of Law & Diplomacy, Tufts University.

THE CONTRIBUTORS

Richard N. Perle is a Resident Fellow, Foreign Policy Studies, at the American Enterprise Institute for Public Policy Research and former Assistant Secretary for International Security Policy, Department of Defense.

Stephen Bryen is Deputy Under Secretary for Trade Security Policy, Department of Defense.

Jack Vorona is Assistant Deputy Director for Scientific and Technical Intelligence, Defense Intelligence Agency.

John P. Hardt is Associate Director, Congressional Research Service, Library of Congress.

Mark Kuchment is a Fellow at the Russian Research Center, Harvard University.

Jan Sejna was former Chief of Staff to the Czechoslovakian Minister of Defense, and former Secretary of the Military Committee of the Communist Party of Czechoslovakia.

Marshall I. Goldman is Professor of Economics, Wellesley College; and Associate Director of the Russian Research Center, Harvard University.

William Schneider, Jr., is President, International Planning Services, Inc.; former Under Secretary for Security Assistance, Science and Technology, Department of State.

Victor Basiuk is Consultant to the U.S. government on Science, Technology, and National Security Policy.

John R. Thomas is a senior Soviet affairs specialist with the Bureau of Science, Department of State.

Denis Fred Simon is Ford International Assistant Professor of Management, Sloan School of Management, Massachusetts Institute of Technology.

Lionel H. Olmer is with Paul, Weiss, Rifkin, Wharton and Garrison; and was formerly Under Secretary for International Trade at the Department of Commerce.

Paul Freedenberg is Assistant Secretary for Trade Administration, Department of Commerce; and former Staff Director, Subcommittee on International Finance and Monetary Policy, Senate Banking Committee.

R. Roger Majak is Washington Representative for Government and Public Affairs, Tektroniks, Inc.; and former Staff Director, Subcommittee on International Economic Policy and Trade, House Foreign Affairs Committee.

Phillip A. Parker was the Deputy Assistant Director, Intelligence Division, Federal Bureau of Investigation.

Vitalij Garber is President, GIA, Inc.; and was formerly NATO's Assistant Secretary General for Defense Support.

Hugh Donaghue is Senior Vice President, Government Programs and International Trade Relations, Control Data Corporation.

Robert Price is Director, Office of East-West Trade, Bureau of Economic and Business Affairs, Department of State.

Manfred Von Nordheim is Vice President for North America, Messerschmitt-Boelkow-Blohm.

Henry R. Nau is Associate Dean, School of International Affairs, George Washington University.